Brilliant Laptops for the Over 50s

Microsoft® Windows 7 edition

Joli Ballew

Prentice Hall
is an imprint of

PEARSON

Harlow, England • London • New York • Boston • San Francisco • Toronto • Sydney • Singapore • Hong Kong
Tokyo • Seoul • Taipei • New Delhi • Cape Town • Madrid • Mexico City • Amsterdam • Munich • Paris • Milan

Pearson Education Limited
Edinburgh Gate
Harlow CM20 2JE
United Kingdom
Tel: +44 (0)1279 623623
Fax: +44 (0)1279 431059
Website: www.pearsoned.co.uk

First published in Great Britain in 2010

ISBN: 978-0-273-73318-8

British Library Cataloguing-in-Publication Data
A catalogue record for this book is available from the British Library

Library of Congress Cataloging-in-Publication Data
A catalog record for this book is available from the British Library of Congress

10 9 8 7 6 5 4 3 2 1
14 13 12 11 10

Typeset in 11pt Arial Condensed by 30
Printed and bound in Great Britain by Scotprint, Haddington, East Lothian

Brilliant guides

What you need to know and how to do it

When you're working on your computer and come up against a problem that you're unsure how to solve, or want to accomplish something that you aren't sure how to do, where do you look? Manuals and traditional training guides are usually too big and unwieldy and are intended to be used as end-to-end training resources, making it hard to get to the info you need right away without having to wade through pages of background information that you just don't need at that moment – and helplines are rarely that helpful!

Brilliant guides have been developed to allow you to find the info you need easily and without fuss and guide you through the task using a highly visual, step-by-step approach – providing exactly what you need to know when you need it!

Brilliant guides provide the quick easy-to-access information that you need, using a table of contents and troubleshooting guide to help you find exactly what you need to know, and then presenting each task or problem, using numerous screenshots to illustrate each step. Added features include 'Did you know?' boxes that point you to relevant expert tips, tricks and advice to further expand your skills and knowledge.

In addition to covering all major office laptop applications, and related computing subjects, the *Brilliant* series also contains titles that will help you in every aspect of your working life, such as writing the perfect CV, answering the toughest interview questions and moving on in your career.

Brilliant guides are the light at the end of the tunnel when you are faced with any minor or major task.

Publisher's acknowledgements

The author and publisher would like to thank the following for permission to reproduce the material in this book:

Microsoft product screen shots reprinted with permission from Microsoft Corporation.

Every effort has been made to obtain necessary permission with reference to copyright material. In some instances we have been unable to trace the owners of copyright material, and we would appreciate any information that would enable us to do so.

Contents

Introduction **xi**

1. Introduction to laptops 1

Introduction 1
Access media and games 3
Watching a DVD 4
Playing games 5
Use the Internet to stay safe on the road 6
Getting directions online 7
Entertain your grandchildren 8
Use your laptop computer ergonomically 9
Get started 10

2. Choosing and using a laptop 11

Introduction 11
Things to consider when shopping for a laptop 12
Visiting a computer store and asking questions 15
Shopping checklist 16
Checking out the manufacturer's website 18
Choosing a rugged laptop 19
Making the purchase 20
Extended warranties 21

3. Exploring the outside of the laptop 23

Introduction 23
Locating and using the power cable 25
Locating and using USB ports 26
Locating and using FireWire ports 27
Locating and using Ethernet ports 28
Locating and using Bluetooth technology 29
Locating and using an external monitor port 30
Locating and using sound ports 31
Locating and using a modem port 32
Locating and inserting or removing the battery 33
Explore additional ports 34

4. Exploring the inside 35
Introduction 35
Basic functionality 36
Locating basic features 37
Using the touchpad 40
Keys common to most keyboards 41
Using common keys 43
Using the arrow keys 45
Using the Function keys 46

5. Instant Windows 7 49
Introduction 49
The Getting Started window 51
Show the Getting Started window 52
Explore the Getting Started window 53
Know your Windows 7 edition 54
Explore the Desktop 58
Discover Windows 7's All Programs menu 61
Discover Windows 7 applications 63
Discover Windows 7 accessories 66
Shut down Windows 7 67

6. Personalising Windows 7 71
Introduction 71
Personalise the Desktop 72
Selecting a theme 73
Changing the background 76
Changing the screensaver 78
Tweaking the Desktop 79
Changing the Windows 7 icons on the Desktop 80
Creating Desktop shortcuts for programs, files and folders 81
Removing icons and shortcuts from the Desktop 83
Configure Desktop and monitor settings 84
Changing the screen resolution 85
Using the Windows Classic theme 87
Adjusting font size 88

7. Configuring accessibility options 91
Introduction 91
Configure the Narrator 92
Using the Narrator 94
Working with the Magnifier 95

Using the Magnifier 96
Using the On-Screen Keyboard 97
Make the keyboard easier to use 99
Explore keyboard shortcuts 101
Exploring additional Ease of Access options 103
Windows Speech Recognition 105
Setting up Windows Speech Recognition 106
Training Windows Speech Recognition 107
Using Windows Speech Recognition 108

8. Safety and security 109

Introduction 109
User accounts and passwords 112
Adding a new user account 113
Protecting your PC 115
Using Windows Update 116
Configuring Windows Update 118
Using Windows Firewall 121
Using Windows Defender 122
Resolving Action Center warnings 124
Protecting your family and your data 125
Setting up Parental Controls 126
Backing up data 127
Creating your first backup 128

9. Connecting to the Internet 131

Introduction 131
Choose from dial-up, broadband, mobile, wireless, satellite 132
Configuring your home Internet connection 134
Creating a connection to the Internet 136
Using free Wi-Fi hotspots 140
Find out if you have wireless hardware 141
Connecting at a free hotspot 142

10. Media applications 143

Introduction 143
Using Windows Media Player 144
Playing media 146
Listening to sample music 147
Rip a CD 148
Ripping your CD collection 149
Burning a CD 150
Download and install Windows Live Essentials 152

Downloading Windows Live 154
Windows Live Photo Gallery 156
Importing pictures from a digital camera, media card or USB drive (and even an iPhone) 158
Editing photos 159
Fixing pictures 160
Sharing photos 162
Emailing pictures 163
Watch DVDs 164
Watch TV using Windows Media Center 165
Watching live TV 167
Record television 168
Recording a TV show or series 170

11. The Mobility Center 171

Introduction 171
Exploring Windows Mobility Center 173
Enhancing battery life 175
Wireless connectivity 178
Turning on and off wireless connectivity 179
Exploring Presentation Settings 180
Turning on Presentation Settings 181
Sync Center 182
Getting started with Sync Center 184
Using an external display 185
Connecting an external display 186

Appendix A: Avoiding laptop disasters 187

Appendix B: Holidaying with a laptop 189

Backup your laptop before you leave 190
Clean up your laptop before leaving on a trip 192
Move sensitive data off the laptop (USB key or external drive) 193
Be sure you need your laptop 194
Packing your laptop 195
Taking your laptop on an aeroplane 197
Preparing for airline travel 199
Changing the time, language or region 200
Getting online access 201
Physically secure your laptop 204

Appendix C: Cleaning and protecting your laptop 205

Maintain your laptop 206
Cleaning the outside of the laptop 207
Cleaning the keyboard and monitor 208
Cleaning the inside of the laptop 209
Using surge protection 210

Jargon buster 211
Troubleshooting guide 221

Introduction

Welcome to *Brilliant Laptops for the Over 50s*, a visual quick-reference book that shows you how to make the most of your laptop computer, particularly if it is your first one, or if you are new to the world of computers! It will give you a solid grounding on how to choose the right laptop for you, how it works and how to get the best out of your laptop – a complete reference for the beginner and intermediate user who hasn't grown up with a laptop.

Find what you need to know – when you need it

You don't have to read this book in any particular order. We've designed the book so that you can jump in, get the information you need, and jump out. To find the information that you need, just look up the task in the table of contents or Troubleshooting guide, and turn to the page listed. Read the task introduction, follow the step-by-step instructions along with the illustration, and you're done.

How this book works

Each task is presented with step-by-step instructions in one column and screen illustrations in the other. This arrangement lets you focus on a single task without having to turn the pages too often.

i

How you'll learn

Find what you need to know – when you need it

How this book works

Step-by-step instructions

Troubleshooting guide

Spelling

Step-by-step instructions

This book provides concise step-by-step instructions that show you how to accomplish a task. Each set of instructions includes illustrations that directly correspond to the easy-to-read steps. Eye-catching text features provide additional helpful information in bite-sized chunks to help you work more efficiently or to teach you more in-depth information. The 'For your information' feature provides tips and techniques to help you work smarter, while the 'See also' cross-references lead you to other parts of the book containing related information about the task. Essential information is highlighted in 'Important' boxes that will ensure you don't miss any vital suggestions and advice.

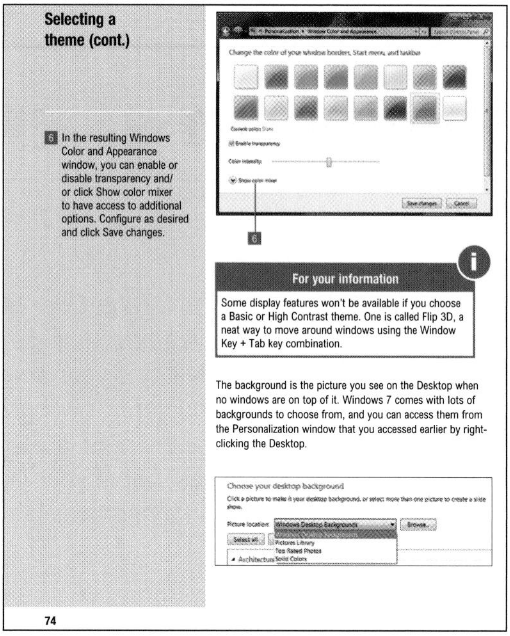
Selecting a theme (cont.)

6 In the resulting Windows Color and Appearance window, you can enable or disable transparency and/or click Show color mixer to have access to additional options. Configure as desired and click Save changes.

For your information

Some display features won't be available if you choose a Basic or High Contrast theme. One is called Flip 3D, a neat way to move around windows using the Window Key + Tab key combination.

The background is the picture you see on the Desktop when no windows are on top of it. Windows 7 comes with lots of backgrounds to choose from, and you can access them from the Personalization window that you accessed earlier by right-clicking the Desktop.

74

Troubleshooting guide

This book offers quick and easy ways to diagnose and solve common problems that you might encounter, using the Troubleshooting guide. The problems are grouped into categories.

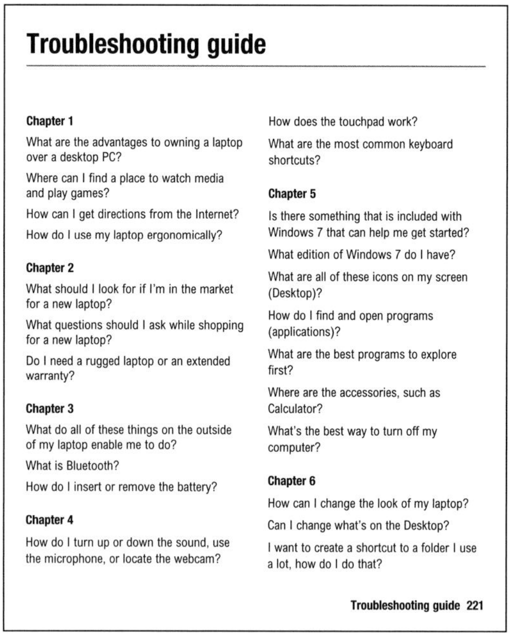
Troubleshooting guide

Chapter 1

What are the advantages to owning a laptop over a desktop PC?

Where can I find a place to watch media and play games?

How can I get directions from the Internet?

How do I use my laptop ergonomically?

Chapter 2

What should I look for if I'm in the market for a new laptop?

What questions should I ask while shopping for a new laptop?

Do I need a rugged laptop or an extended warranty?

Chapter 3

What do all of these things on the outside of my laptop enable me to do?

What is Bluetooth?

How do I insert or remove the battery?

Chapter 4

How do I turn up or down the sound, use the microphone, or locate the webcam?

How does the touchpad work?

What are the most common keyboard shortcuts?

Chapter 5

Is there something that is included with Windows 7 that can help me get started?

What edition of Windows 7 do I have?

What are all of these icons on my screen (Desktop)?

How do I find and open programs (applications)?

What are the best programs to explore first?

Where are the accessories, such as Calculator?

What's the best way to turn off my computer?

Chapter 6

How can I change the look of my laptop?

Can I change what's on the Desktop?

I want to create a shortcut to a folder I use a lot, how do I do that?

Troubleshooting guide 221

Spelling

We have used UK spelling conventions throughout this book. You may therefore notice some inconsistencies between the text and the software on your computer which is likely to have been developed in the USA. We have however adopted US spelling for the words 'disk' and 'program' as these are commonly accepted throughout the world.

Introduction to laptops

1

What you'll do

Watch a DVD

Play games

Get directions online

Introduction

Laptop computers are smaller versions of their desktop counterparts. They often do everything a desktop will, and offer portability. If you travel a lot now or are planning to in the future, a laptop is certainly something to consider. With a laptop, you'll always have access to your favourite games, music and media (pictures and video), as well as email, the Internet, and travel directions (provided you have an Internet subscription). If these are things you want to have handy when you travel, a laptop is the way to go.

You may wish to purchase a laptop even if you don't travel though. You can take a laptop with you anywhere, including hospitals, friends' and relatives' homes, the local senior centre, or even just your back garden.

In addition to being portable and offering access to personal data and the Internet, there are other advantages to having a laptop. These include but are not limited to:

- Disconnecting from a power source and using the laptop where power is not available, such as in aeroplanes, cars and trains.
- Storing and travelling with pictures, videos and documents.
- Having access to a music player and DVD player.
- Being able to play your favourite games when there's nothing else to do.

- Installing a GPS so you always know where you are and how to get where you're going.
- Having the option to always have access to Internet and email.
- Having something to keep your grandchildren busy on long car rides.

Yes, you can take it with you! With a laptop you can bring along your favourite photos, necessary documents, address books, journals, videos and any other digital data you keep. Having this information at your fingertips makes travelling safer, and also allows you to show pictures of your children and grandchildren to people you meet along the way. You can also bring data with you to share. You can bring pictures, videos, movies you've made and more.

With a laptop, you'll also have access to Windows Media Player for playing music and videos, Windows Journal for taking notes and keeping a diary, Windows Paint for creating drawings, and games such as Solitaire, just to name a few. Here's Windows Media Player, where you can listen to music and watch DVDs.

Windows Media Player
« Music ▸ All music
Play
Burn
Sync
Organize
Stream
Search
Album
Title
Library
Playlists
Music
Artist
Album
Genre
Videos
Pictures
Recorded TV
SnagIt (D:)
E:\
Other Libraries
Media Guide
Bob Acri
Bob Acri
Bob Acri
Jazz
2004
Sleep Away
Mr. Scruff
Ninja Tuna
Mr. Scruff
Electronic
2008
Kalimba
Richard Stoltzman
Fine Music, Vol. 1
Richard Stoltzman
Classical
2008
Maid with the Flaxen Hair

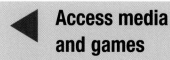

It's simple to watch a DVD too; no experience is necessary.

Access media and games

Watching a DVD

1. Press the button on the outside of your laptop that opens the DVD drive.
2. Carefully place a DVD in the drive.
3. If prompted, choose Play DVD Movie using Windows Media Player. You may not be prompted; the movie may simply begin to play.

In addition to watching DVDs, you can also play games. You don't need to bring your own games though, Windows 7 comes with plenty! To find the games on your laptop, click the Start button and click Games.

US NAVY
CARRIERS
Play film
Scene selection

Playing games

1 Click Start.

2 Click Games.

3 Double-click any game to start it.

Did you know?

You may have additional games. Sometimes the manufacturers add games of their own.

Getting Started
Windows Media Center
Calculator
Sticky Notes
Snipping Tool
Paint
Magnifier
Solitaire
All Programs
Search programs and files
Joli
Documents
Pictures
Music
Games
Computer
Control Panel
Devices and Printers
Default Programs
Help and Support
Shut down
2

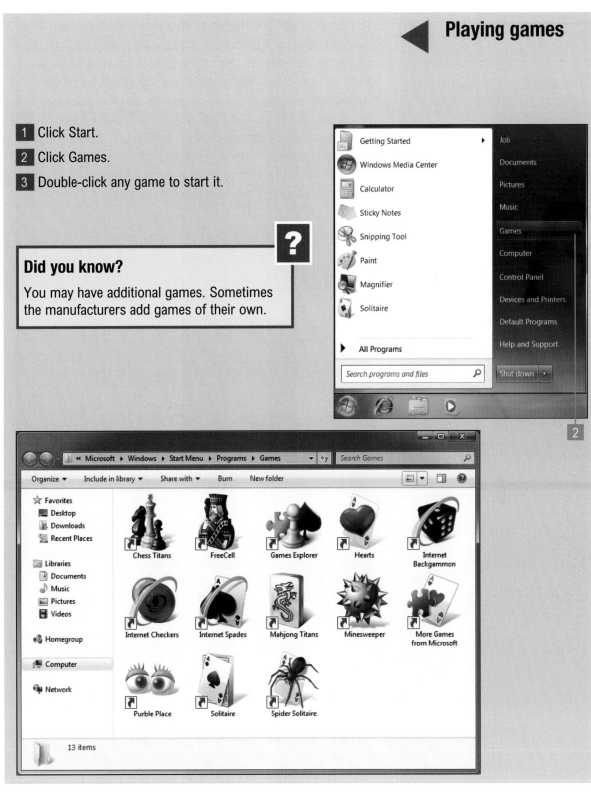

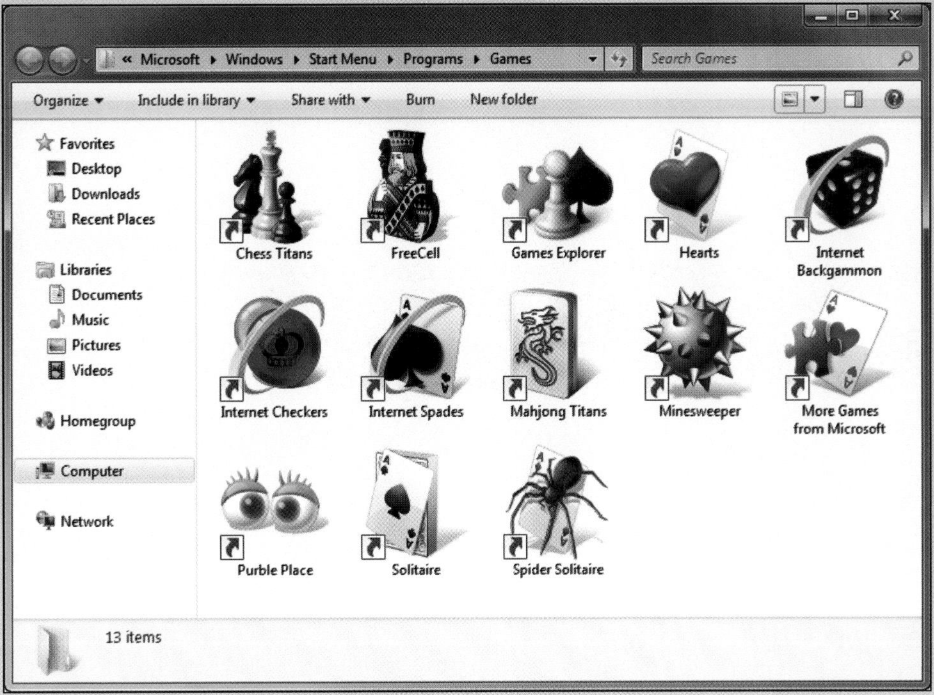
« Microsoft ▸ Windows ▸ Start Menu ▸ Programs ▸ Games
Search Games
Organize
Include in library
Share with
Burn
New folder
Favorites
Desktop
Downloads
Recent Places
Libraries
Documents
Music
Pictures
Videos
Homegroup
Computer
Network
Chess Titans
FreeCell
Games Explorer
Hearts
Internet Backgammon
Internet Checkers
Internet Spades
Mahjong Titans
Minesweeper
More Games from Microsoft
Purble Place
Solitaire
Spider Solitaire
13 items

Use the Internet to stay safe on the road

You can also use your laptop to stay safe while travelling. You can get directions from sites such as www.mapquest.com and access phone numbers from sites such as www.yellowpages.com. You can follow the weather. You can check local petrol prices, read reviews of local restaurants, and find out what places are safe to visit and which are not. You can make air and hotel reservations, check flight arrivals and departures, and read reviews of hotels and camp parks. If you opt for a GPS add-on, you can have your laptop read directions aloud while you drive. You can even download maps.

Getting directions online

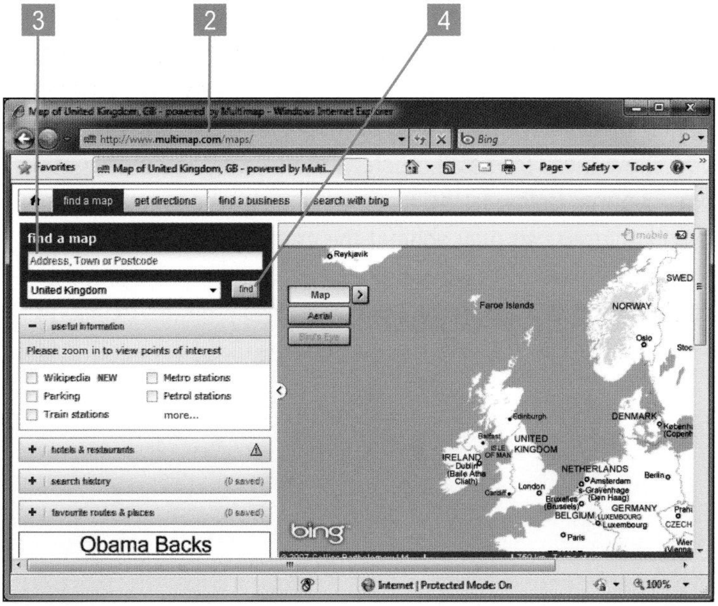

3
2
4
Map of United Kingdom, GB - powered by Multimap - Windows Internet Explorer
http://www.multimap.com/maps/
find a map
get directions
find a business
search with bing
Address, Town or Postcode
United Kingdom
find
useful information
Please zoom in to view points of interest
Wikipedia NEW
Metro stations
Parking
Petrol stations
Train stations
more...
hotels & restaurants
search history
favourite routes & places
Obama Backs
Map
Aerial
Internet | Protected Mode: On
100%

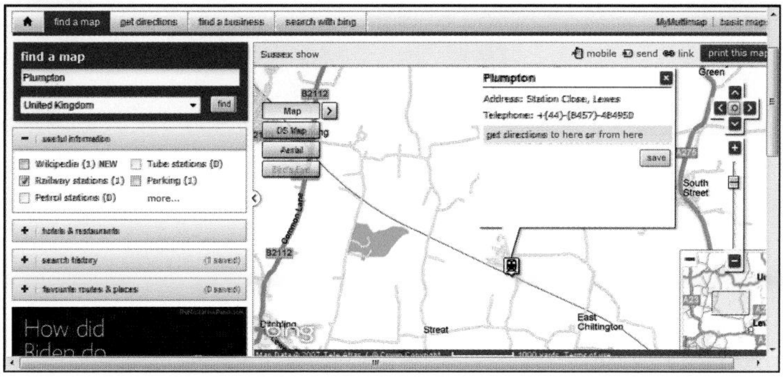

find a map
get directions
find a business
search with bing
Plumpton
United Kingdom
find
useful information
hotels & restaurants
search history
favourite routes & places
How did Biden do
Plumpton
Address: Station Close, Lewes
get directions to here or from here
save
Map
Aerial
South Street
East Chiltington
Streat

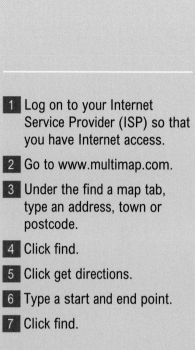

1. Log on to your Internet Service Provider (ISP) so that you have Internet access.
2. Go to www.multimap.com.
3. Under the find a map tab, type an address, town or postcode.
4. Click find.
5. Click get directions.
6. Type a start and end point.
7. Click find.

Entertain your grandchildren

You can use a laptop to entertain your grandchildren too. They can play games, of course, but they can also use Paint to 'draw', Windows Live Mail to send email, Windows Media Center to work with any type of media, and use any programs you allow them to install, such as their own games or applications. Below is the game of Chess, where you or your grandchildren can play against the computer.

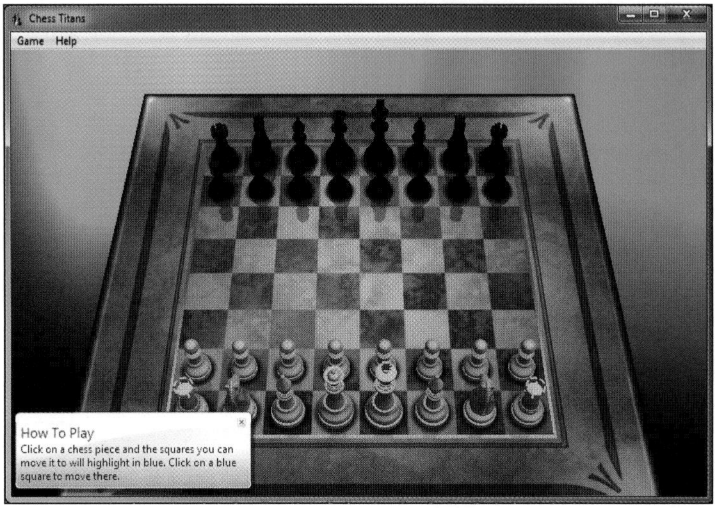
Chess Titans
Game Help
How To Play
Click on a chess piece and the squares you can move it to will highlight in blue. Click on a blue square to move there.

Use your laptop computer ergonomically

Because laptops are small, in general they are harder to use than desktops. Keyboards aren't ergonomic and it's hard sometimes to find a comfortable position for long-term use. For best results, try the following:

- Sit in a chair that is comfortable and that you can lean back in.
- If possible, purchase a laptop 'desk'. You place the desk on your lap, and the laptop on top of it. Men, note that the heat from a laptop can decrease sperm count, which is another plus for a laptop desk.
- Angle the laptop's screen so that you don't have to strain your neck or eyes to see it.
- When working at a desk at home or in the office, consider a computer monitor pedestal and use a 'real' keyboard and mouse. You can connect these via a universal serial bus (USB).

Get started

A laptop is a great piece of equipment. It's awesome for travel, and lets you keep in touch with friends and family no matter where you are or where you're going. And Windows 7 is a great operating system. In this book we'll cover both of these topics.

Next, you'll learn about laptops, including what each port on the outside of the laptop does. Then you'll also learn about things specific only to a laptop keyboard. With that done, you'll explore Windows 7, including the applications you'll need to use your laptop effectively. You'll also learn about what's missing in Windows 7 and how to get it free. If you're ready, let's get started!

Choosing and using a laptop

2

Introduction

If you've yet to purchase a laptop or are considering replacing the laptop you have, read through the tips in this chapter. There are lots of things to consider, including the weight and size of the laptop, its cost and related features, Internet connection options, and things like the amount of (random-access memory) RAM, hard-drive space and processor speed. You'll also want to consider things such as laptop bags, additional batteries, extended warranties and set-up services. Some of these aren't necessary and are a waste of money.

What you'll do

Visit a computer store and ask questions

Check out the manufacturer's website

Make the purchase

Things to consider when shopping for a laptop

If you're shopping for a laptop or if you're considering replacing an older laptop or desktop PC, there are several things to consider before you buy. If you're planning to travel via aeroplane, for instance, you'll want to research the laptop's weight and size. The smaller and lighter the laptop is, the easier it will be to travel with. If you travel mostly in a motorhome or car, weight and size may not be an issue. In both cases though, the laptop needs to be large enough so that you can use it easily, making these factors even more complex. You'll also want to consider cost, features, speed and how the keyboard feels when you type on it.

Weight and size

A typical laptop weighs between 1.8 and 3.6 kilos. You can get 'ultralight' models that weigh about 1.4 kilos, but they can be much more expensive and often lack features other laptops have, such as DVD drives. When purchasing a laptop, make sure it's not too heavy if you plan to travel with it in tow, such as on an aeroplane. However, if your main mode of travel is a cruise ship, car or motorhome, a heavier laptop may actually be an asset, because it will be less likely to fall when you're in motion.

When a laptop is small, it may be hard to use the keyboard and pointing device. You might consider carrying a small mouse with you on your travels.

Ergonomics

You'll want to test the keyboard before you buy a laptop. The finest laptop will become a burden if you can't type effectively. This happens more often than you think; I have a laptop whose keyboard is so hard to use that I actually bring along an external keyboard and mouse, and connect them using the laptop's USB ports. This defeats the main purpose of the laptop: portability and convenience.

A laptop's small size can make it less comfortable to use too. Often, your laptop's display is not set at eye level, and the keyboard is not properly positioned for best posture.

Things to consider when shopping for a laptop (cont.)

If possible, try to improve your position by putting the laptop on a hotel room's desk, raising or lowering your chair, or building a special table or tray for your motorhome.

Cost and features

PC desktops are less expensive than laptops, and are more easily upgraded if you need or want additional features later. Because it's nearly impossible to add features internally to a laptop, like a DVD drive, FireWire port, or larger hard drive, it's important to find a laptop you really like, that offers the features you want right from the beginning. I'll spell out later what you should look for, but make sure you save enough money to get the laptop you need, and not the laptop you can afford.

One thing you'll need to decide is if you like the touchpad offered in many laptops, or if you'd like to shop for something else. Many people have a touchpad but connect a mouse. It's up to you.

Reliability

Laptops are more prone to accidents than PCs because you take them with you, and can be damaged if they are exposed to too much heat, humidity or vibration. Of course, a laptop can be stolen, lost or even damaged, making it unavailable. When considering a laptop, know that you'll have to be

Things to consider when shopping for a laptop (cont.)

extremely careful with it, and keep it safe from harm. Make sure, when you purchase a laptop, that you can secure it with a lock, preferably a Kensington lock.

Connectivity

When purchasing a laptop, make sure it includes Ethernet and wireless networking. You don't know where your travels will take you, and it's best to be prepared for any type of connection. An Ethernet cable looks like a phone cord, only the ends are slightly larger.

Visiting a computer store and asking questions

1 If you're close to a computer store, visit it in person.

2 At the store ask the following questions:
   a. What is your least expensive laptop?
   b. What is your most expensive laptop?
   c. What are the differences?
   d. What features are absolutely necessary?
   e. What features are not necessary?

3 Tell the salesperson how you plan to use the laptop.

4 Ask the salesperson the following questions:
   a. What laptop would you suggest?
   b. Will a less expensive model work?
   c. Is this laptop rugged enough for what I want to do?
   d. Can you show me any independent reviews of this laptop?

5 Leave the store without buying anything.

Shopping checklist

I can't tell you exactly what you'll need in a laptop, but I can help you choose one by providing a list of things you'll probably want. Here are some things to consider:

- A capable processor. Almost all laptops have a processor that is fast enough to handle email, web surfing, uploading and viewing photos, and keeping a journal. That said, you may not need to purchase a laptop with the fastest processor to get a laptop you'll love. If you plan to render movies in Movie Maker though, or if you need to use Photoshop or other high-end graphics programs, you'll need a faster processor than what you'll find in your basic laptop.
- Additional processors. If you play games that require lots of calculations, create your own movies or perform other resource-intensive tasks (you'll know if you do), consider additional processors. Some laptops come with dual processors or graphics cards with processors built in.
- More RAM. RAM (random access memory) is where your laptop will temporarily store information while it processes it. You should get a laptop that has at least 2 gigabytes (GB) of memory. Get more if you can afford it.
- Hard drive space. A hard drive is where your data are stored. Digital music, photos and video take up a surprisingly large amount of hard drive space. Make sure you get at least 160 GB of hard drive space and get more if you can afford it.
- Size and weight. Carefully consider a laptop's weight. Although 3.2 kilos may not feel like a heavy piece of equipment now, after carrying it, along with a power cable, adapters, computer case and other peripherals from your car to the airport terminal, you'll be wishing you'd opted for the 1.8 kilo model. Trust me on this.
- Battery life. Always look at battery life, and if you can't afford a model that offers long battery life, buy an extra battery.
- Wireless – the laptop should have Ethernet and connectivity capabilities.
- Dimensions – the size of the screen is a big part of selecting a laptop. It may seem like a 17- or 19-inch screen is the way to go, until you try to use it on an aeroplane. And, a 12.5 or 15-inch screen may seem perfect for you too, until you want

Did you know?

The best way to compare battery life, weight, processor speed, RAM and other components is to go to an electronics store where laptops are offered for sale side-by-side, and where you can compare price and features.

Shopping checklist (cont.)

to do some image-editing. Of course, it's likely the larger screen size will cause the weight of the laptop to increase. You'll have to weigh carefully where and how you'll use your laptop before deciding on a screen size.

- DVD drive – opt for a laptop that can, at the very least, play DVDs. If possible, spend the extra money to get a DVD writeable drive.

To sum up, here's what you'll want to look for if:

- you only want to check email, surf the web, keep a journal and upload a picture or two. Compare prices of brand name computers. Any laptop these days can handle these tasks, no matter how slow the processor or how little RAM (provided it's new, that is). Make sure, if you buy a lower-end laptop, that it comes with Ethernet and wireless capabilities.
- you travel a lot. Focus on weight, battery life and how well the keyboard responds to your typing style. Make sure you get at least 2 GB of RAM, 160 GB hard drive and wireless capabilities.
- you play a lot of games. Make sure you get a high end graphics chip, graphics card and a powerful processor. You'll also want a 17-inch or larger high-resolution monitor. If you focus on this, you'll get plenty of RAM and other features.
- you love all things media and/or want to create home movies. Focus on getting a large hard drive (500 GB), dual core processor and 4 GB+ of RAM. You may even want to purchase an external hard drive, shown here.

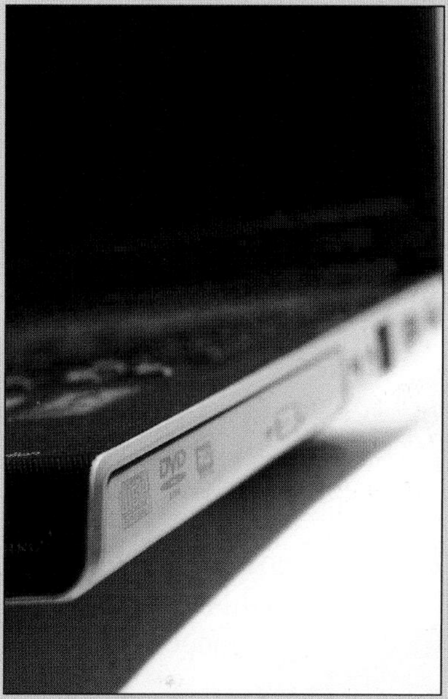

USB2.0
1394

Checking out the manufacturer's website

1. After you've selected the laptop you want to buy, or have narrowed it down to a few makes and models, visit the manufacturer's website(s).
2. Browse through the site. Look for Support and/or Help pages.
3. See if there is an online or chat option for getting support.
4. Call the manufacturer's help line to see how long it takes to talk to a support person.
5. See how expensive additional components are, such as additional RAM, external speakers and the like.
6. See how much it would cost to purchase the laptop through this website versus the store.

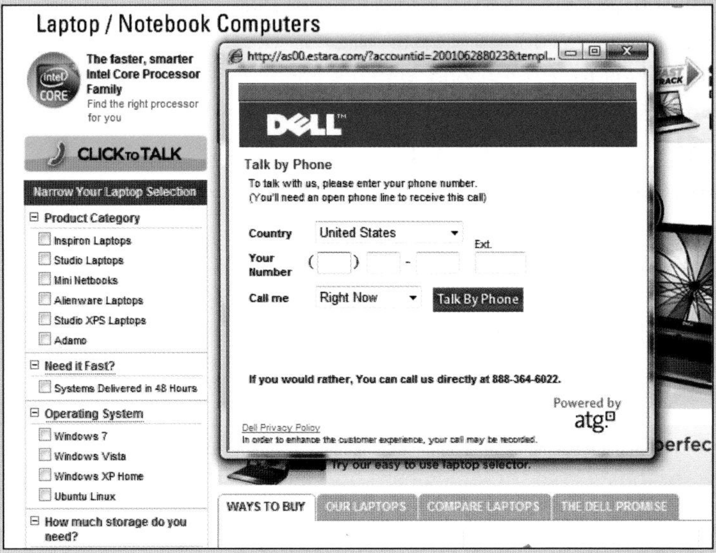

Laptop / Notebook Computers
The faster, smarter Intel Core Processor Family
Find the right processor for you
CLICK TO TALK
Narrow Your Laptop Selection
Product Category
Inspiron Laptops
Studio Laptops
Mini Netbooks
Alienware Laptops
Studio XPS Laptops
Adamo
Need it Fast?
Systems Delivered in 48 Hours
Operating System
Windows 7
Windows Vista
Windows XP Home
Ubuntu Linux
How much storage do you need?
DELL
Talk by Phone
To talk with us, please enter your phone number.
(You'll need an open phone line to receive this call)
Country
United States
Your Number
Ext.
Call me
Right Now
Talk By Phone
If you would rather, You can call us directly at 888-364-6022.
Powered by atg
Dell Privacy Policy
In order to enhance the customer experience, your call may be recorded.
Try our easy to use laptop selector.
WAYS TO BUY
OUR LAPTOPS
COMPARE LAPTOPS
THE DELL PROMISE

Choosing a rugged laptop

Yes, there is such a thing as a rugged laptop. You'll want to consider a rugged laptop if you plan to take your laptop with you on a safari or mountain climbing excursion, for instance. Rugged laptops have sealed keyboards and casings and are thus better protected from water, humidity, sand and dust. Even the external ports are protected with plastic covers.

Rugged laptops also have a stronger outer shell, offering internal protection for the central processing unit (CPU), hard disk drive and optical drives. This means, if you drop it, it's less likely to be damaged, and it's less susceptible to shock and vibration than regular laptops are. Many rugged laptops can also repel rain, snow, sleet, hail, wind, fog, dust, sand, extreme cold and heat, salt spray and/or humidity.

If your travels will take you to places where a normal laptop would fail, consider a rugged laptop. (A rugged laptop may be just what your clumsy spouse needs too!)

Making the purchase

1. Make sure the laptop meets your needs.
2. Do not purchase an additional warranty or sign up for any 'services'. You can load anti-virus software, configure a screensaver and input your user name.
3. Purchase an additional battery if you think you will be travelling away from power sources often.
4. Purchase an Ethernet cable and keep it with you.
5. If you have a motorhome, consider purchasing a second power supply so you don't have to pack it when you leave.
6. Consider purchasing a laptop desk.
7. Look over Internet subscription plans if you don't have one. Don't purchase a plan at the store, though; just look at your options.
8. Look at computer bags. Before purchasing one, read the information in Appendix B of this book.
9. If you don't already have one, purchase a surge protector.

Extended warranties

There's no doubt you'll be asked to purchase an extended warranty when you purchase your laptop. This warranty is supposed to cover everything from drops to spills to hard drive crashes to mechanical failures. Don't fall for this scam. It's highly unlikely you'll need the coverage, and highly unlikely you'll be covered if something does happen.

An extended warranty is supposed to act as an insurance package. The multi-page document you'll sign when you purchase it will explain what the extended warranty covers. If you really are sold on the idea of an extended warranty, ask to see the agreement. Read it carefully, ask questions, and beware of vague references to what 'damage' is covered. If you really want to insure your laptop, consider your own home or car insurance company, or opt for a company that is in the business of covering electronics.

Exploring the outside of the laptop

3

What you'll do

- Locate and use the power cable
- Locate and use USB ports
- Locate and use FireWire ports
- Locate and use Ethernet ports
- Locate and use Bluetooth technology
- Locate and use an external monitor port
- Locate and use sound ports
- Locate and use a modem port
- Locate and insert or remove the battery

Introduction

A laptop is much smaller than a desktop PC, but the ports you'll have access to are basically the same. Like a desktop PC you'll likely have access to USB ports, an Ethernet port and an external monitor port. You'll probably also see a place to connect speakers or headphones. There might also be a place to plug in a phone cord to access the Internet via dial-up, a FireWire port, or even a slot for inserting a SD card from a digital camera. Depending on the make and model, there may be other options too, such as a serial port or additional USB ports. Practically all laptops come with a disk drive for viewing and/or burning CDs/DVDs too. You may even have a Bluetooth connection. It's a lot to explore.

The best way to find out what's available on your laptop is to read the documentation that came with it. If you can't find the physical guide, there might be one installed on your laptop. To find out, click Start, and in the Start Search window, type User Guide (or User's Guide). If you find one, click it in the Start menu results to open it.

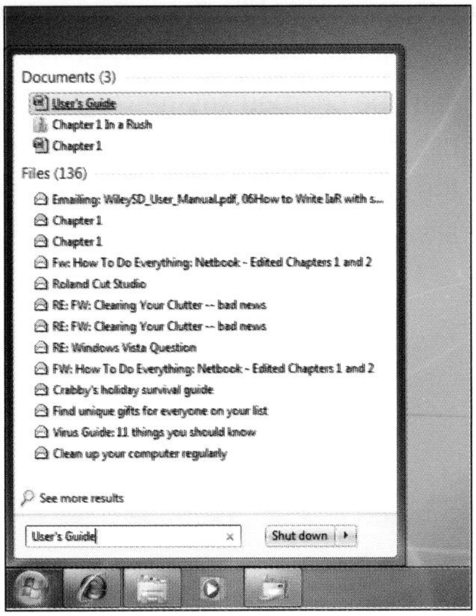

Documents (3)
User's Guide
Chapter 1 In a Rush
Chapter 1
Files (136)
Chapter 1
Chapter 1
Roland Cut Studio
RE: FW: Clearing Your Clutter -- bad news
RE: FW: Clearing Your Clutter -- bad news
RE: Windows Vista Question
Crabby's holiday survival guide
Find unique gifts for everyone on your list
Virus Guide: 11 things you should know
Clean up your computer regularly
See more results
User's Guide
Shut down

Did you know?

If a User's Guide is not available, you can probably visit the manufacturer's website and download one.

A User's Guide will help you discover more about the laptop. The User Guide will show what is available on the outside of the laptop, detail features specific to it, and offer tips for using it safely, among other things.

You can also find out what's installed using Device Manager or System Information, both included with Windows 7 and both equally cryptic when it comes to discovering what's physically installed on your computer. However you discover what is available on your laptop, even if it's simply eyeing what's on the outside, you need to know what each of these ports looks like, what they do, and how to use them.

A power cable is the cable that you will use to connect the laptop to the wall outlet (power outlet). You can connect and disconnect the power cable at any time, even when the computer is running. When you connect the power cable both to the laptop and the power outlet, the laptop will use the power from the outlet and charge the battery at the same time. When you unplug the laptop from the power outlet, the laptop will run on stored battery power.

If you always use your laptop at home, and it's always plugged in, you can remove the battery so that it does not continually charge itself. You can then insert the battery and charge it when you need to. This will lengthen the life of the battery; because a battery can only be charged so many times and then can't be charged any more, it'll last longer. However, if you use the laptop a lot while it's running on battery power, leave the laptop plugged in when you can; that way the battery will always be fully charged when you need it.

USB ports, or Universal Serial Bus ports, offer a place to connect USB devices. USB devices include mice, external keyboards, mobile phones, digital cameras and other devices, including USB flash drives. You may have a small USB printer or scanner for instance, or a USB flash drive that you use for backing up data. USB cables don't always come with USB devices you purchase, so, although you may have a USB device, unless you've purchased a USB cable separately, you may not have a USB cable.

The universal symbol for USB is shown here. Two USB ports are shown as well. The picture of the USB port was taken from my laptop's User Guide, and you may be able to find a similar user guide with pictures of your laptop. USB ports are rectangular and small. Your laptop probably includes at least two of these ports but may have four or more.

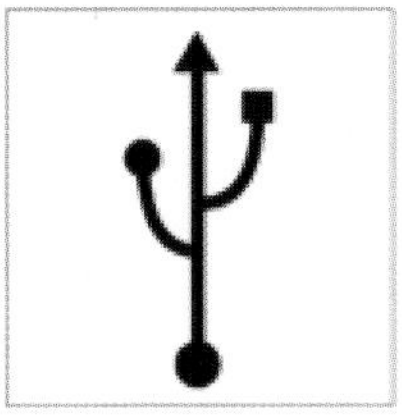

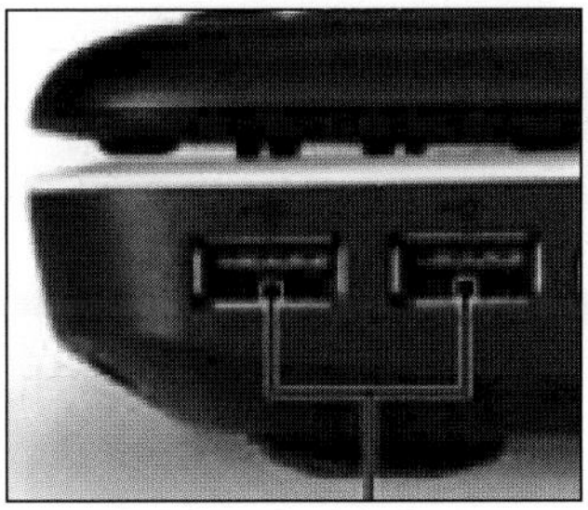

Locating and using the power cable

1. Locate the power cord. It may consist of two pieces that need to be connected. One end will be small and plug into the power port on your PC; the other end will plug into a wall outlet.
2. Connect the power cord to the back or side of the laptop as noted in the documentation. In almost all cases, there is only one port that a power cord can fit in to. It if doesn't fit, it's not the right port. You may see a symbol similar to the one shown here.

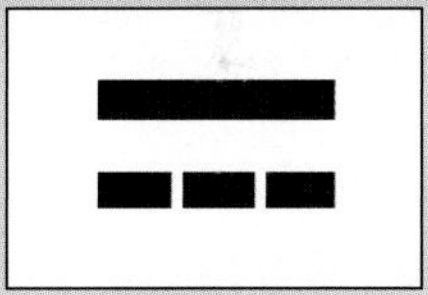

3. Plug the power cord into the wall outlet.

3

Locating and using USB ports

1. Locate a USB cable. It is sometimes rectangular on one end and almost square on the other. Both ends will likely look the same though; small and rectangular.
2. Plug the proper end of the USB cable into an empty USB port on your laptop. If it fits, it's the proper end.
3. Connect the other end to the USB device.
4. Often, you'll need to turn on the USB device to have Windows 7 recognise it but not always. You do not generally have to 'turn on' USB storage units, such as flash drives.
5. Most of the time you can see USB devices in the computer window. Just click Start and then Computer. Here, an empty USB flash drive is shown as Removable Disk (E:).

FireWire, also called IEEE 1394, is often used to connect digital video cameras, professional audio hardware and external hard drives to a laptop. FireWire connections are much faster than USB, and are better than anything else when you need to transfer large amounts of data, such as digital video.

Unlike USB devices, many devices that require a FireWire cable often come with one. When searching for a FireWire port on your newer laptop, look for an extremely small, rectangular port, with the numbers 1394 beside it, or a symbol similar to this. On an older laptop, the FireWire port may be larger, but often these larger FireWire ports were used only on older desktop PCs.

Did you know?

The images in this book have been made to appear larger than they do by default. You'll learn how to make your computer easier to see and use throughout the book.

Computer
Search Computer
Organize
System properties
Favorites
Desktop
Downloads
Recent Places
Libraries
Documents
Music
Pictures
Videos
Homegroup
Computer
Network
Hard Disk Drives (1)
Local Disk (C:)
Devices with Removable Storage (2)
DVD
DVD RW Drive (D:)
Removable Disk (E:)
JOLI-PC Workgroup: WORKGROUP
Memory: 2.00 GB
Processor: AMD Turion(tm) 64 X2 ...

Ethernet, also called RJ-45, is used to connect a laptop to a local, wired, network. If you have a cable modem, router or other high-speed Internet device at home, you'll likely use Ethernet to connect to it. If you want to connect to a hotel network, you may use Ethernet to do that too. An Ethernet cable looks like a telephone cable, except both ends are slightly larger. Both ends of an Ethernet cable are the same though, which is unlike some of the other cables we've discussed so far. The universal symbol for Ethernet is shown here.

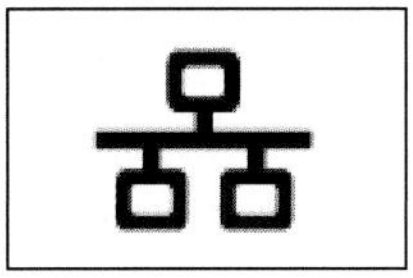

When looking for an Ethernet port on your laptop, look for this symbol and/or an almost square port. The Ethernet cable will snap in.

Locating and using FireWire ports

1. Locate your FireWire cable.
2. Plug the appropriate end of the cable into the FireWire device.
3. Plug the other end of the cable into the FireWire port on the laptop. (Not all laptops have this port.)
4. Often, you'll have to turn on the FireWire device for Windows 7 to recognise it.

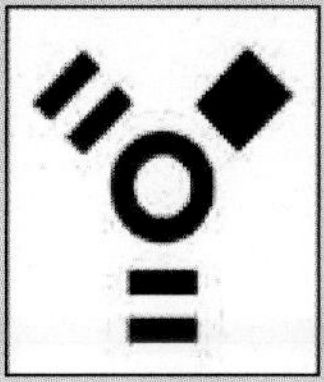

Locating and using Ethernet ports

1. Locate an Ethernet cable. You should have one if you've installed a local network at home. You may have to borrow one from the front desk if you're using a hotel network.
2. Connect the cable to both the laptop and the Ethernet outlet on a router or cable modem (or a wall in a hotel).

If you've seen people talking on their mobile phones using a headset (while leaving their mobile phones in their pockets or purses), you've seen Bluetooth technology in action. Bluetooth is used to create 'personal' networks, to connect devices that are in close range. A laptop may come with built-in Bluetooth capabilities (although this is not very common), or you can add it by purchasing and installing a USB Bluetooth dongle. A Bluetooth dongle is a small device, about the size of a USB flash drive, and it connects directly to a USB port on the outside of the laptop.

Once a Bluetooth dongle is installed, Bluetooth connections can be made between your laptop and any of the following Bluetooth enabled devices (and this is not a complete list): mobile phones, other laptops, PCs, printers, GPS receivers, digital cameras and game consoles. The universal symbol for Bluetooth is shown here.

My Bluetooth
Places

Did you know?

Bluetooth is best used when the two devices are close together and very little data needs to be transferred (as is the case with a mobile phone and Bluetooth headset).

Most laptops come with an external monitor port. With this port you can connect your laptop to a secondary monitor or network projector where you can mirror what you see on the laptop's screen or extend the screen to the second monitor. If you travel with a laptop in a motorhome, and watch DVDs or TV using it, consider purchasing and storing a secondary display.

The universal symbol for an external display (VGA) port is shown here, above the actual 15-pin VGA port.

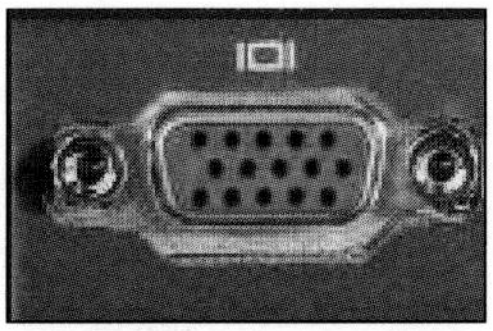

?

Did you know?

When a VGA is used as a second monitor, it can be used to duplicate or extend what's on the screen.

Locating and using Bluetooth technology

1. If necessary, insert the Bluetooth dongle and install any drivers required.
2. On the laptop, click My Bluetooth Places, or whatever icon represents the Bluetooth device you installed.
3. Turn on the external Bluetooth device.
4. Work through the set-up wizard as prompted.

Locating and using an external monitor port

1 Locate a port on your laptop that is in the shape of a trapezoid and contains 15-pin holes. Look for this icon.

2 Configure a secondary display to this port using the cable attached to the display.

3 Turn on the display.

4 When prompted, select how to use the display. Computer only is the default, and you can click Duplicate, Extend or Projector only as desired.

Did you know?

If you are not prompted to configure the display as shown here, press and hold the Windows key and press P.

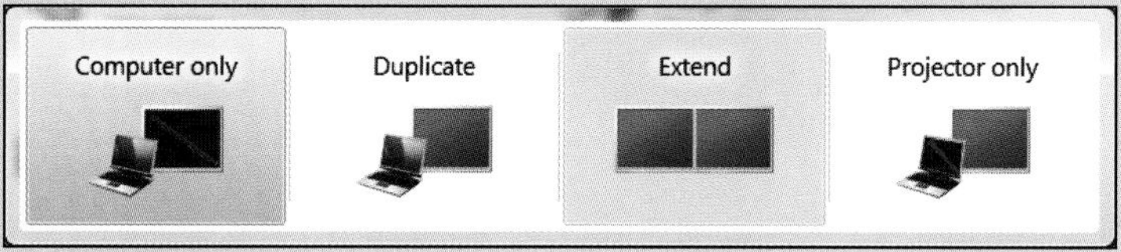
Computer only
Duplicate
Extend
Projector only

If there are any external sound ports, you'll probably see three. Most of the time you have access to a line-in jack, a microphone-in jack and a headphones/speaker/line-out jack. The symbols for these are shown here.

	Line-in jack
	Microphone-in jack
SPDIF	Headphones/speaker/ line-out jack with SPDIF support

A line-in jack accepts audio from external devices, such as CD players. A microphone-in jack accepts input from external microphones. A headphones/speaker/line-out jack lets you connect your laptop to an external source for output, including but not limited to speakers and headphones.

Locating and using sound ports

1. If necessary, plug the device into an electrical outlet (speakers) or insert batteries (portable music players).
2. If necessary, turn on the device.
3. Insert the cables that connect to the device to the laptop in the proper port. Remember, line-in jacks bring data into the laptop; line-out jacks port data out to external devices such as speakers or headphones.
4. If prompted, work through any set-up processes.

Locating and using a modem port

1. Connect the laptop to a phone jack using a telephone cord.
2. Connect using your dial-up Internet connection.

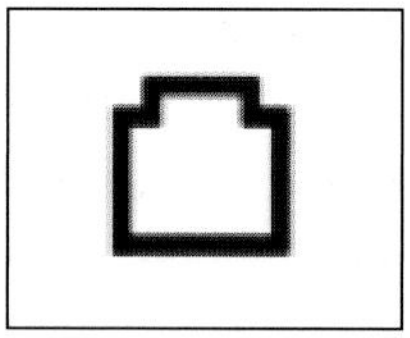

A modem port lets you connect your laptop to a phone jack using a standard telephone cord. Once connected, you can connect to the Internet using a dial-up connection, provided you've signed up for a dial-up Internet subscription. The telephone cable must be connected to both the wall and the laptop to connect. Here's the universal symbol for a dial-up modem.

There are several items that have to do with the battery, and they're probably all located on the underside of your laptop. Before you turn the laptop upside-down to look at them, make sure to turn off the laptop and unplug it.

You'll probably find the following items on the back of the laptop, at least regarding the battery:

- Battery bay – this holds the computer battery. Sometimes you have to use a screwdriver to get inside the battery bay, other times you simply need to slide out the compartment door.
- Battery release latch – this latch holds the battery in place, even after the battery bay's door has been opened. You'll need to release this latch to get to the battery.
- Battery lock – this locks the battery in position.

at&t Communication Manager
Windows Live Mail
Connect to a Projector
Remote Desktop Connection
Sticky Notes
Snipping Tool
Paint
Calculator
Getting Started
XPS Viewer
Windows Fax and Scan
All Programs
Search programs and files
Joli
Documents
Pictures
Music
Computer
Control Panel
Devices and Printers
Default Programs
Help and Support
Shut down
1

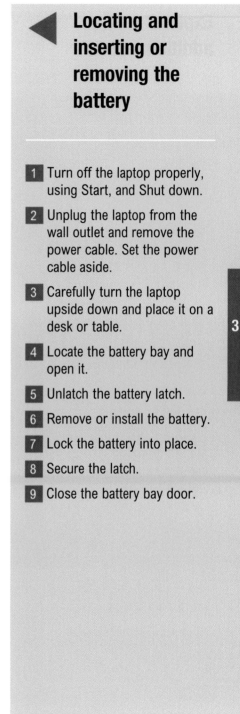

Locating and inserting or removing the battery

1. Turn off the laptop properly, using Start, and Shut down.
2. Unplug the laptop from the wall outlet and remove the power cable. Set the power cable aside.
3. Carefully turn the laptop upside down and place it on a desk or table.
4. Locate the battery bay and open it.
5. Unlatch the battery latch.
6. Remove or install the battery.
7. Lock the battery into place.
8. Secure the latch.
9. Close the battery bay door.

Explore additional ports

The ports detailed in this chapter are common ports you'll see on most laptops. However, high-end laptops have other ports. You may have one or more of the following:

- Kensington lock slot – to connect the laptop to a lock to prevent it from being stolen from a hotel or motorhome.
- DVI port – used to connect the laptop to a television set or other DVI device.
- S-video – used to connect the laptop to a television or other display that also offers s-video connectivity.
- SD card slots or card readers – used to accept digital memory cards found in digital cameras and similar technologies.
- ExpressCard – used to insert an ExpressCard where you can expand your laptop's capabilities by offering additional ways to connect devices. ExpressCards are often used to offer wireless capabilities.
- AV-in – accepts input from various audio/video devices.
- RF-in – accepts input signal from digital TV tuners.

4

Exploring the inside

What you'll do

Locate basic features

Use the touchpad

Use common keys

Use the arrow keys

Use the function keys

Introduction

When you open your laptop for the first time, you'll likely be able to find the power button, keyboard keys, touchpad or trackball, and the display screen, but you can be sure there are plenty of hidden features. There may be a microphone, webcam, speakers and 'easy-launch' buttons, for starters. To get the most out of your laptop you should be aware of all of the features, and if configurable, personalise them.

Your laptop is probably not the same make and model as mine, nor is it the same as other readers' models, so this chapter may seem a bit generic. All laptops do have display screens, keyboards, arrow keys, specialised keys and function keys. Most have buttons that you configure too, buttons that will open, with a single click, your email application, web browser, music program or favourite application. We'll look at all of this here, starting with basic functionality.

Important

The best way to find out what's available inside your laptop is to read the documentation that came with it, as noted in Chapter 3. If you can't find the physical guide, there might be one installed on your laptop. To find out, click Start, and in the Start Search window, type User Guide (or User's Guide). If you find one, click it in the Start menu results to open it. If a User's Guide is not available, you can probably visit the manufacturer's website and download one.

Basic functionality

Some features are included in all laptops. There's some sort of a latch for opening the laptop, a power button for turning it on, some sort of pointing device (often a touchpad) and, of course, the display. There may also be a microphone or webcam. Let's find them.

2

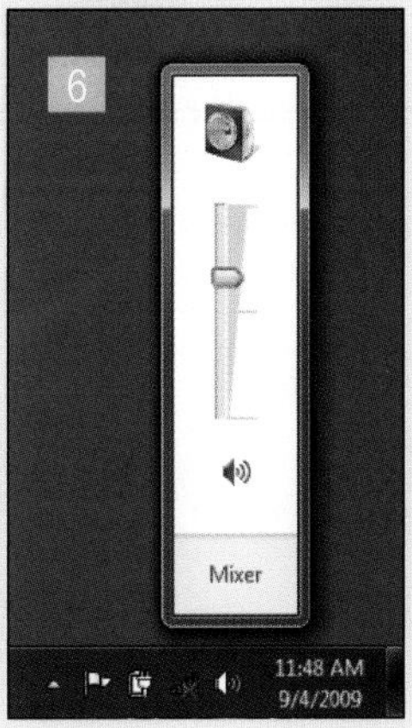
6
Mixer
11:48 AM
9/4/2009

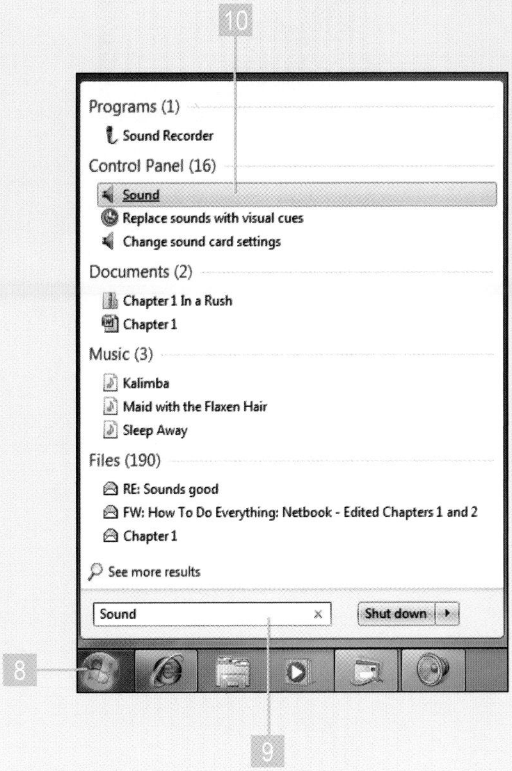
10
Programs (1)
Sound Recorder
Control Panel (16)
Sound
Replace sounds with visual cues
Change sound card settings
Documents (2)
Chapter 1 In a Rush
Chapter 1
Music (3)
Kalimba
Maid with the Flaxen Hair
Sleep Away
Files (190)
RE: Sounds good
FW: How To Do Everything: Netbook - Edited Chapters 1 and 2
Chapter 1
See more results
Sound
Shut down
8
9

Locating basic features

1 Locate the latch on the outside of the laptop to open the lid.

2 Locate the power button. It may have the universal power button symbol on it. Press it to boot the computer.

3 Watch the computer's progress on the display screen.

4 When the computer has finished its startup tasks, look to the bottom of the display screen. Locate the Volume icon in the Notification area.

5 Click the Volume icon one time.

6 Use the slider to increase or decrease the volume.

7 Follow the sound to locate the speakers.

8 Click Start.

9 In the Start Search window, type sound.

10 In the results list, under Control Panel, click Sound.

Locating basic features (cont.)

11 Click the Recording tab.

12 Locate a working microphone. Here, one microphone is active.

13 Click OK.

14 Look for a small camera eye, which should be located at the top of the display. This is the webcam. You may or may not see a webcam lens and/or a webcam may not be included with your laptop. To find out, complete steps 15–18.

15 Click Start.

16 In the Start Search window, type Devices.

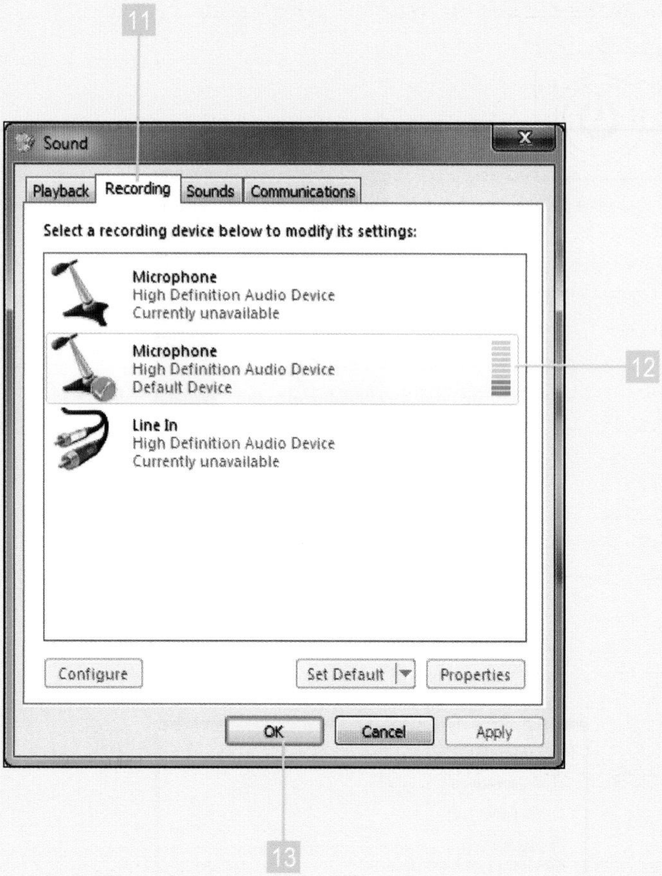

11
Sound
Playback
Recording
Sounds
Communications
Select a recording device below to modify its settings:
Microphone
High Definition Audio Device
Currently unavailable
Microphone
High Definition Audio Device
Default Device
Line In
High Definition Audio Device
Currently unavailable
12
Configure
Set Default
Properties
OK
Cancel
Apply
13

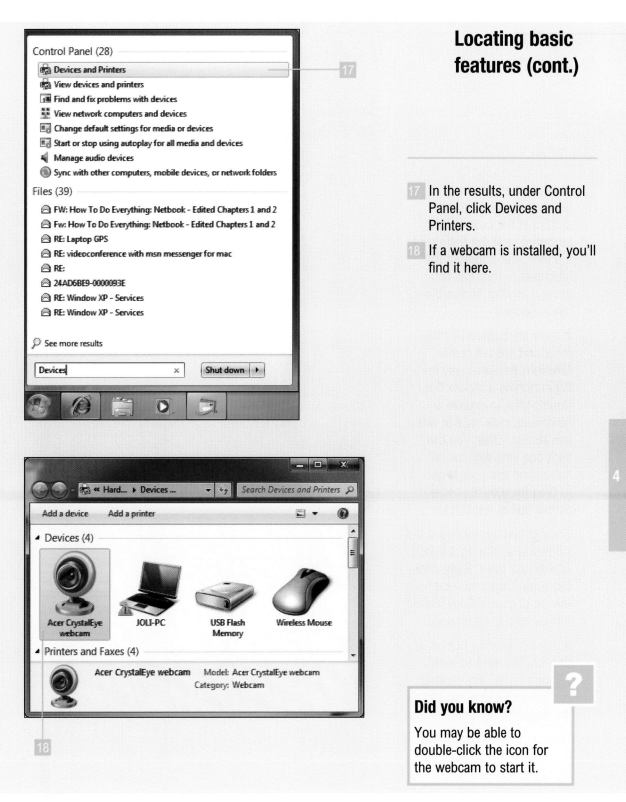

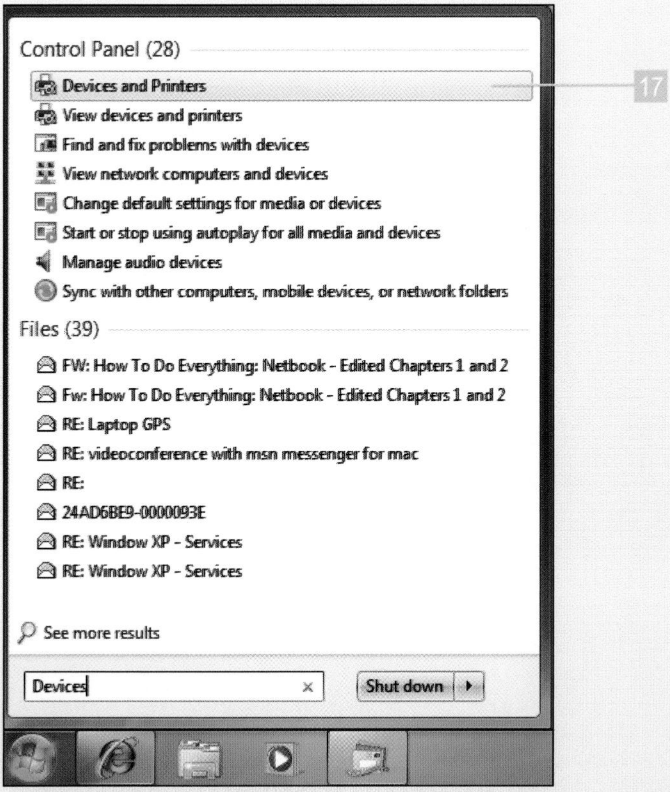
Control Panel (28)
Devices and Printers
View devices and printers
Find and fix problems with devices
View network computers and devices
Change default settings for media or devices
Start or stop using autoplay for all media and devices
Manage audio devices
Sync with other computers, mobile devices, or network folders
Files (39)
FW: How To Do Everything: Netbook - Edited Chapters 1 and 2
Fw: How To Do Everything: Netbook - Edited Chapters 1 and 2
RE: Laptop GPS
RE: videoconference with msn messenger for mac
RE:
24AD6BE9-0000093E
RE: Window XP - Services
RE: Window XP - Services
See more results
Devices
Shut down
17

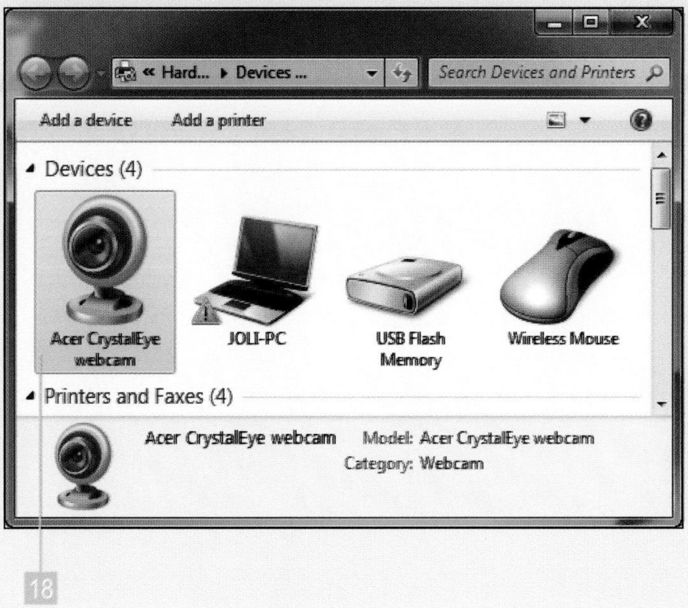
« Hard... ▸ Devices ...
Search Devices and Printers
Add a device
Add a printer
Devices (4)
Acer CrystalEye webcam
JOLI-PC
USB Flash Memory
Wireless Mouse
Printers and Faxes (4)
Acer CrystalEye webcam
Model: Acer CrystalEye webcam
Category: Webcam
18

Locating basic features (cont.)

17 In the results, under Control Panel, click Devices and Printers.

18 If a webcam is installed, you'll find it here.

Did you know?

You may be able to double-click the icon for the webcam to start it.

Using the touchpad

Important

Keep your fingers and hands clean when using the touchpad. It has a sensitive surface.

1. The touchpad or other pointing device is usually located in the centre of the keyboard or at the bottom of it. Place your finger on the touchpad or trackball and move it around. Notice the mouse moves.
2. If there are buttons, for the most part, the left button functions the same way the left button on a mouse does. Double-click to execute a command, click once to select something. (Often you can click one time with the left button and use your finger to drag the mouse pointer across text to select it.)
3. The right button functions the same way as the right button of a mouse does. Right-click one time to open context menus to access Copy, Select All and similar commands.
4. If there is a centre button, this is often used to scroll through pages. Try clicking and holding it to move up, down, left or right on a page.

Keys common to most keyboards

Most laptop keyboards have more than a few universal keys and, much of the time, these keys offer the same things across makes and models. For instance, pressing F1 almost always opens a Help window for the open application. The Windows key opens the Start menu, and the Windows key in combination with other keys will do other things, such as minimise all windows (Start + M) or lock your computer (Start + L). The Caps Lock key makes sure anything you type appears in capital letters only, and the Num Lock key makes sure your number pad offers numbers and nothing else.

There are arrow keys too, which you can use to move around in a web page, document or other window. Page Up and Page Down keys let you move around as well. And there are always Function keys, which offer shortcuts to specific computer-related functions, most of which are make and model specific.

There are literally hundreds of keyboard shortcuts, and my goal in this chapter does not include listing them or suggesting you learn them. However, the Windows Start key, also called the Windows Logo key, can be a real time saver if you can get in the habit of using it regularly. That said, here are a few shortcuts you can commit to memory:

- Windows Logo key – open the Start Menu.
- Windows Logo key + E – open Computer.
- Windows Logo key + D – Show Desktop (and minimise all open windows).
- Windows Logo key + M – minimise all windows.
- Windows Logo key + Shift + M – maximise all minimised windows.
- Windows Logo key + L – switch between users or lock the laptop.
- Windows Logo key + F – open Search.
- Windows Logo Key + F1 – open Help and Support.

Keys common to most keyboards (cont.)

Additionally, here are some general keys and their common uses:

- Ctrl – this key rarely does anything by itself, but when pressed with other keys, does. Ctrl + Alt + Del opens a new screen where you can lock the computer, switch users, log off, change a password or start Task Manager, for instance. Here are a few options you may like to explore:
  - Ctrl + O – opens the Open window where you can search for and open a file, folder or program.
  - Ctrl + P – opens the Print dialog box.
  - Ctrl + S – saves the current document.
  - Ctrl + T – opens a new tab in Internet Explorer.
- Esc – stops the current activity, usually.
- Tab – advances the cursor to the next tab stop.
- Shift – like the Ctrl key, generally does nothing by itself, but when used with other keys, performs tasks. Here are a few options you may like to explore:
  - Shift + F10 – opens a context menu you'd normally get by right clicking.
  - Shift + Delete – deletes the selected item permanently.
  - Shift + any letter – in a Word document, capitalises the letter you type.
- Home/End – Home moves the cursor to the beginning of a paragraph, line or document, depending on the current placement of the cursor. End moves the cursor to the end of the paragraph, line or document.
- Fn – like Shift and Ctrl, doesn't do anything by itself, but instead is used to access items listed on the F1, F2, F3, etc. keys. The items listed are laptop specific and may offer options to change the volume, lock the laptop, put the laptop to sleep, set Num Lock or Scroll Lock and more.
- Scroll Lock – varies depending on the application open and is rarely used on today's laptops.

Using common keys

1 Click the Windows Logo key to the Start menu.

2 Click the Windows Logo key (which I'll call the Start key from here forward) to close the Start menu.

3 Click the Start key + E to open Computer.

4 Click the Start key + F to open a Search window.

5 Click the Start key + F1 to open Help and Support.

6 Click the Start key + D to show the Desktop.

7 Click the Start key + Shift + M to maximise all minimised windows.

8 Click the X at the top of each of the open windows to close each one.

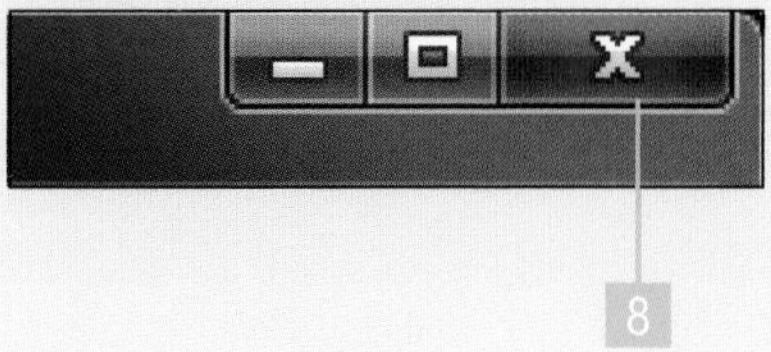

X
8

4

Using common keys (cont.)

9 Locate the button for Internet Explorer on the Taskbar. The Taskbar runs across the bottom of your screen and the Internet Explorer button looks like a big, blue e.

10 Click Ctrl + T to open a new tab (where you can type an Internet address).

11 Click Shift + F10 to open a context menu you'd normally get by right-clicking inside Internet Explorer.

12 Close Internet Explorer.

9

Using the arrow keys

2

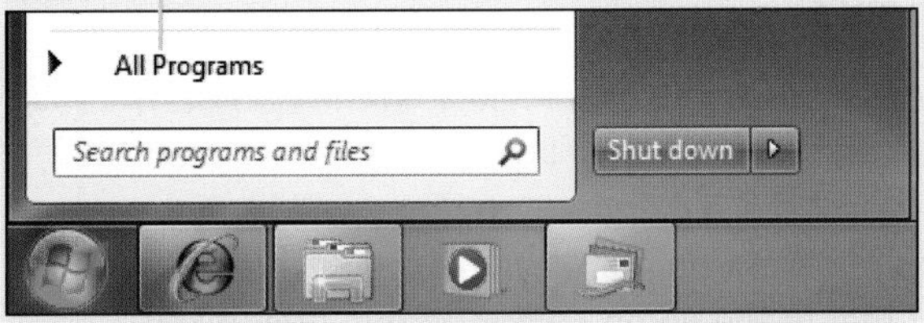

All Programs
Search programs and files
Shut down

4

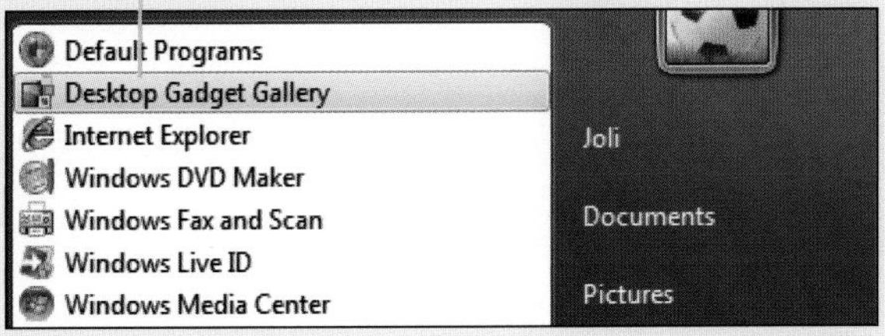

Default Programs
Desktop Gadget Gallery
Internet Explorer
Windows DVD Maker
Windows Fax and Scan
Windows Live ID
Windows Media Center
Joli
Documents
Pictures

1. Click Start.
2. Click All Programs.
3. Click Desktop Gadget Gallery to open it.
4. Use the arrow keys on the keyboard to move through the gadgets.
5. Click the X in the top right corner of the Gadget Gallery to close it.

4

?

Did you know?

A 'gadget' is a small program icon you can drag to your Desktop for up-to-date information on things such as the weather, the time or the news.

Using the Function keys

1. Locate the Fn key on your keyboard. If you do not see an Fn key, read the 'Did you know?' note here.
2. Notice the colour of the text or images under F1, F2, F3 and other function keys. It may be blue, green or any colour other than the colour of the keyboard letters. Under F1 you may see a blue question mark, for instance. This alternate-coloured information tells you what will happen when you press the Fn key and this key at the same time.
3. Press Fn + F1. This will most likely open Help.
4. Press Fn + F2. Make a note of what happens as well as what is listed under F2 on the key itself.
5. Continue in this manner until you've explored all the function keys, up to F12. (Some keys might not do anything.)

Did you know?

Although most laptops offer an Fn key, some do not. If you don't see an Fn key, take a look at the items listed underneath F1, F2, F3, F4 and so on. They will likely be a different colour from default keys on the keyboard. Locate a key that is the same colour as this one, a key that has an F on it or something similar. This is most likely the Fn key we're talking about here.

Using the Function keys (cont.)

6 Look for other keys on the keyboard that have additional information on them other than letters or punctuation. For instance, you may see additional functionality on the arrow keys (which is where you might access the volume or brightness), or on the Page Up and Page Down keys (where you may find options to scroll left or right). Explore these keys.

?

Did you know?

All of the laptops I've seen recently come with specialised buttons that you can configure. These often include buttons for Mail, Web Browser, Bluetooth or Music Player, among others. Each manufacturer offers different ways to use and configure these buttons, so you'll need to access your User Guide to find out exactly how to do this. For the most part, all you need to do is press the proper key on the keyboard and follow the configuration directions, or access the Keyboard option in Control Panel to configure the available buttons.

Instant Windows 7

5

What you'll do

Explore the Getting Started window

Know your Windows 7 Edition

Explore the Desktop

Discover Windows 7 applications

Discover Windows 7 accessories

Shut down Windows 7

Introduction

Now that you know a little about the outside and inside of your computer, let's talk about Windows 7. Windows 7 is the most important software installed on your computer. Although you likely have other software programs (such as Microsoft Office or Photoshop Elements), Windows 7 is your computer's *operating system* and, thus, it's what allows *you* to *operate* your computer's *system*. You will use Windows 7 to find things you have stored on your computer, connect to the Internet, send and receive email and surf the web, among other things.

You don't need to be a computer guru or have years of experience to use Windows 7. Its interface is intuitive. The Start button offers a place to access just about everything you'll need, from photos to music to email; the Recycle Bin holds stuff you've deleted; and the Desktop Gadget Gallery offers *gadgets* you'll likely need to access, such as a clock, the weather and news headlines. In this chapter you will discover how little you need to know (and learn) to get started with Windows 7.

!

Important

Windows 7 comes in several editions and computer manufacturers often add their own touches. As a result, your screen may not look exactly like what you'll see in the screenshots in this book (but it'll be close).

One of Windows 7's main jobs is to serve as a liaison between you and your laptop. When you physically move the mouse cursor, Windows 7 helps the laptop to move the cursor virtually on the laptop's screen. When you save a file, Windows 7 interacts with the hard drive to offer a place to save the information and remembers where it is stored. If you want to print a web page, Windows 7 communicates with the printer and sends the required information to it. And, when you want to burn a CD or DVD, Windows 7 communicates with those drives too, making sure what you want to do is completed successfully. This all occurs behind the scenes, making sure that you never have to worry about how anything technically works. That's the job of the *operating system*.

Windows 7 also offers applications to help you be more productive and do more things. For instance, Windows DVD Maker helps you create DVDs, Windows Fax and Scan lets you, well, fax and scan, and Media Center and Media Player let you manage, organise, obtain, watch and listen to media. You also get Internet Explorer for surfing the web and the Sync Center for synching portable players for music, photos, videos and ebooks, among other applications. There are some applications you'll need to download though, such as Windows Live Essentials and perhaps a PDF reader such as Adobe Reader, but these things are free, and you'll learn all about them later.

The Getting Started window

The first time you started Windows 7, the Getting Started window may have opened. It is here you can learn quite a lot about Windows 7 in very short order. There are options to find out what's new, personalise Windows, add new users and more. Often computer manufacturers add their own listings and links to help you learn about your computer and the applications they've installed on it, as well as links to their own Help files or website.

You can learn many things from the Getting Started options, but the items you'll be most interested in now are:

- Discover Windows 7 – access information regarding what's been added since Windows Vista, including but not limited to using the Action Center to keep your computer secure and maintained, taking advantage of new navigation features, using the new Windows HomeGroup to set up your home network, using DeviceStage to see device status, using Internet Explorer 8, and accessing new features such as Windows Touch.
- Personalise Windows – Change the picture that appears on your Desktop, change your screensaver, personalise sounds and change fonts.
- Transfer your files – learn about and use Windows Easy Transfer, an application included with Windows 7 that helps you transfer user accounts, files and folders, program settings, Internet settings and Favorites, and email settings, contacts and messages from an older computer to your new one.
- Backup your files – open Windows Backup and backup important files once or on a schedule.
- Add new users – learn how to secure your computer with user accounts for each person who will access it. If two people share one laptop, each can have his or her own user account, where documents, email, photos and other data are secure. You can also customise settings and set up parental controls here.

Show the Getting Started window

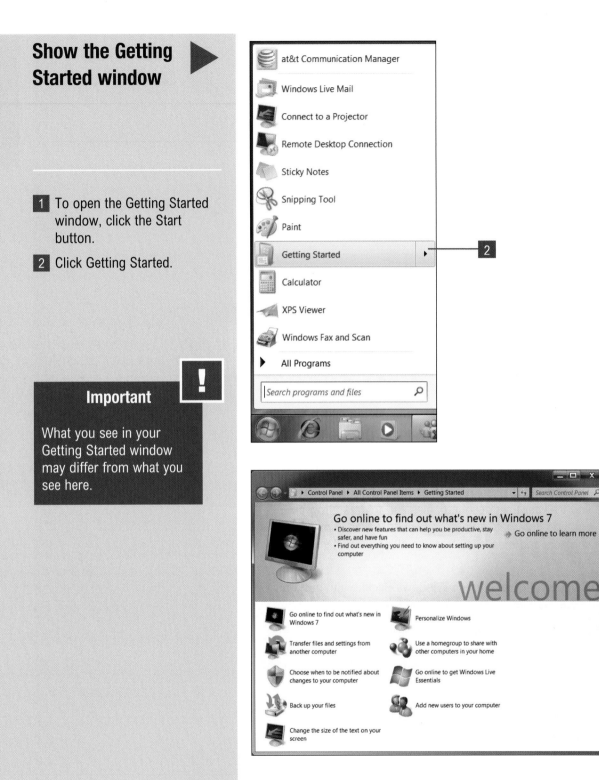

1. To open the Getting Started window, click the Start button.
2. Click Getting Started.

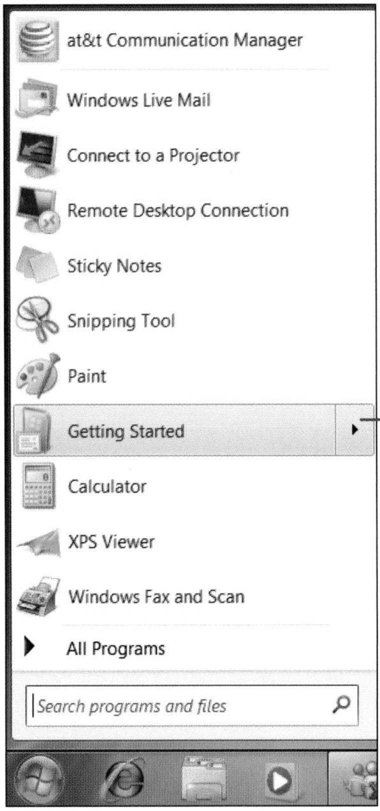
at&t Communication Manager
Windows Live Mail
Connect to a Projector
Remote Desktop Connection
Sticky Notes
Snipping Tool
Paint
Getting Started
Calculator
XPS Viewer
Windows Fax and Scan
All Programs
Search programs and files
2

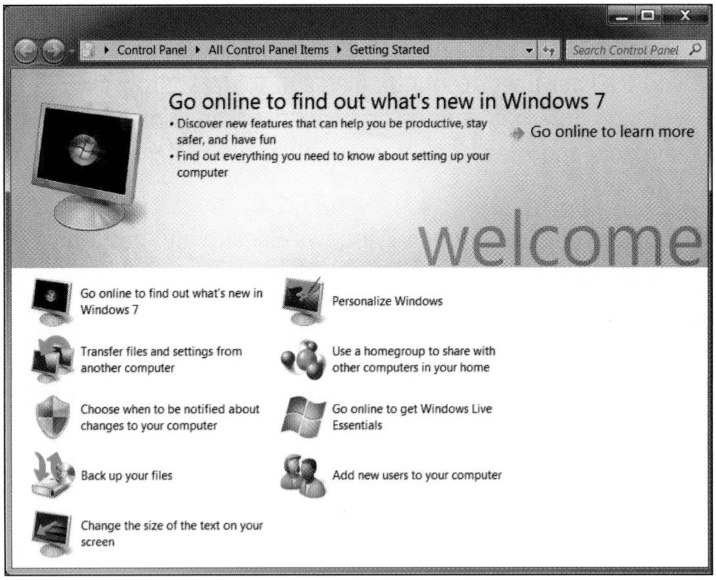
Control Panel ▸ All Control Panel Items ▸ Getting Started
Search Control Panel
Go online to find out what's new in Windows 7
• Discover new features that can help you be productive, stay safer, and have fun
• Find out everything you need to know about setting up your computer
Go online to learn more
welcome
Go online to find out what's new in Windows 7
Personalize Windows
Transfer files and settings from another computer
Use a homegroup to share with other computers in your home
Choose when to be notified about changes to your computer
Go online to get Windows Live Essentials
Back up your files
Add new users to your computer
Change the size of the text on your screen

Important

What you see in your Getting Started window may differ from what you see here.

Explore the Getting Started window

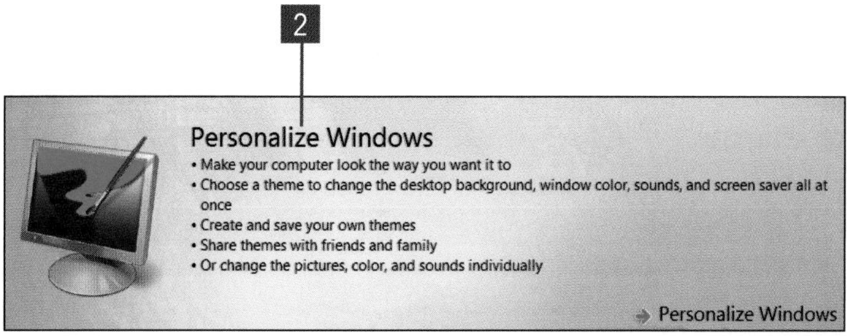
2
Personalize Windows
• Make your computer look the way you want it to
• Choose a theme to change the desktop background, window color, sounds, and screen saver all at once
• Create and save your own themes
• Share themes with friends and family
• Or change the pictures, color, and sounds individually
Personalize Windows

1. With the Getting Started window open, click Personalize Windows.
2. Notice the top pane changes to reflect your choice.
3. Later, you could click Personalize Windows to modify your copy of Windows 7, although you'll learn how to do that in Chapter 6.

Did you know?

To close any window, click the X in the top right corner.

Know your Windows 7 edition

You may or may not know what edition of Windows 7 is installed on your laptop. This information is available from the System window. Here, the computer is running Windows 7 Enterprise. You probably have Home Premium, Professional or Ultimate.

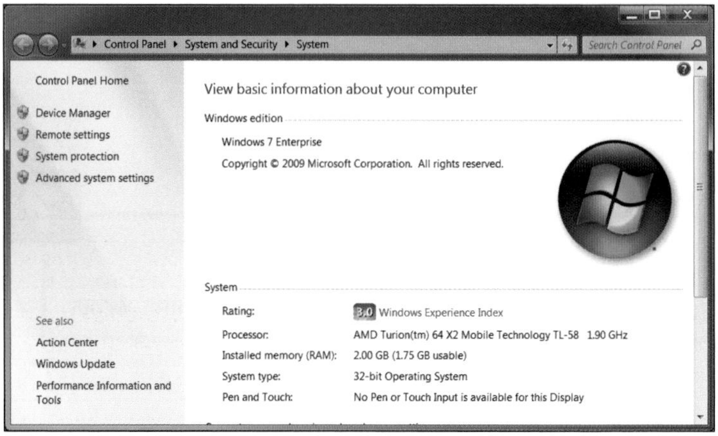
Control Panel ▸ System and Security ▸ System
Search Control Panel
Control Panel Home
Device Manager
Remote settings
System protection
Advanced system settings
View basic information about your computer
Windows edition
Windows 7 Enterprise
Copyright © 2009 Microsoft Corporation. All rights reserved.
System
Rating:
3.0 Windows Experience Index
Processor:
AMD Turion(tm) 64 X2 Mobile Technology TL-58 1.90 GHz
Installed memory (RAM):
2.00 GB (1.75 GB usable)
System type:
32-bit Operating System
Pen and Touch:
No Pen or Touch Input is available for this Display
See also
Action Center
Windows Update
Performance Information and Tools

Although Microsoft offers many editions to meet the needs of users worldwide, the two editions built specifically for consumers are:

- Windows 7 Home Premium – this edition was created for the home user. It offers all of the Windows 7 features you want and need, offers a full-function PC experience, and is a visually rich environment. This edition comes with Media Player, Media Center, Internet Explorer 8, the Action Center, DeviceStage, and accessories such as the Calculator, Notepad, Paint, Sync Center and more. The key features are: Aero Glass, Aero Background, Windows Touch, Home Group creation, Media Center, DVD playback and authoring, and premium games.
- Windows 7 Professional – this edition was created for small businesses and for people who work at home. It offers business-related tools along with the applications you'll need to function in a business environment where security and productivity are critical. Key features are: Domain join, Remote Desktop host, location aware printing, EFS, Mobility Center, Presentation Mode and Offline Folders.

Jargon buster

EFS stands for encrypting file system and is an encryption and decryption technology available on certain Microsoft computers to help protect your files and folders from unauthorised access.

Did you know?

There are other versions of Windows 7 you might hear about, but they are geared towards large corporations (Windows 7 Enterprise), emerging countries (Windows 7 Starter) and those users who simply must have an edition that has everything (Windows 7 Ultimate).

Did you know?

Windows 7 Starter is an affordable way for emerging markets to gain access to Windows 7. Windows 7 Starter is not available in high income markets like the US, the European Union, Australia and the Netherlands, though. This version of Windows 7 is designed for users with little or no computer experience and in countries where PCs have previously been unavailable or unwarranted due to price and/or lack of user experience.

Know your Windows 7 edition (cont.)

Know your Windows 7 edition (cont.)

1. Click the Start button.
2. Right-click Computer.
3. Click Properties.
4. Read the system information. You'll see your Windows edition at the top of the window, information about your PC's processor, RAM and system type in the middle, and your computer name, workgroup name and activation information at the bottom.

Did you know?

Programs that have been recently installed appear highlighted in the Start menu.

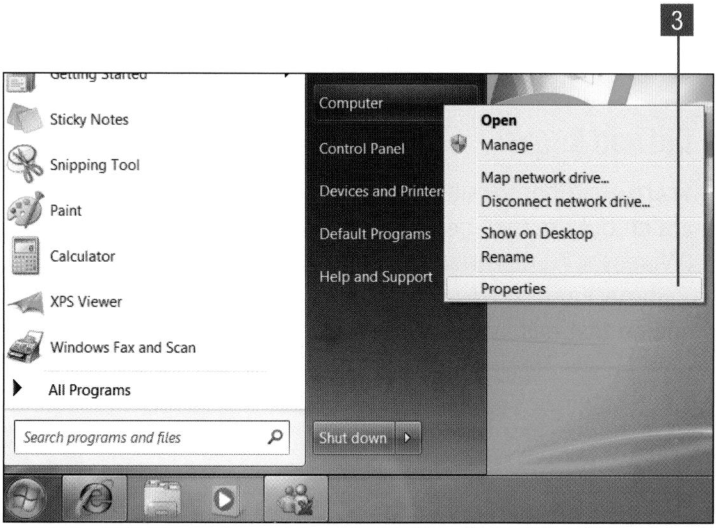
3
Getting Started
Sticky Notes
Snipping Tool
Paint
Calculator
XPS Viewer
Windows Fax and Scan
All Programs
Search programs and files
Computer
Control Panel
Devices and Printers
Default Programs
Help and Support
Shut down
Open
Manage
Map network drive...
Disconnect network drive...
Show on Desktop
Rename
Properties

Did you know?

You can right-click Computer and select Manage to open the Computer Management window where you can view system tools such as Device Manager and Task Scheduler.

Did you know?

Click Windows Experience Index to see how you can rate and improve your computer's performance. Tips for improving performance include adjusting visual effects, using Disk Cleanup, adjusting power settings and more.

Jargon buster

Processor – short for microprocessor, it's the silicon chip that contains the central processing unit (CPU) inside a computer. Generally, the terms CPU and processor are used interchangeably. A CPU does almost all of the computer's calculations and is the most important piece of hardware in a computer system.

RAM – short for random access memory, it's the hardware inside your computer that temporarily stores data that is being used by the operating system or programs. Although there are many types of RAM, all you need to know is that the more RAM you have, the faster your computer will (theoretically) run and perform.

System type – you'll either have a 32-bit operating system or a 64-bit operating system. Stating the difference would require a few pages of explanation, but suffice it to say that 64-bit computers are faster than 32-bit computers because they can process more data, more quickly.

Know your Windows 7 edition (cont.)

Explore the Desktop

What you see on the Desktop will vary depending on how long you've been using your computer and which manufacturer created it. If it's brand new, you may only see the Recycle Bin. If you've been using Windows 7 for a while, you may see other things, including Computer, Network, Control Panel or a folder with your name on it (for storing your personal files). You might even see icons with names of applications or Internet service providers written on them. If you've worked with gadgets, you may have those too. Here you can see a sample Desktop. This Desktop has really been 'personalised', something you'll learn about in Chapter 6.

Control Panel
Joli
Recycle Bin
Network
Computer
58°
Norden, DEU
Music
Pictures
Music + Pictures
Windows Media Center
1:51 PM
9/4/2009

Here are just a few of the things you might find on the Desktop:

- Recycle Bin – the Recycle Bin holds deleted files until you decide to empty it. The Recycle Bin serves as a safeguard, allowing you to recover items accidentally deleted, or items you thought you no longer wanted but later decide you need. Note that once you empty the Recycle Bin, the items in it are gone forever. (You can empty the Recycle Bin by right-clicking it and choosing Empty Recycle Bin.)
- Gadgets – gadgets are desktop components you manually select from the Desktop Gadget Gallery. The gallery includes several gadgets you can add to the Desktop including but not limited to a calendar, clock, currency converter, picture puzzle and up-to-the-minute weather information. You can find the Desktop Gadget Gallery from the All Programs menu.

Explore the Desktop (cont.)

5

- Network – double-clicking this icon opens the Network window, where you can view the computers on your network.
- Computer – double-clicking this icon opens the Computer window, shown here. You can see your hard disk drive(s) where the operating system, installed applications and personal data are stored, along with CD or DVD drives.

For your information

The icons on the desktop in the figures here are enlarged so they're easier to see. You'll learn how to enlarge your icons in the next chapter.

- Your personal folder – the name of this folder is the user name you created when you set up Windows 7. Every user account has a personal folder. Double-clicking the folder icon opens it, and inside are subfolders named My Documents, My Music, My Pictures, Downloads, Searches, My Videos and more. You'll use these folders to store your personal data.

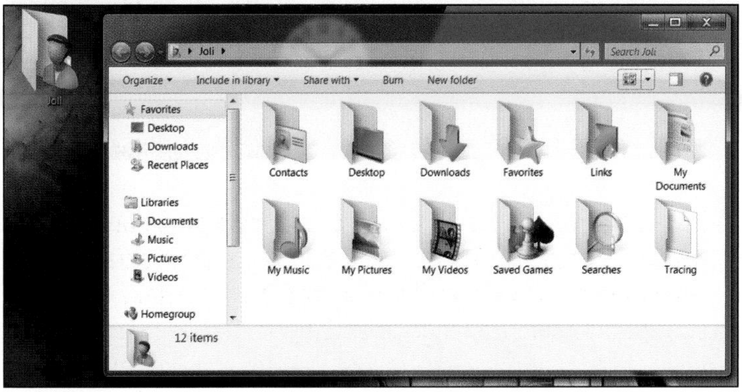
Joli
Search Joli
Organize
Include in library
Share with
Burn
New folder
Favorites
Desktop
Downloads
Recent Places
Libraries
Documents
Music
Pictures
Videos
Homegroup
Contacts
Desktop
Downloads
Favorites
Links
My Documents
My Music
My Pictures
My Videos
Saved Games
Searches
Tracing
12 items

Explore the Desktop (cont.)

1. Locate the Recycle Bin.
2. Notice any other icons including Network or Computer, or your personal file folder (the one with your name on it). You may only see the Recycle Bin.
3. Locate the Start button. It's located on the bottom left corner. The Start button is round and is on the Taskbar.
4. Locate the Internet Explorer icon, your personal folder icon and the Media Player icon. You may see others.
5. Locate the clock and volume. (You may see additional icons.)

Jargon buster

Start Button – you'll use the Start button to locate programs installed and data stored on your computer. Click it once to open the Start menu, right-click it to see additional options.

Taskbar – the blue or transparent bar that runs across the bottom of the screen. The Taskbar holds icons for running programs, applications you use often, and icons for network, volume, and time and date.

Recycle Bin
Start Button
Internet Explorer
Media Player
Volume
Clock

Discover Windows 7's All Programs menu

Just about anything you want to access on your computer can be accessed through the Start menu. You can access office applications, graphics applications, games and even your personal folders. You can access Computer, Help and Support, and Control Panel too. In this section, though, we'll only look at one part of the Start menu, and that part is the All Programs menu.

Windows 7 comes with just about everything you need when it comes to applications and software. There's Internet Explorer for surfing the web, Windows DVD Maker for burning your own DVDs and Media Player for listening to music. But there's a myriad more features than that. In this section you'll learn a little about many of the available Windows 7 features, and you can decide if it's something you want to explore and use or not. With that out of the way, you can then skip around in the book for the information you need on using and applying the feature, and ignore those you don't need or want to use.

Here are some of the more commonly used Windows 7 features, all available by clicking the Start button and then clicking All Programs:

- Internet Explorer 8 – one software option for accessing and surfing the web. Internet Explorer offers tabbed browsing, meaning you can have several web pages open at the same time, a place to store links to your favourite pages, a pop-up blocker, and the ability to zoom, change the text size, print and subscribe to RSS feeds among other things. You'll learn more about Internet Explorer in Chapter 9.

Important

Some features are only available in certain editions. For instance, while Internet Explorer 8 is available in every Windows 7 edition, Domain Join, a feature that enables simple and secure server networking, is not.

Did you know?

You don't have to click All Programs to see the list; you can simply hover your mouse over it for a second and it will appear automatically.

Discover Windows 7's All Programs menu (cont.)

Jargon buster

RSS – stands for really simple syndication and is a format used to publish data that changes frequently, such as blog posts and web feeds.

- Windows Media Center – an application that allows you to watch, record, fast-forward and (after recording or pausing a TV show) rewind live TV. You can also listen to music stored on your PC, locate and watch sports programmes, view, download and/or purchase online media, burn CDs and DVDs, sync portable music devices, view and organise your personal pictures and videos, and more. To have access to all of Media Center's features, though, you'll need a TV tuner, CD and DVD burner, Internet connection, large hard drive and lots of RAM. You'll learn a little about Media Center in Chapter 10.
- Windows Media Player – an application that enables you to store, access, play and organise the music stored on your PC. You can also 'rip' music (that means copying music CDs you own to your PC's hard drive), burn CDs, sync portable devices and more. Media Player is covered briefly in Chapter 10.
- Windows DVD Maker – an application that lets you create DVDs easily by working through a series of steps, offered by the Windows DVD Maker wizard.
- Windows Fax and Scan – an application that lets you scan and then fax documents, or simply fax documents created on your PC.
- Windows Update – an application that allows you manually or automatically to obtain and install updates to your computer to keep it secure. You'll learn about Windows Update in Chapter 8.

Important

The applications introduced here are not all of the applications that ship with Windows 7. There are many we did not list in the interest of time, space and importance, or because the features are better introduced independently in other chapters.

As you saw in Step 5, Windows 7 comes with a lot of accessories. Two examples are the calculator and notepad. The accessories in the Accessories folder include:

- Calculator – a standard calculator you can use to perform basic mathematical tasks. Click the View menu and choose Scientific to see the calculator shown here.
- Command Prompt – opens a command prompt that you can use to communicate with Windows 7's operating system, a task you'll likely never need to do.
- Connect to a Network Projector – enables you to connect to a network project when giving a presentation.
- Notepad – an application that enables you to type notes and save them. Using this application you can also print, cut, copy and paste, find and replace words, and select a font, font size and script.
- Paint – a program you can use to create drawings either on a blank canvas or on top of a picture. You can use the toolbar to draw shapes, lines, curves and input text. You can use additional tools including paintbrushes, pencils,

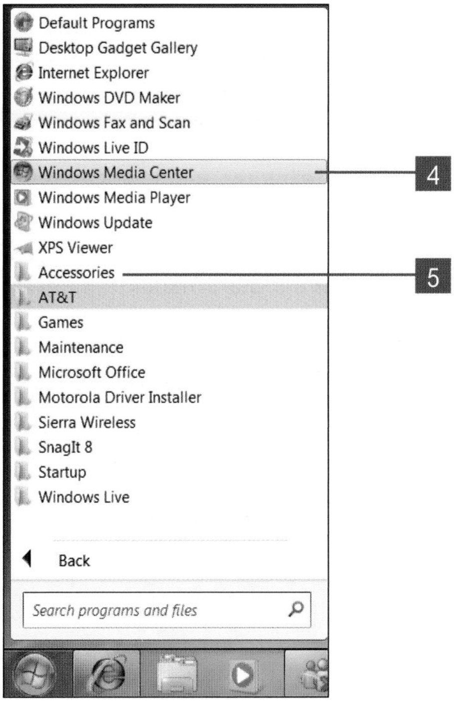

Default Programs
Desktop Gadget Gallery
Internet Explorer
Windows DVD Maker
Windows Fax and Scan
Windows Live ID
Windows Media Center
Windows Media Player
Windows Update
XPS Viewer
Accessories
AT&T
Games
Maintenance
Microsoft Office
Motorola Driver Installer
Sierra Wireless
SnagIt 8
Startup
Windows Live
Back
Search programs and files
4
5

Discover Windows 7 applications

5

1 Click the Start button.

2 Click All Programs.

3 If necessary, use the scroll bar to move to the top of the All Programs list.

4 Locate Windows Media Center. Do not click it or it will open.

5 Locate Accessories. Click it once to see the available accessories. A scroll bar will likely appear so that you can scroll through the items no longer in view.

6 Continue down the list, noting what programs and applications are available in your edition of Windows 7.

airbrushes and the like, as well as choose colours for objects you draw.

- Run – a dialog box where you can type a command. There are many commands; one example is sfc /scannow, which will cause Windows 7 to find and fix problems with the operating system, and msconfig, which opens a dialog box where you can control what programs load when you start Windows, among other things.
- Snipping Tool – a tool you can use to copy any part of any screen, including information from a web page, part of your Desktop or even part of a picture.
- Sound Recorder – a recording program that you can use to record your own voice. You can use the voice clips as reminders for tasks and you can add them to Movie Maker files or a web page, among other things.

Sound Recorder
Start Recording
0:00:00

- Sync Center – an application that lets you set up partnerships between Windows 7 and external devices such as portable media players, e-book readers and portable PCs or phones. After a partnership is set up, each time you connect the device to your PC, the information that has changed is synced per your instructions during set-up.
- Windows Explorer – opens an 'explorer' window where you can browse for files, programs, pictures, music, videos and more. However, it's generally easier to locate these items in their respective folders or from the Start menu.
- WordPad – a word processing program where you can create, edit, save and print files. Like Notepad, you can cut, copy and paste, find and replace words, and select a font, font size and script. However, you also have access to a formatting toolbar, a ruler and additional options. You can insert the date and time into a document, and an object, such as a graph or chart, or a compatible picture.

There are some other folders available inside the Accessories folder. These subfolders include:

- Ease of Access folder – allows you to access tools that make using the computer easier for those with disabilities. Items include things such as a magnifier and narrator. You'll learn more about Ease of Access tools in Chapter 7.
- System Tools – allows you to access tools you'll need to maintain your computer's health. These include but are not limited to Disk Cleanup, Disk Defragmenter and System Restore.
- Tablet PC – accessories in this folder include tools related to mobile PCs such as the Tablet PC input panel and Windows Journal, among other things.

Discover Windows 7 accessories

1. Click the Start button. Click All Programs.
2. Use the scroll bar to move down the list until you see Accessories.
3. Click Accessories.
4. Click Calculator. Close the Calculator program by clicking the red X in the top right corner.
5. Repeat steps 1–4 and click Paint. Close the Paint program by clicking the red X in the top right corner.
6. Repeat steps 1–4, and click Sound Recorder. Close the program by clicking the red X in the top right corner.
7. Continue as desired, exploring additional features.

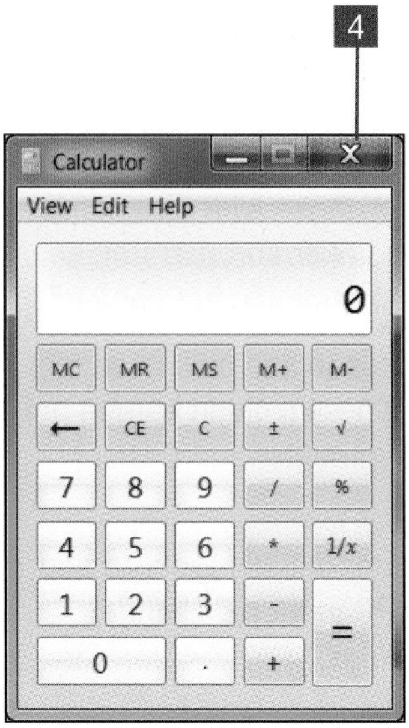
4
Calculator
View Edit Help
0
MC MR MS M+ M-
← CE C ± √
7 8 9 / %
4 5 6 * 1/x
1 2 3 -
0 . + =

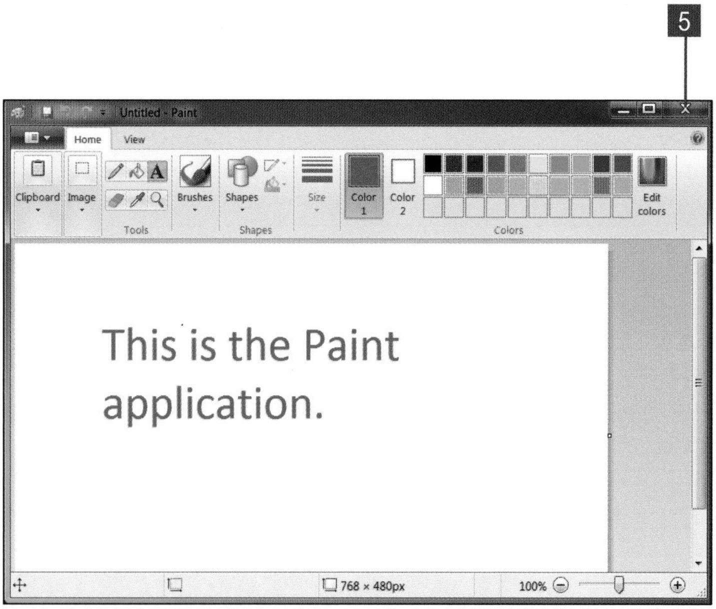
5
Untitled - Paint
Home View
Clipboard Image Tools Brushes Shapes Size Color 1 Color 2 Colors Edit colors
This is the Paint application.
768 × 480px
100%

By default, Windows 7 will turn off the display and put the computer to sleep after a specific amount of idle time. The amount of time that must elapse before this happens depends on the power settings that you've configured for the laptop, the settings configured by the manufacturer, or the operating system's settings default. It's important to note that, when the computer goes to sleep, it uses very little power. Because of this, there's often no need actually to turn off the laptop, unless you plan to move it, not use it for a few days, or if you're extremely energy-conscious.

Important

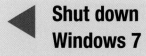

If you do want to turn off your laptop, don't just hit the power button. You need to let Windows 7 handle the shutting down process. Remember, Windows 7 is an operating system, and is here to help you operate your computer system safely and properly.

Shut down Windows 7

Shut down Windows 7 (cont.)

1 Click the Start button.

2 Click Shut down.

?

Did you know?

You can also choose to put the computer to sleep, restart the computer, switch users, log off or lock the computer. Just click the right arrow next to the Shut down button.

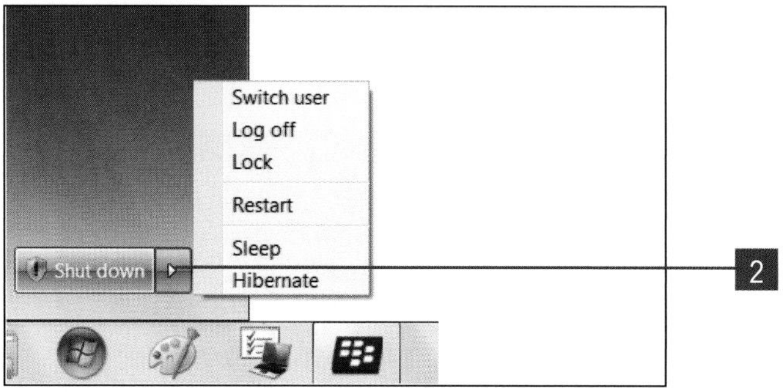
Switch user
Log off
Lock
Restart
Sleep
Hibernate
Shut down
2

The options available in the list shown here include the following:

- Switch user – if more than one user account is available on the laptop, select Switch user to switch to another user. Switching users is different from logging off. When you choose to switch users, the current user's program, files, folders and open windows remain intact. When you switch back you do not need to reopen these items. Switching users has nothing to do with putting the computer to sleep or turning it off.
- Log off – choose this option when you want to log out of your computer session. This does not shut down or put the computer to sleep, but will bring up the login screen. Once logged off, you'll need to log back on, usually by inputting your user name and/or password.
- Lock – use this option to lock the computer. You'll have to input your password to unlock the laptop if one is assigned. If a password is not assigned, you'll simply click your user name.
- Restart – use this option to restart the PC. You should restart your laptop any time you're prompted to (usually

after a Windows 7 update or the installation of a program), when you know an application has stopped working, or the computer seems slow or unresponsive.

- Sleep – use this option to put the laptop or computer to sleep. Windows 7's Sleep State uses very little energy and is a better option than turning the computer off completely, unless of course you do not plan to use the laptop for a couple of days or longer.
- Hibernate – this option is similar to sleep but 'deeper'. Use Hibernate if you plan to use your laptop or computer again in 12–24 hours.

?

Did you know?

Many computers now come with a Sleep button on the outside of the PC tower or on the inside of a laptop. Clicking the Sleep button puts the computer to sleep immediately.

Shut down Windows 7 (cont.)

Personalising Windows 7

6

Introduction

One of the first things many people like to do when they get a new laptop or upgrade an older one is to personalise the Desktop, select a screensaver and create shortcuts to their favourite programs or folders so they are easily accessible. You may also wish to select a new theme, or change the screen resolution, colour or appearance. That's what we'll do here. This isn't a must-read chapter, though; either you want to change how Windows 7 looks or you like it just the way it is. You can always come back here if you decide you want to change the theme or apply a screensaver. However, if you're ready to explore personalisation options, read on!

What you'll do

Select the theme

Change the background

Change the screensaver

Change the Windows Desktop

Create Desktop shortcuts for programs, files and folders

Remove icons and shortcuts from the Desktop

Change the screen resolution

Use the Windows Classic theme

Adjust font size

Personalise the Desktop

Did you know?

You don't have to use a theme that includes Aero features. If the fancy graphics distract you or you prefer the Windows Classic look, you can certainly turn it off by selecting a non-Aero theme.

Windows 7 includes themes you can choose from to personalise your computer. The Windows 7 theme is the one selected by default, and includes the Aero features introduced in Windows Vista. Aero offers a clean, sleek interface and Windows 7 experience. You can only use Aero if your computer hardware supports it, meaning that the hardware installed on your computer meets Aero's minimum requirements. Windows Aero offers a high-performing Desktop experience that includes (among other things) the translucent effect of Aero Glass. Aero Glass offers visual reflections and soft animations too, making the interface quite 'comfortable'.

You can see Aero in action here. Note that you can see 'underneath' the title bar of the Games window, making out the background underneath. This is just one of Aero's features.

ms ▸ Games
Search Games
New folder
Games Explorer
Hearts
Internet Backgammon

You can personalise your laptop by selecting a different theme. As noted, Windows 7 is the default theme but there are others. You may like to try Landscapes, Nature, Scenes, Windows Basic or one of the high contrast options.

Did you know?

You enable or disable the Aero feature by selecting a theme that does or does not offer it, like Windows 7 Basic.

Selecting a theme

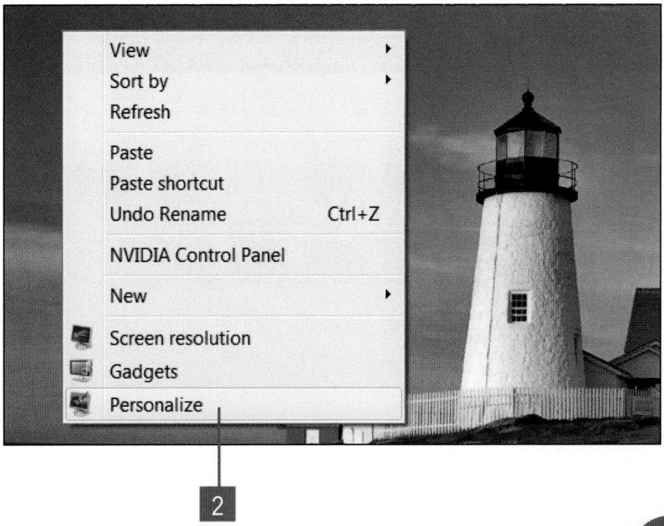

View
Sort by
Refresh
Paste
Paste shortcut
Undo Rename Ctrl+Z
NVIDIA Control Panel
New
Screen resolution
Gadgets
Personalize
2

For your information

You may see items in this list that are not shown here, or vice-versa.

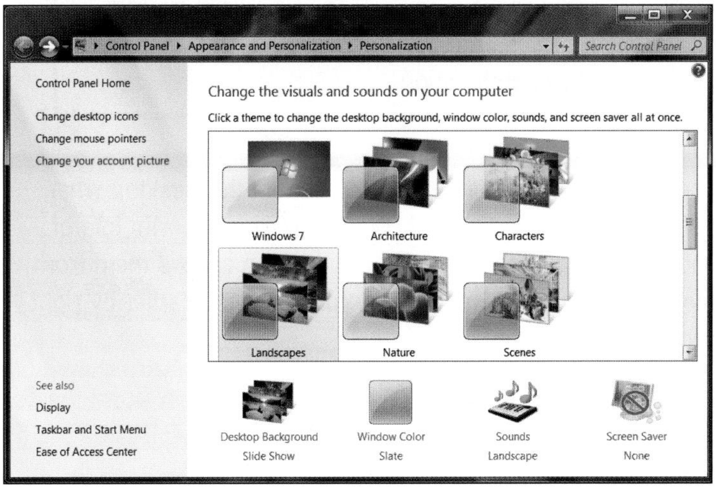

Control Panel ▸ Appearance and Personalization ▸ Personalization
Search Control Panel
Control Panel Home
Change desktop icons
Change mouse pointers
Change your account picture
Change the visuals and sounds on your computer
Click a theme to change the desktop background, window color, sounds, and screen saver all at once.
Windows 7
Architecture
Characters
Landscapes
Nature
Scenes
See also
Display
Taskbar and Start Menu
Ease of Access Center
Desktop Background
Slide Show
Window Color
Slate
Sounds
Landscape
Screen Saver
None

For your information

Choosing an Ease of Access theme will disable Aero.

1. Right-click an empty area of the Desktop.
2. Click Personalize.
3. Under Aero Themes, click each theme one time. Notice how the Desktop and window colours change.
4. Under Basic and High Contrast Themes, click each theme one time.
5. To tweak the theme, click Window Color Slate at the bottom of the Personalization window.

Selecting a theme (cont.)

6 In the resulting Windows Color and Appearance window, you can enable or disable transparency and/ or click Show color mixer to have access to additional options. Configure as desired and click Save changes.

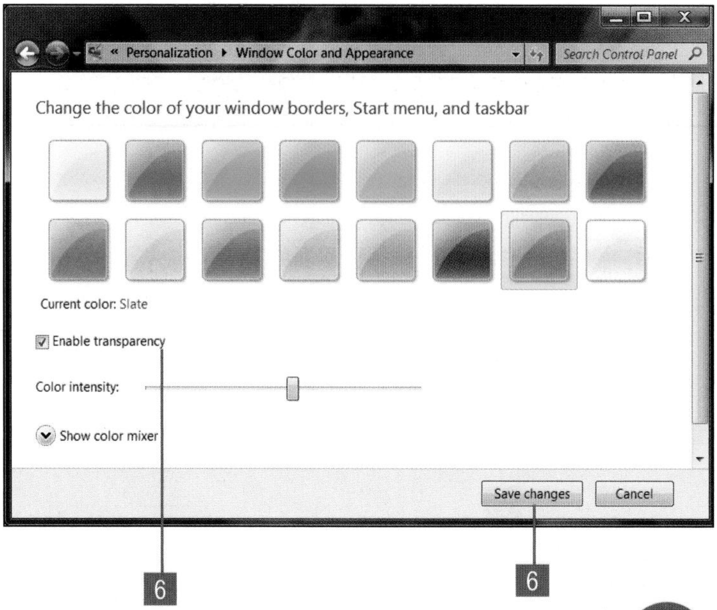

Personalization ▸ Window Color and Appearance
Search Control Panel
Change the color of your window borders, Start menu, and taskbar
Current color: Slate
Enable transparency
Color intensity:
Show color mixer
Save changes
Cancel
6
6

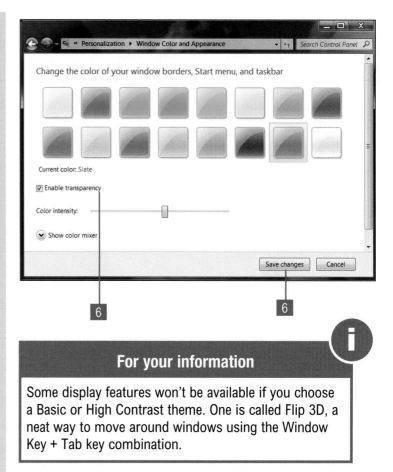

For your information

Some display features won't be available if you choose a Basic or High Contrast theme. One is called Flip 3D, a neat way to move around windows using the Window Key + Tab key combination.

The background is the picture you see on the Desktop when no windows are on top of it. Windows 7 comes with lots of backgrounds to choose from, and you can access them from the Personalization window that you accessed earlier by right-clicking the Desktop.

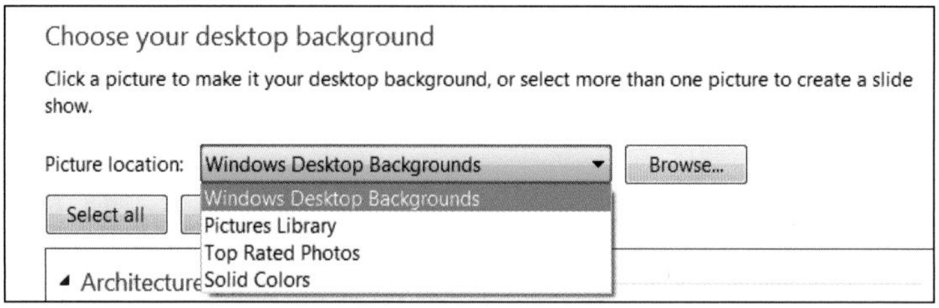

Choose your desktop background
Click a picture to make it your desktop background, or select more than one picture to create a slide show.
Picture location:
Windows Desktop Backgrounds
Browse...
Select all
Windows Desktop Backgrounds
Pictures Library
Top Rated Photos
Solid Colors
Architecture

There are many kinds of backgrounds including:

- Windows Desktop Backgrounds – the images included with Windows 7, which are categorised by their subject matter.

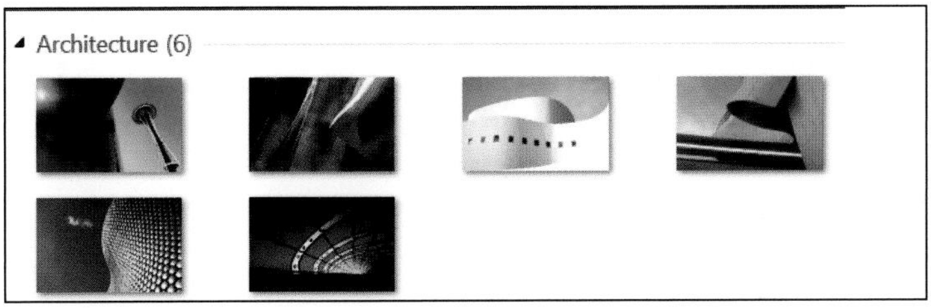
Architecture (6)

- Pictures Library – the images here by default are those in the Sample Pictures folder, but you can click the Browse button to locate a picture you've taken, acquired or otherwise saved to your computer.
- Top Rated Photos – this folder contains the images in the Sample Pictures folder by default, but pictures you take and rate will also appear here.
- Solid Colors – solid backgrounds of a single colour are the only options here.

Note that you can also position the background you select to fill the entire screen, to fit exactly, to stretch, to tile across the screen or to appear in the centre of the screen. Finally, you can select every picture available and choose to change the picture often (the settings range from 10 seconds to once a day).

Changing the background

1 Right-click an empty area of the desktop.

2 Click Personalize.

3 Click Desktop Background.

4 For Location, select Windows Desktop Backgrounds. You can repeat these steps and the remaining ones using other options, if desired.

5 Use the scroll bars to locate the wallpaper to use as your Desktop background. You can select as many as you like. If you select more than one, you'll also have the option to change the picture on a schedule.

6 Select a Picture position option (Fill is the best choice).

7 If you selected more than one background, choose how often to change it. Shuffle means to mix up the order the pictures appear. Click that too, if desired.

8 Click Save changes.

Did you know?

If you can't access all of the options in the window, click and drag from the bottom right corner of the Personalization window to resize it.

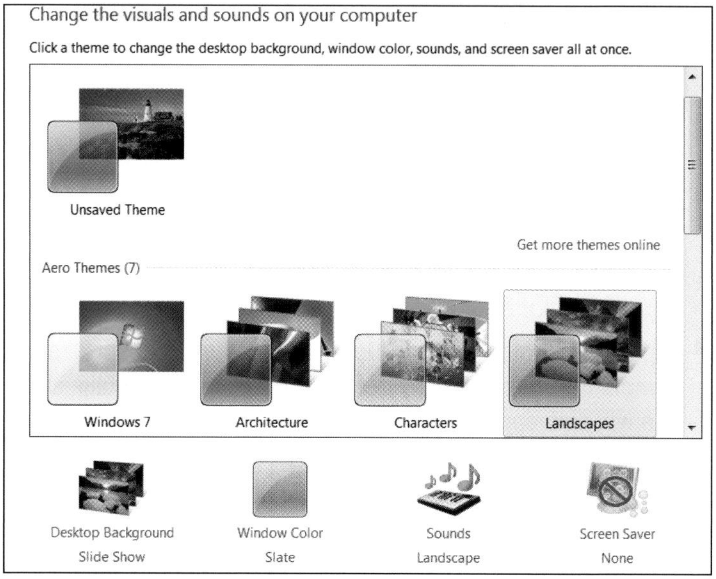

Change the visuals and sounds on your computer
Click a theme to change the desktop background, window color, sounds, and screen saver all at once.
Unsaved Theme
Get more themes online
Aero Themes (7)
Windows 7
Architecture
Characters
Landscapes
Desktop Background
Slide Show
Window Color
Slate
Sounds
Landscape
Screen Saver
None

« Appearance and Personalization ▸ Personalization ▸ Desktop Background
Search Control Panel
Choose your desktop background
Click a picture to make it your desktop background, or select more than one picture to create a slide show.
Picture location: Windows Desktop Backgrounds
Browse...
Select all
Clear all
Landscapes (6)
Picture position:
Fill
Change picture every:
30 minutes
Shuffle
When using battery power, pause the slide show to save power
Save changes
Cancel
8

Changing the background (cont.)

6

For your information

If you don't find what you want in the Desktop Background options, you can click Browse in any option to locate and find a file stored on your computer.

A screensaver is a picture or animation that covers your screen and appears after your computer has been idle for a specific amount of time that you set. It used to be that screensavers 'saved' your computer screen from image burn-in, but that is no longer the case. Now, screensavers are used for either visual enhancement or as a security feature. As an extra measure of security, you can configure your screensaver to require a password on waking up, which happens when you move the mouse or hit a key on the keyboard. Requiring a password means that once the screensaver is running, no one can log into your computer but you, by typing in your password when prompted.

Screensavers come in many flavours, and Windows 7 comes with several; the Bubbles screensaver is one of my favourites. As with enabling Aero or changing the Desktop background, you access the settings by right clicking an empty area of the Desktop and selecting Personalize.

You can also get screensavers online and from third-party retailers. However, screensavers from these places are notorious for containing, at the very least, annoying pop-ups or purchasing ads and, at worst, malicious code or even viruses. Before you download and install a screensaver from a third party, make sure you've read the reviews and are positive it's from a worthy and reliable source.

Changing the screensaver

1. Right-click an empty area of the Desktop.
2. Click Personalize.
3. Click Screen Saver.

Screen Saver
None

4. Click the arrow to see the available screensavers.
5. Select any screensaver from the list.
6. Use the arrows to change how long to wait before the screensaver is enabled.
7. If desired, click On resume, display logon screen to require a password to log back into the computer.
8. Click OK.

Did you know?

Select Photos and your screensaver will be a slideshow of photos stored in your Pictures folder.

Did you know?

If you click Settings after selecting a screensaver you may be able to configure it. In the case of 3D text, you can create custom text and set the size, style, colour and rotation speed.

For your information

Click Preview to see what the screensaver will look like. Press any key on the keyboard to disable the preview.

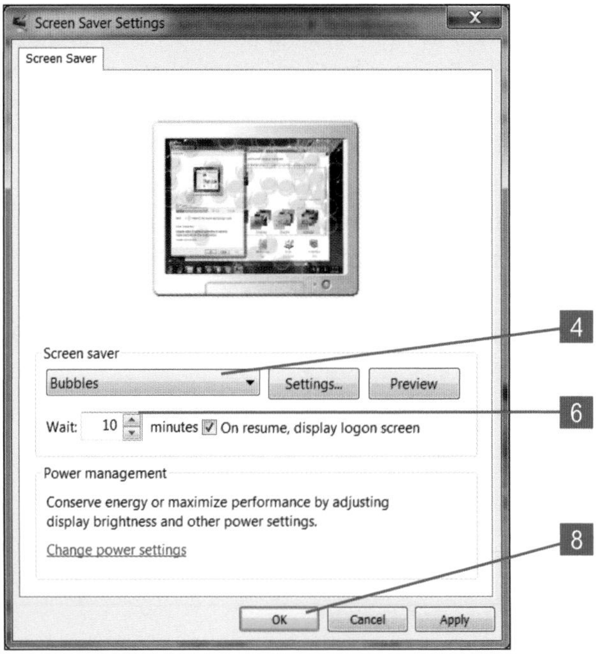
Screen Saver Settings
Screen Saver
Screen saver
Bubbles
Settings...
Preview
Wait: 10 minutes On resume, display logon screen
Power management
Conserve energy or maximize performance by adjusting display brightness and other power settings.
Change power settings
OK
Cancel
Apply
4
6
8

Tweaking the Desktop

When Windows 7 started the first time, it may have had only one item on the Desktop: the Recycle Bin. Alternatively, it may have had 20 or more. What appears on your Desktop the first time Windows boots up depends on a number of factors:

- If you installed Windows 7 yourself, and you chose not to upgrade from another version of Windows but instead to perform a 'clean' installation, you will likely only see one icon: the Recycle Bin.
- If you installed Windows 7 as an upgrade from another operating system version, such as Windows Vista, then you'll see the Windows 7-related icons you had on your computer prior to the upgrade. These may include Documents, Pictures or even shortcuts to your favourite programs.
- If you purchased a new laptop with Windows 7 installed, you could have icons on your desktop for Internet Service Providers (ISPs) such as AOL, Verizon, Time Warner or any number of others. You may also see icons for anti-virus software such as McAfee or Semantic. There may also be any number of links to what's called OEM software, or software that comes preinstalled on your PC that you may or may not want, including image editing applications, music players and word processing or database applications.

Whatever the case, it's likely the desktop doesn't match your needs exactly, and so needs to be tweaked. Thus, adding and deleting Desktop icons is a pretty common task, and will be discussed in depth.

Besides the icons that are on the Desktop by default depending on the installation configuration, there are Windows 7 icons that you can add or remove. You can choose to view or hide Computer, Recycle Bin, Control Panel, Network and your personal user folder.

You can also choose to add shortcuts to programs you use frequently. Often, people add shortcuts to the Desktop for folders they create, programs they use often or network places, such as folders stored on other computers.

Changing the Windows 7 icons on the Desktop

1. Right-click an empty area of the desktop.
2. Click Personalize.
3. Click Change desktop icons.
4. Select the Desktop icons you would like to appear on your Desktop.
5. Click OK.

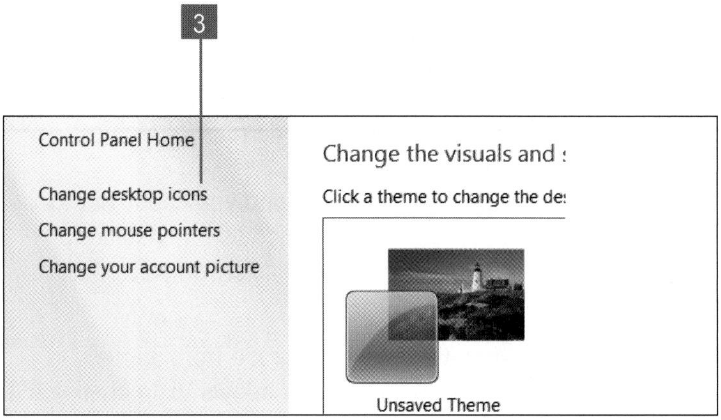
3
Control Panel Home
Change desktop icons
Change mouse pointers
Change your account picture
Change the visuals and
Click a theme to change the de
Unsaved Theme

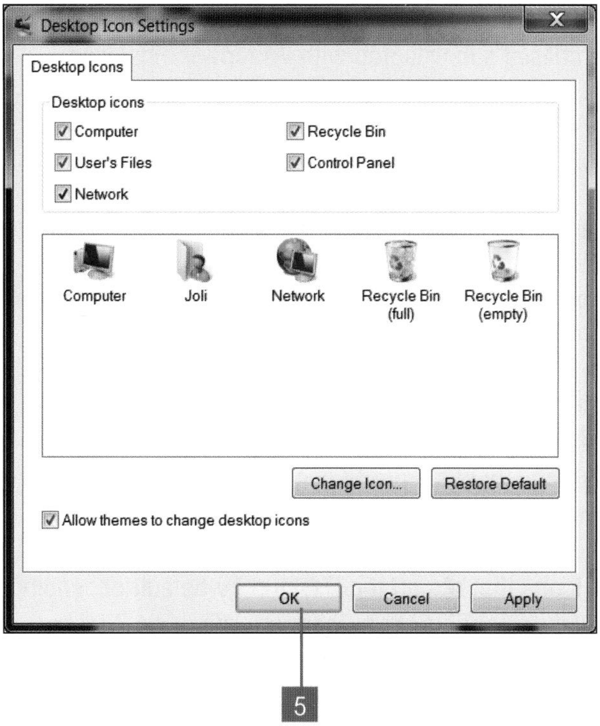
Desktop Icon Settings
Desktop Icons
Desktop icons
Computer
Recycle Bin
User's Files
Control Panel
Network
Computer
Joli
Network
Recycle Bin (full)
Recycle Bin (empty)
Change Icon...
Restore Default
Allow themes to change desktop icons
OK
Cancel
Apply
5

?

Did you know?

If you have more than one user account on your computer, all users can configure their Desktop as they wish.

A shortcut always appears with an arrow beside it (or on it, actually). Shortcuts enable you to access folders, files, programs and other items stored on your laptop without the hassle of drilling into the Start menu, accessing the folder on a network or using the Start Search dialogue box. You can create shortcuts from the Start menu.

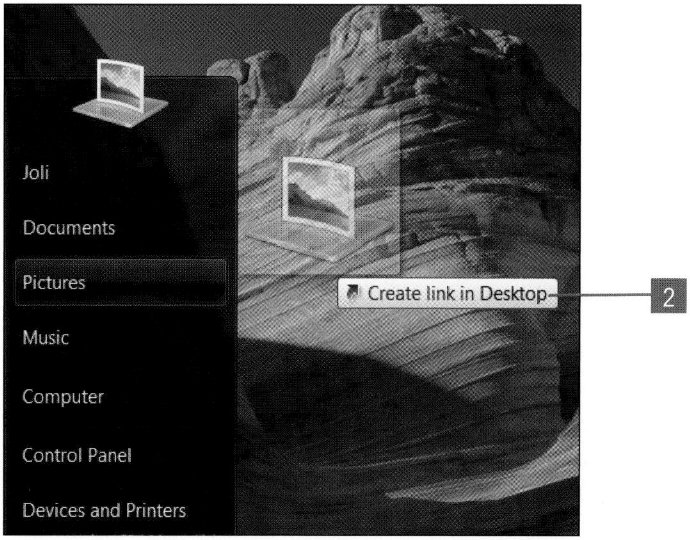
Joli
Documents
Pictures
Music
Computer
Control Panel
Devices and Printers
Create link in Desktop
2

Did you know?

You can add a shortcut to the Taskbar in the same manner. Instead of Create Shortcut Here, choose Pin to Windows Explorer.

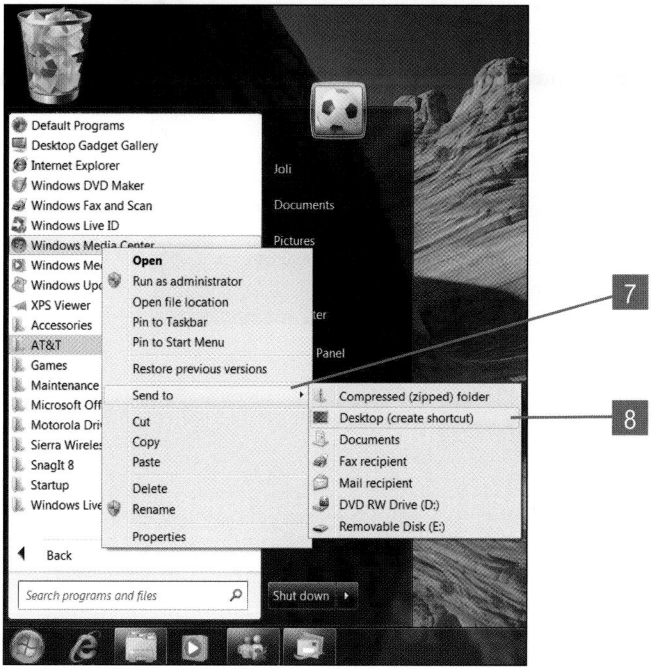
Default Programs
Desktop Gadget Gallery
Internet Explorer
Windows DVD Maker
Windows Fax and Scan
Windows Live ID
Accessories
AT&T
Games
Maintenance
Startup
Back
Open
Run as administrator
Open file location
Pin to Taskbar
Pin to Start Menu
Restore previous versions
Send to
Cut
Copy
Paste
Delete
Rename
Properties
Compressed (zipped) folder
Desktop (create shortcut)
Documents
Fax recipient
Mail recipient
DVD RW Drive (D:)
Removable Disk (E:)
Joli
Documents
Pictures
Search programs and files
Shut down
7
8

Creating Desktop shortcuts for programs, files and folders

6

1. Click Start.
2. If you see the item for which you want to create a shortcut, drag it to the desktop. Note that as you drag a shortcut arrow appears.
3. When you let go, the shortcut will appear. If you're ever prompted, click Create Shortcut here.
4. To add a shortcut for a program, in the Start menu, click All Programs.
5. In the All Programs list, locate the program for which to create a shortcut.
6. Right-click the program name. (Note this is a right-click, not a left-click.)
7. Click Send to.
8. Click Desktop (create shortcut).

Creating Desktop shortcuts for programs, files and folders (cont.)

For your information

You can drag any shortcut on the Desktop to the Recycle Bin to remove it from the Desktop.

When you right-click a shortcut on the Desktop, you'll see lots of choices. One is to create a shortcut, interestingly. When you click Delete, you are prompted to move the shortcut to the Recycle Bin. Since it's a shortcut, that's just fine; you can delete any shortcut without worrying about deleting actual data. You're not going to delete the Pictures folder or the pictures in it; you are simply deleting the shortcut.

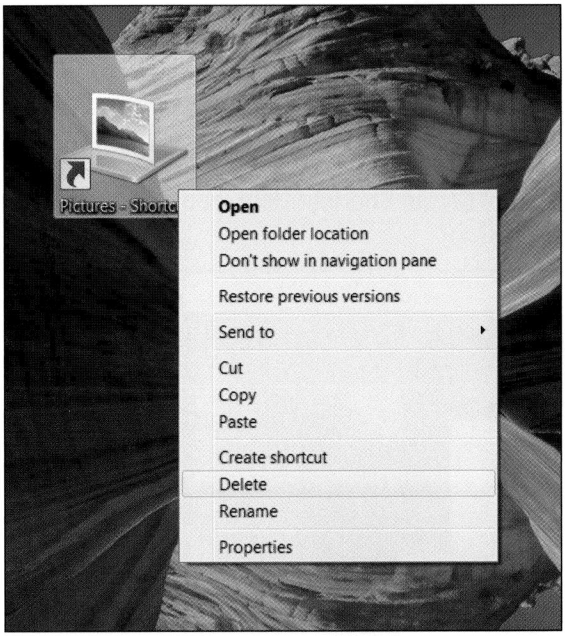

Pictures - Shortc
Open
Open folder location
Don't show in navigation pane
Restore previous versions
Send to
Cut
Copy
Paste
Create shortcut
Delete
Rename
Properties

Important

If the item you want to delete does not have an arrow by it, and it's data you have created such as a picture or file, deleting it from the Desktop will delete the actual data. You should only delete items that have the shortcut arrow on them, just to be safe.

Delete Shortcut
Are you sure you want to move this shortcut to the Recycle Bin?
Pictures - Shortcut
Location: Pictures
(C:\Users\Joli\AppData\Roaming\Microsoft\Windov
Yes
No
3

For your information

If you are deleting a shortcut, you might still see a warning that you are moving a file to the Recycle Bin, when in reality you are not. Remember, you can always delete a shortcut, even if prompted it's a file.

Removing icons and shortcuts from the Desktop

1. Right-click the icon to remove.
2. Click Delete.
3. Carefully read the information in the resulting dialogue box. Click Yes to delete or No to cancel.

Configure Desktop and monitor settings

There are even more ways to change how Windows 7 looks. One is to change the screen resolution. While the science behind resolution is rather complex, suffice it to say that the lower the resolution, the larger your material appears on the monitor; the higher the resolution, the smaller your material appears on the monitor. With a higher resolution, you can have more items on your screen; with a lower resolution, fewer.

Here's what my screen looks like at the lowest resolution offered: 800 by 600 pixels.

Recycle Bin
3:04 PM
9/4/2009

In this figure the icons and Taskbar items are really large. Compare this with what you see on your own laptop. Your icons are likely much smaller. If you're interested in seeing the resolution options, follow the steps here.

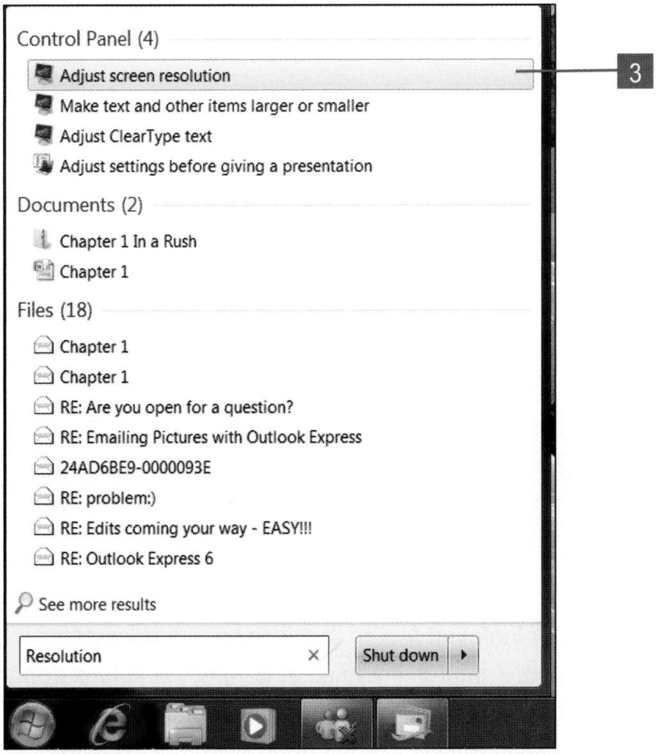

Control Panel (4)
Adjust screen resolution
Make text and other items larger or smaller
Adjust ClearType text
Adjust settings before giving a presentation
Documents (2)
Chapter 1 In a Rush
Chapter 1
Files (18)
Chapter 1
Chapter 1
RE: Are you open for a question?
RE: Emailing Pictures with Outlook Express
24AD6BE9-0000093E
RE: problem:)
RE: Edits coming your way - EASY!!!
RE: Outlook Express 6
See more results
Resolution
Shut down
3

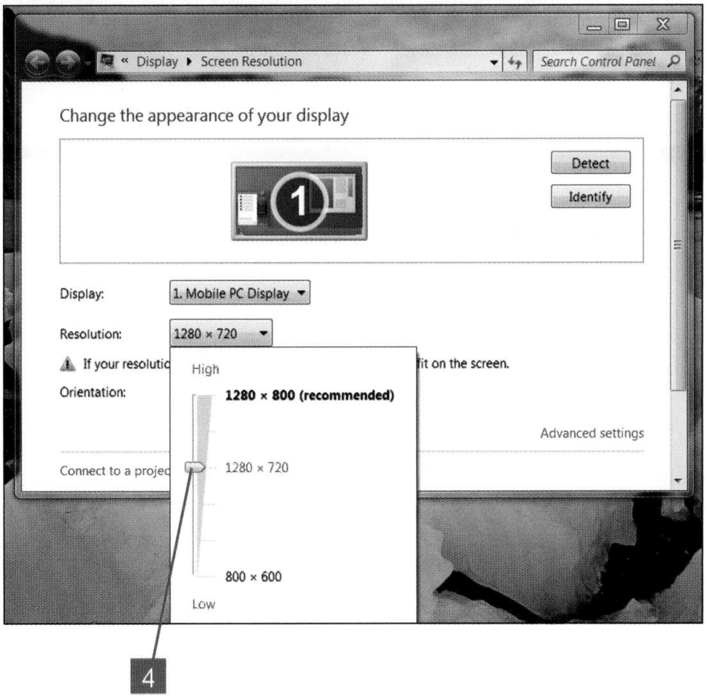

Display ▸ Screen Resolution
Search Control Panel
Change the appearance of your display
Detect
Identify
1
Display:
1. Mobile PC Display
Resolution:
1280 × 720
If your resolutio
fit on the screen.
Orientation:
High
1280 × 800 (recommended)
1280 × 720
800 × 600
Low
Advanced settings
Connect to a projec
4

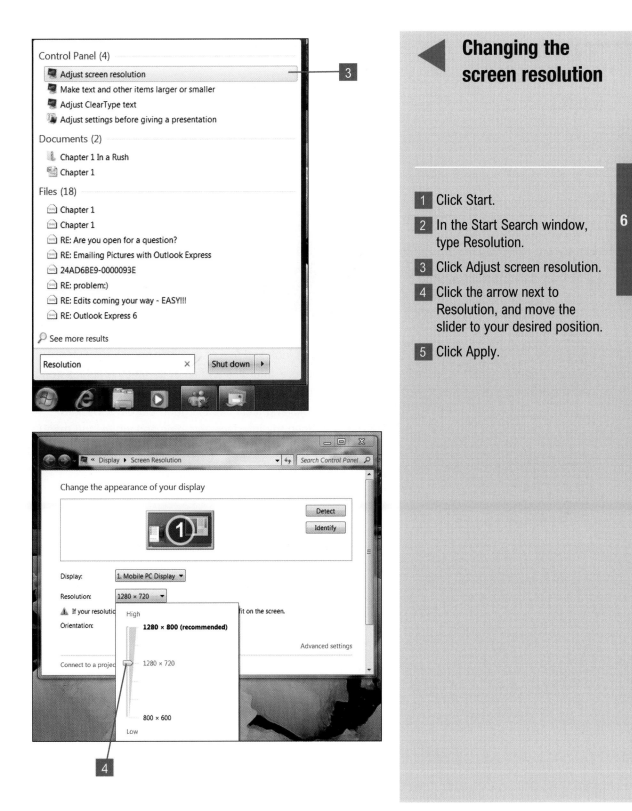

Changing the screen resolution

1 Click Start.

2 In the Start Search window, type Resolution.

3 Click Adjust screen resolution.

4 Click the arrow next to Resolution, and move the slider to your desired position.

5 Click Apply.

Changing the screen resolution (cont.)

6 If prompted to keep these settings, click Yes. Note how the appearance of the screen changes. Click Yes or No.

7 Repeat these steps as desired, and select the resolution that is best for you.

?

Did you know?

If the screen goes black after selecting a new resolution, it means your video card does not support that resolution. This rarely happens, especially on new PCs.

!

Important

If you don't see anything and the screen goes black, don't touch anything. Your screen will return to its previous resolution in a few seconds.

If you prefer the look and feel of an older operating system and the Windows 7 interface and all of its fancy graphics don't do anything for you, you can use the Windows Classic theme. This theme looks and feels like the good old days, back in 2000 or so, when the interface was blue and white, and menu bars were grey. You really can go back in time.

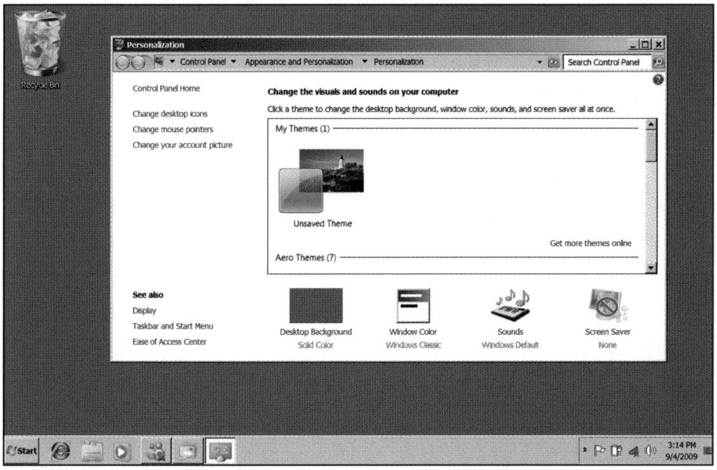
Personalization
Control Panel
Appearance and Personalization
Personalization
Search Control Panel
Control Panel Home
Change desktop icons
Change mouse pointers
Change your account picture
Change the visuals and sounds on your computer
Click a theme to change the desktop background, window color, sounds, and screen saver all at once.
My Themes (1)
Unsaved Theme
Get more themes online
Aero Themes (7)
See also
Display
Taskbar and Start Menu
Ease of Access Center
Desktop Background
Solid Color
Window Color
Windows Classic
Sounds
Windows Default
Screen Saver
None
Recycle Bin
Start
3:14 PM
9/4/2009

Using the Windows Classic theme

1. Right-click an empty area of the desktop.
2. Click Personalize.
3. Click the Windows Classic theme under Basic and High Contrast Themes.

Did you know?

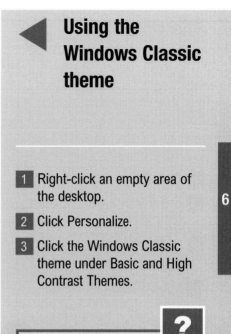

If you want your screen to match the screen shots in this book, work through the steps again, this time choosing the Windows 7 theme. That's what I use most.

Adjusting font size

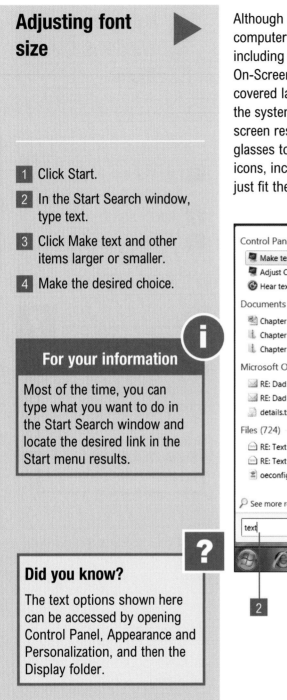

1 Click Start.

2 In the Start Search window, type text.

3 Click Make text and other items larger or smaller.

4 Make the desired choice.

For your information

Most of the time, you can type what you want to do in the Start Search window and locate the desired link in the Start menu results.

Did you know?

The text options shown here can be accessed by opening Control Panel, Appearance and Personalization, and then the Display folder.

Although Windows 7 includes many features to make the computer more easily accessible for those with disabilities, including applications such as Magnifier, Narrator and On-Screen Keyboard (available from the Ease of Access Center covered later in Chapter 7), there is a way simply to increase the system font and icon size if need be. If you've changed the screen resolution to 800 by 600 and still have to wear reading glasses to make out what's on the monitor, including Desktop icons, increasing the size of the system icons and fonts may just fit the bill.

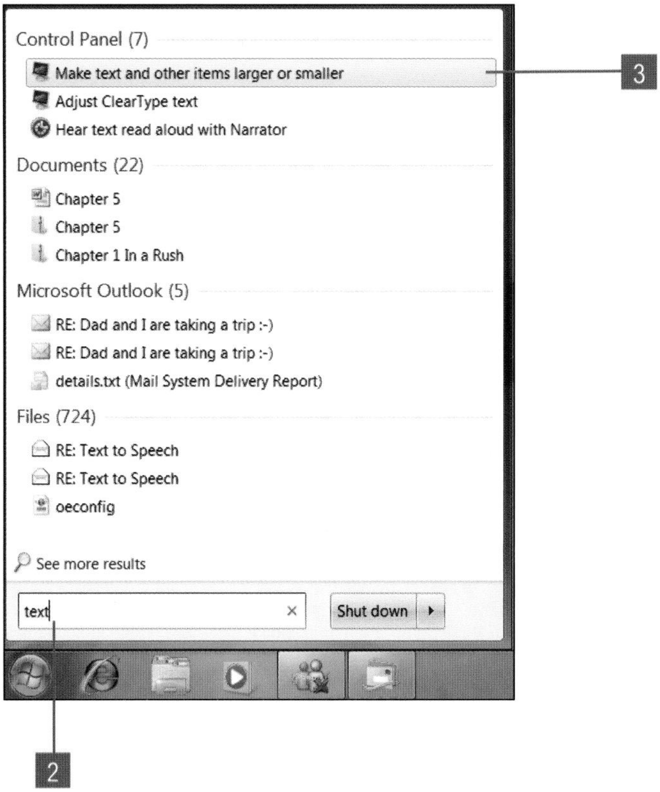

Control Panel (7)
Make text and other items larger or smaller
Adjust ClearType text
Hear text read aloud with Narrator
Documents (22)
Chapter 5
Chapter 5
Chapter 1 In a Rush
Microsoft Outlook (5)
RE: Dad and I are taking a trip :-)
RE: Dad and I are taking a trip :-)
details.txt (Mail System Delivery Report)
Files (724)
RE: Text to Speech
RE: Text to Speech
oeconfig
See more results
text
Shut down
3
2

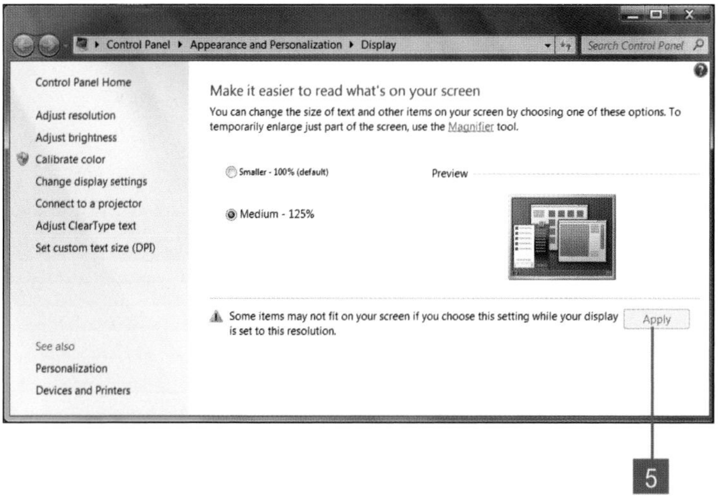
Control Panel ▸ Appearance and Personalization ▸ Display
Search Control Panel
Control Panel Home
Adjust resolution
Adjust brightness
Calibrate color
Change display settings
Connect to a projector
Adjust ClearType text
Set custom text size (DPI)
See also
Personalization
Devices and Printers
Make it easier to read what's on your screen
You can change the size of text and other items on your screen by choosing one of these options. To temporarily enlarge just part of the screen, use the Magnifier tool.
Smaller - 100% (default)
Preview
Medium - 125%
Some items may not fit on your screen if you choose this setting while your display is set to this resolution.
Apply
5

Jargon buster

Boot up – when a computer is powered on, it goes through a sequence of tasks before you see the Desktop. This process is called the boot up process. Computers can be rated by many factors, and one of those factors is how long the 'boot up process' takes.

Browse – browsing for a file, folder or program is the process of drilling down into Windows 7's folder structure to locate the desired item.

Adjusting font size (cont.)

5 Click Apply.

6 If required, click Log off now to apply the settings. (You'll have to log back on after logging off.)

Configuring accessibility options

7

Introduction

Windows 7 offers the Ease of Access Center to help you turn on and configure settings that will make using the laptop easier if you have a disability. You can optimise the display for blindness, or just make the items on the screen easier to see. You can use the computer without a mouse or keyboard by using an On-Screen Keyboard or the built-in speech recognition program. You can make the keyboard easier to use by configuring sticky keys, toggle keys, filter keys and more. And you can use the built-in Narrator application to read what's on the screen out loud, so you don't have to squint to read it yourself.

Did you know? After turning 50, two-thirds of us experience vision, hearing or dexterity problems that impact how well we use our computers. Getting older doesn't mean the end of using a computer, though; laptops can be customised to meet the needs of those who are blind, deaf and quadriplegic, as well as those with the usual over-50 vision, hearing and manual deftness problems.

What you'll do

Use the Narrator

Use the Magnifier

Use the On-Screen Keyboard

Make the keyboard easier to use

Explore keyboard shortcuts

Set up Windows Speech Recognition

Train Windows Speech Recognition

Use Windows Speech Recognition

Configure the Narrator

The Narrator is a basic screen reader. This means that the application will read text that appears on the screen to you, while you navigate using the keyboard and mouse. You can choose what text Narrator reads, change the Narrator's voice and even configure it to describe events, such as error messages (or not). There isn't much to configuring in Narrator; the art of Narrator lies in learning to use it properly.

Narrator is not a cure-all for those who want to have everything read to them. It's not designed to read content in every program you have; it's really just a *screen reader*. Additionally, Narrator may not pronounce all words correctly, cannot read certain parts of the screen and has various other limitations. However, in the absence of a third-party accessibility program, Narrator will do in a pinch.

Although Narrator is part of the Ease of Access group of applications, you can open Narrator by searching for it from the Start menu. As soon as you click the Narrator link, it starts reading to you. In fact, it talks and talks and talks. It first announces that Microsoft Narrator is running, and then continues on by reading the dialogue box shown earlier. Once it stops reading that, it announces each thing you do with the mouse or keyboard. For instance, if you hover the mouse over the Internet Explorer icon, it says 'Launch Internet Explorer Browser. Finds and displays information and websites on the Internet. Tooltip'. It may also say things like 'Window opened' or 'Window closed'. Now all of this is great, except that you might not need every little thing read to you. That's what keyboard shortcuts are for. Clicking Ctrl will cause the reading to stop, at least for the current event. Other things may interrupt Narrator too, like changing the volume or opening a new window.

It first announces that Microsoft announces that Microsoft Narrator is running and then continues reading the dialogue box and other on-screen items:

- Contents of the open window.
- Menus and menu options.
- Text you have typed.

- Tooltips.
- Events such as minimising and maximising windows.
- Some email in Windows Live Mail.
- Various other on-screen items.

Narrator doesn't read much else, although it will read the names of folders, the tooltip that appears when you hover your mouse over something, and what you are clicking with the mouse, such as the Start button or minimise or maximise buttons. It won't read a document, but it will read the title of the document as it appears on the screen.

!

Important

According to Microsoft, the Narrator will read documents, PDFs, web pages and more. But I can't get it to work that way. Sure, it will read anything I click on, what I'm doing to the windows, and if I'm scrolling or not, but getting it to read documents is another story. Lots of people have difficulties with it, too, not just you and me. If you find you're having problems making Narrator work, consider a third-party program.

?

Did you know?

Microsoft offers help for those with disabilities at www.microsoft.com/enable.

Using the Narrator

1. Click Start.
2. In the Start Search dialogue box, type Narrator.
3. Select or deselect options to configure Narrator to your needs. The default, shown here, is a good place to start.
4. Click the Start button. If you can't hear the Narrator, which will start talking immediately, turn up or plug in your speakers.
5. Click inside the Start Search dialogue box while Narrator reads what's on the Start menu.
6. Type Internet Explorer.
7. Click the Ctrl key to stop Narrator from continuing to read.
8. Click Exit to turn Narrator off and exit the program.

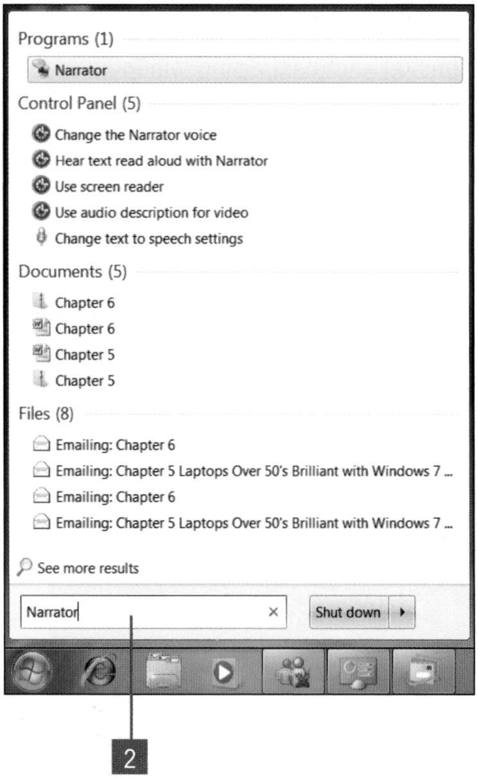

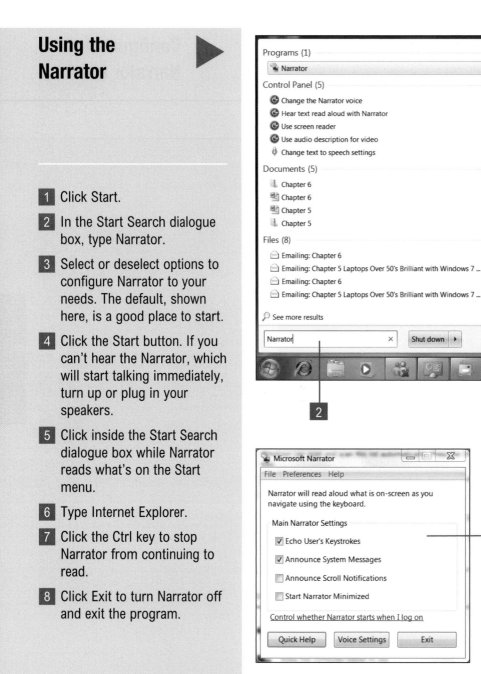

Programs (1)
Narrator
Control Panel (5)
Change the Narrator voice
Hear text read aloud with Narrator
Use screen reader
Use audio description for video
Change text to speech settings
Documents (5)
Chapter 6
Chapter 6
Chapter 5
Chapter 5
Files (8)
Emailing: Chapter 6
Emailing: Chapter 5 Laptops Over 50's Brilliant with Windows 7 ...
Emailing: Chapter 6
Emailing: Chapter 5 Laptops Over 50's Brilliant with Windows 7 ...
See more results
Narrator
Shut down
2

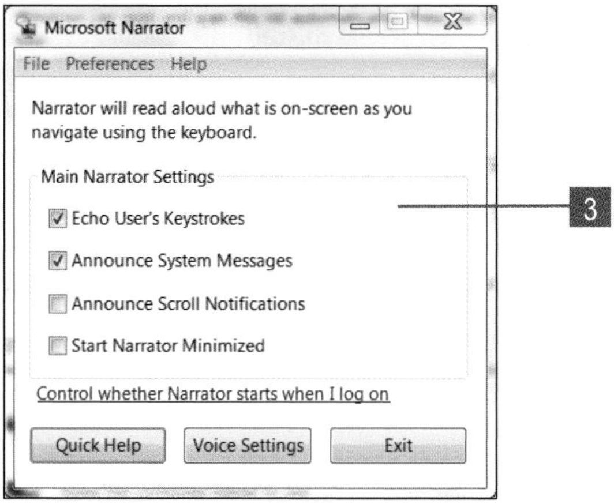

Microsoft Narrator
File Preferences Help
Narrator will read aloud what is on-screen as you navigate using the keyboard.
Main Narrator Settings
Echo User's Keystrokes
Announce System Messages
Announce Scroll Notifications
Start Narrator Minimized
Control whether Narrator starts when I log on
Quick Help
Voice Settings
Exit
3

Working with the Magnifier

The Magnifier is another tool in the Ease of Access suite of applications. As with Narrator, you can access Magnifier from the Start Search dialogue box, by typing Magnifier. There isn't anything to configure in Magnifier. As with Narrator, the art of Magnifier lies in your ability to use it.

When you start Magnifier, you'll immediately notice a difference. You will only be able to see an enlarged part of the screen. As you move the mouse around, different parts of the screen will be magnified. This application works much better than Narrator. You are in complete control of the mouse, and, thus, what is magnified on screen.

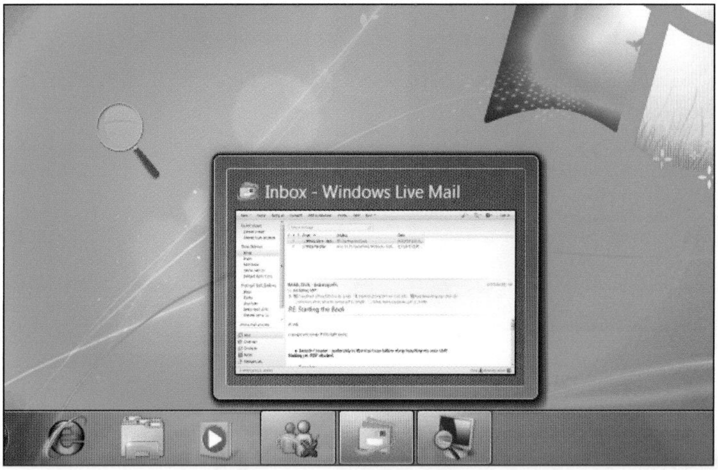
Inbox - Windows Live Mail

Using the Magnifier

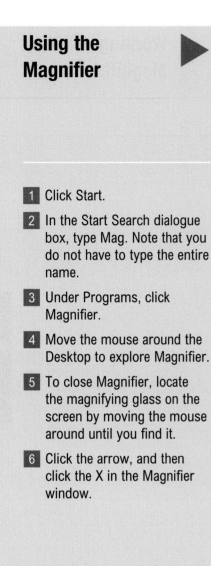

1. Click Start.
2. In the Start Search dialogue box, type Mag. Note that you do not have to type the entire name.
3. Under Programs, click Magnifier.
4. Move the mouse around the Desktop to explore Magnifier.
5. To close Magnifier, locate the magnifying glass on the screen by moving the mouse around until you find it.
6. Click the arrow, and then click the X in the Magnifier window.

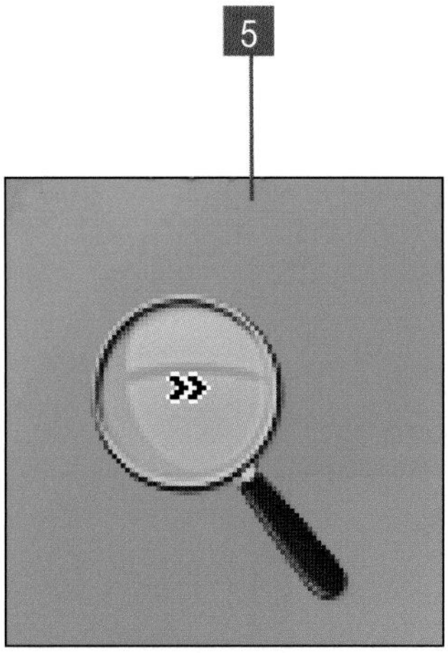

5

Magnifier
200% Views
Close
6

Using the On-Screen Keyboard

If you can't use a mouse, don't like the touchpad and you can't use a keyboard, you can still input data to your computer. You can use a joystick, trackball, modified switch, touch screen, electronic pointing device or any other available input method to input data using the Windows 7 On-Screen Keyboard feature. If your hands shake too badly to use traditional hardware, if your fingers are just too big for the tiny keyboard keys, or if you can't use your hands at all due to arthritis or a similar condition, there are certainly options. A large joystick is one of them. If you're a quadriplegic there are options too. One is the sip/puff switch. This switch lets a mobility impaired person control mouse clicks with a sip or a puff on a device that is kept at the mouth. Every week there seem to be advancements in input devices. Whatever hardware you choose to input data it can be with Microsoft's On-Screen Keyboard, although some hardware may come with its own software. To use the On-Screen Keyboard feature, you use whatever pointing device that works for you to click the keys desired on the screen.

On-Screen Keyboard
Esc
Bksp
Home
PgUp
Tab
Del
End
PgDn
Caps
Insert
Pause
Shift
Shift
PrtScn
ScrLk
Ctrl
Alt
Alt
Ctrl
Fn
Options
Help

Using the On-Screen Keyboard (cont.)

1. Click Start.
2. In the Start Search dialogue box, type On-Screen.
3. Under Programs, click On-Screen Keyboard.
4. Click Options on the On-Screen Keyboard. There are a few things you may like to configure, such as whether or not to use a 'click sound' when typing, if you actually want to click the keys or simply hover over them and more. Configure as desired and click OK.
5. Click Start, and in the Start Search dialogue box, use your mouse to type the word Internet. Note the results.
6. To close the On-Screen Keyboard, click the X in the top right corner.

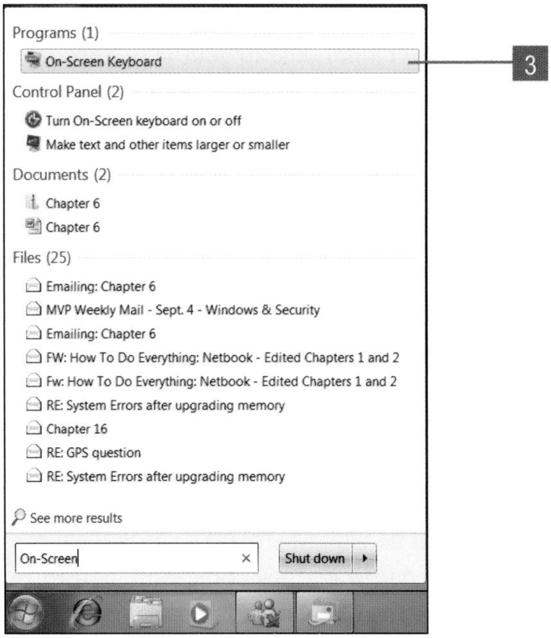

Programs (1)
On-Screen Keyboard
3
Control Panel (2)
Turn On-Screen keyboard on or off
Make text and other items larger or smaller
Documents (2)
Chapter 6
Chapter 6
Files (25)
Emailing: Chapter 6
MVP Weekly Mail - Sept. 4 - Windows & Security
Emailing: Chapter 6
FW: How To Do Everything: Netbook - Edited Chapters 1 and 2
Fw: How To Do Everything: Netbook - Edited Chapters 1 and 2
RE: System Errors after upgrading memory
Chapter 16
RE: GPS question
RE: System Errors after upgrading memory
See more results
On-Screen
Shut down

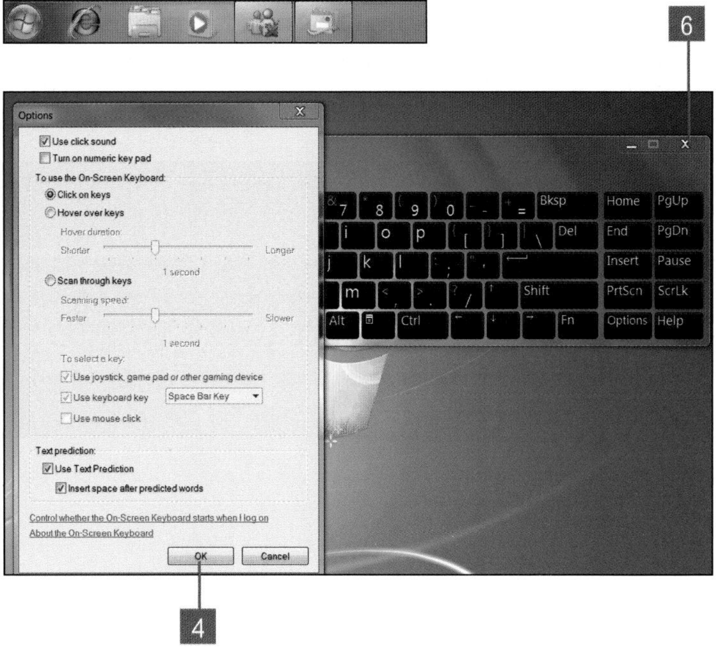

6
Options
Use click sound
Turn on numeric key pad
To use the On-Screen Keyboard:
Click on keys
Hover over keys
Hover duration:
Shorter
Longer
1 second
Scan through keys
Scanning speed:
Faster
Slower
1 second
To select a key:
Use joystick, game pad or other gaming device
Use keyboard key
Space Bar Key
Use mouse click
Text prediction:
Use Text Prediction
Insert space after predicted words
Control whether the On-Screen Keyboard starts when I log on
About the On-Screen Keyboard
OK
Cancel
Bksp
Home
PgUp
Del
End
PgDn
Insert
Pause
Shift
PrtScn
ScrLk
Alt
Ctrl
Fn
Options
Help
4

Make the keyboard easier to use

There are several ways to make the keyboard easier to use, including options such as Mouse Keys, Sticky Keys, Toggle Keys and Filter Keys. Each of these offer different accessibility options.

- Mouse Keys let you forgo using the mouse; instead, you can use the arrow keys on your keyboard or the numeric keypad to move the mouse pointer on the Desktop or inside programs or documents.
- Sticky Keys allow you to configure the keyboard so that you never have to press three keys at once (such as when you must press the Ctrl, Alt and Delete keys together to log into Windows). With Sticky Keys, you can use one key to perform these tasks. You configure the key to use for three-key tasks.
- Toggle can be configured to sound an alert when you press the Caps Lock, Num Lock or Scroll Lock keys. These alerts can help prevent the aggravation of unintentionally pressing a key and not realising it.
- Filter Keys let you configure Windows to ignore keystrokes that occur in rapid succession, such as when you accidentally leave your finger on a key for too long.
- Underline keyboard shortcuts and access keys. This option makes dialogue boxes easier to work with by highlighting the access keys used to control them.
- Prevent windows from being automatically arranged when moved to the edge of the screen. This allows you to move windows without having them snap into place.

Make the keyboard easier to use (cont.)

1. Click Start.
2. Type Change keyboard.
3. Select Change how your keyboard works from the results.
4. Place a check mark in the accessibility options to enable.
5. Click Apply.

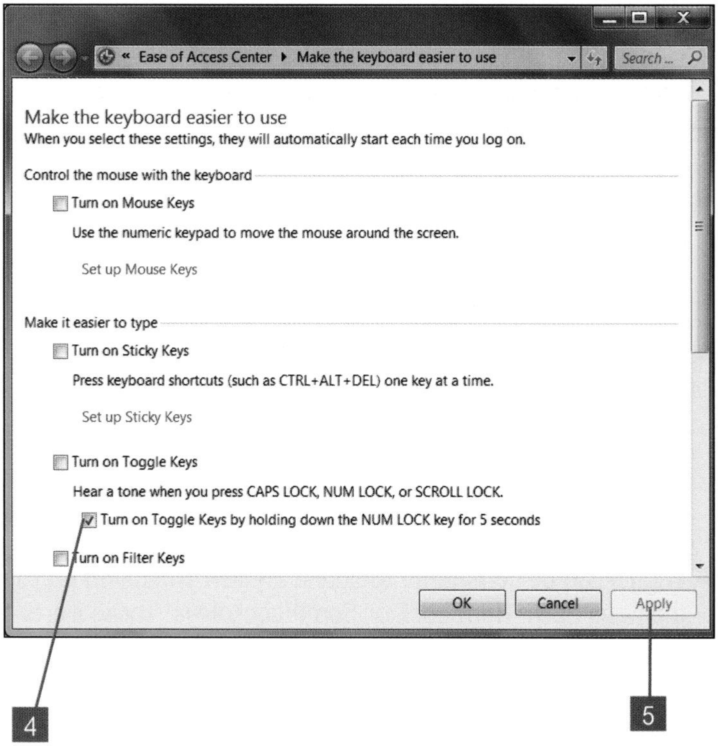

« Ease of Access Center ▸ Make the keyboard easier to use
Search...
Make the keyboard easier to use
When you select these settings, they will automatically start each time you log on.
Control the mouse with the keyboard
Turn on Mouse Keys
Use the numeric keypad to move the mouse around the screen.
Set up Mouse Keys
Make it easier to type
Turn on Sticky Keys
Press keyboard shortcuts (such as CTRL+ALT+DEL) one key at a time.
Set up Sticky Keys
Turn on Toggle Keys
Hear a tone when you press CAPS LOCK, NUM LOCK, or SCROLL LOCK.
Turn on Toggle Keys by holding down the NUM LOCK key for 5 seconds
Turn on Filter Keys
OK
Cancel
Apply
4
5

There are keyboard shortcuts that go along with these options. They include:

Left Alt + Left Shift + Num Lock – turn Mouse Keys on or off.

Num Lock for five seconds – turn Toggle Keys on or off.

Right Shift for eight seconds – turn Filter Keys on or off.

Shift five times – turn Sticky Keys on or off.

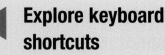

Explore keyboard shortcuts

It doesn't matter if you're over 50, disabled, have arthritis in your hands or are just a little lazy, learning and using keyboard shortcuts can be one of the best ways to spend your time. Keyboard shortcuts let you do things more quickly than you could with multiple keystrokes. For instance, to open Help and Support you could click Start, and then Help and Support, or you could do it with one finger by clicking the F1 key on the keyboard. Instead of highlighting text in a document and searching for the menu or button that makes that text bold, just click Ctrl + B. And there's more where this came from. In the following sections I'll list my favourite keyboard shortcuts but, if you want more, just search the Internet for 'Windows keyboard shortcuts'.

General keyboard shortcuts

Alt + Esc – cycle through items in the order in which they were opened.

Alt + F4 – close the active item or exit the active program.

Alt + Print Screen – copies an image of the selected window to the clipboard.

Alt + Tab – switch between open items.

Ctrl + A – select all items in a document or window.

Ctrl + Alt + Delete – displays options for: Lock This Computer, Switch User, Log Off, Change a Password and Start Task Manager.

Ctrl + Alt + Tab – use the arrow keys to switch between open items.

Ctrl + C – copy the selected item.

Ctrl + Esc – open the Start menu (the Windows Logo key works too).

Ctrl + V – paste the selected item.

Ctrl + X – cut the selected item.

Ctrl + Y – redo an action.

Ctrl + Z – undo an action.

Delete – delete the selected item and move it to the Recycle Bin.

Esc – cancel the current task.

Explore keyboard shortcuts (cont.)

1. Click the Windows key on the keyboard. If you don't see a Windows key, click the Start key. The Start menu opens.
2. Click the Tab key on the keyboard. Notice what is selected in the Start menu.
3. Use the arrow keys on the keyboard to move through the Start menu items.
4. Press the Enter key to open the selected item.

F1 – display Help.

F5 – refresh the active window.

Print Screen – copies an image of the entire screen to the clipboard.

Shift + F10 – display the shortcut menu for the selected item.

Dialogue box shortcuts

Dialogue boxes appear when you have to make choices before applying a command. For instance, in a Print dialogue box you have to choose how many copies and the quality of the print. You can apply the following shortcuts while in a dialogue box:

Alt + underlined letter – perform the command (or select the option) that goes with that letter.

Arrow keys – select a button if the active option is a group of option buttons.

Backspace – open a folder one level up if a folder is selected in the Save As or Open dialogue box.

Ctrl + Shift + Tab – move back through tabs.

Ctrl + Tab – move forward through tabs.

Enter – replaces clicking the mouse for many selected commands.

Shift + Tab – move back through options.

Spacebar – select or clear the check box if the active option is a check box.

Tab – move forward through options.

Exploring additional Ease of Access options

There are far too many accessibility options in Windows 7 to cover each and every one. But now that you're familiar with some of them, configuring and using the features we haven't covered will be a little more intuitive.

One of the options is to make the mouse easier to use. It is easy to select a different colour or size for your mouse. Another option is to use text or visual alternatives for sounds. This allows you to turn on visual notifications of sounds that play on your computer as well as text captions for spoken dialogue.

You can also opt to use the computer without a display. Here, you can turn on Narrator and Audio Description. The latter lets you hear descriptions of what's happening in the videos you watch, if it's available.

And, although there are many other options, perhaps the most helpful is the one that helps you get recommendations to make your computer easier to use. A wizard asks questions about your current abilities (and disabilities), and helps you decide what accessibility options are best for you.

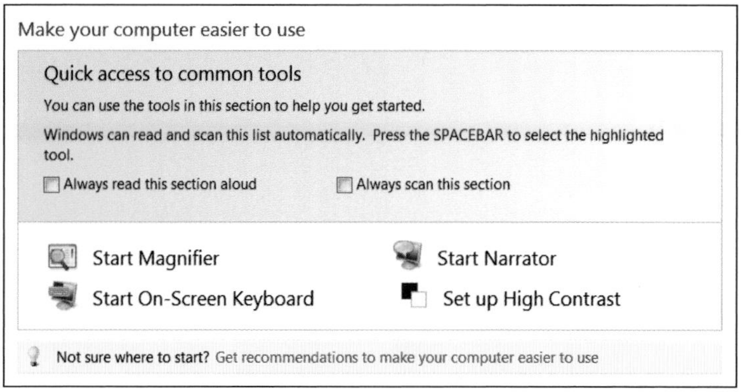
Make your computer easier to use
Quick access to common tools
You can use the tools in this section to help you get started.
Windows can read and scan this list automatically. Press the SPACEBAR to select the highlighted tool.
Always read this section aloud
Always scan this section
Start Magnifier
Start Narrator
Start On-Screen Keyboard
Set up High Contrast
Not sure where to start? Get recommendations to make your computer easier to use

Statements you can select include but are not limited to:

- I am blind.
- I have another type of vision impairment (even if glasses correct it).
- A physical condition affects the use of my arms, wrists, hands or fingers.

7

Exploring additional Ease of Access options (cont.)

- Pens and pencils are difficult to use.
- Conversations are difficult to hear (even with a hearing aid).
- I am deaf.
- I have a speech impairment.
- It is often difficult for me to concentrate.
- It is often difficult for me to remember things.
- I have a learning disability, such as dyslexia.

After filling out the questionnaire, you'll receive information regarding the settings recommended for you.

Windows Speech Recognition

Last, but certainly not least, is the Windows 7 Speech Recognition program. This program does a good job of allowing you to control your computer with your voice. From the Speech Recognition options you can set up your microphone, take a speech tutorial, train your computer to understand you better and more.

With Speech Recognition you can:

- start programs
- open menus
- click buttons
- click objects
- dictate documents
- write and send email
- do almost anything you can do with a keyboard and mouse.

You have to work through the Speech Recognition wizard before you can use Speech Recognition and that takes a little bit of time, so let's start there.

Setting up Windows Speech Recognition

1. Click Start.
2. In the Start Search dialogue box, type Speech Recognition.
3. Select Windows Speech Recognition from the results.
4. Read the introductory page and click Next.
5. Select your input device Choose from Headset Microphone, Desktop Microphone or Other. Click Next.
6. Read the informational page and, if necessary, place your microphone at the suggested distance and click Next.
7. Read the sentences as suggested, in a natural speaking voice. Reposition the microphone, if necessary, so that when you speak the lower bar appears in the green area of the upper bar. Click Next to continue.
8. Click Next to continue setting up Speech Recognition.
9. Continue to work through the wizard to the end.
10. When prompted, click Start Tutorial or Cancel. I suggest you choose Start Tutorial and work through it now.

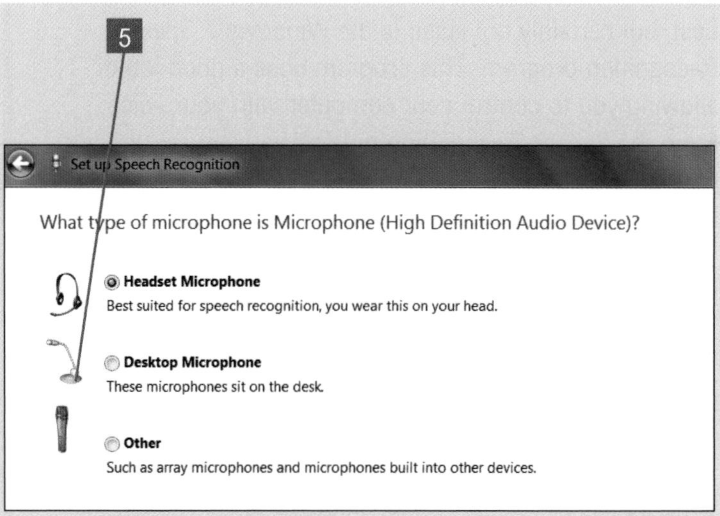
5
Set up Speech Recognition
What type of microphone is Microphone (High Definition Audio Device)?
Headset Microphone
Best suited for speech recognition, you wear this on your head.
Desktop Microphone
These microphones sit on the desk.
Other
Such as array microphones and microphones built into other devices.

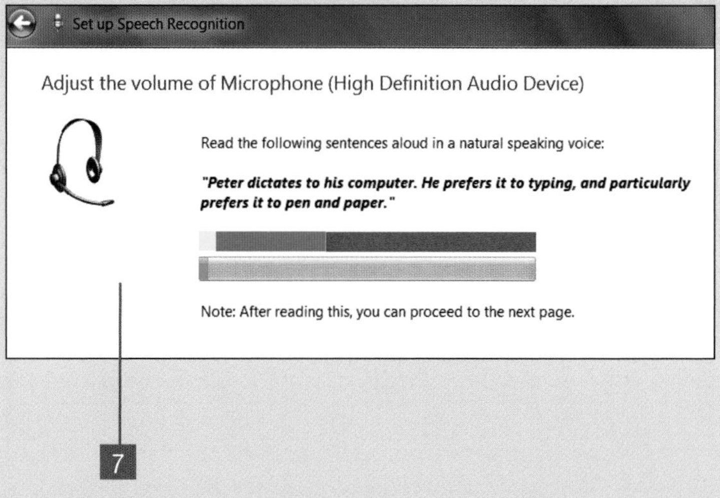
Set up Speech Recognition
Adjust the volume of Microphone (High Definition Audio Device)
Read the following sentences aloud in a natural speaking voice:
"Peter dictates to his computer. He prefers it to typing, and particularly prefers it to pen and paper."
Note: After reading this, you can proceed to the next page.
7

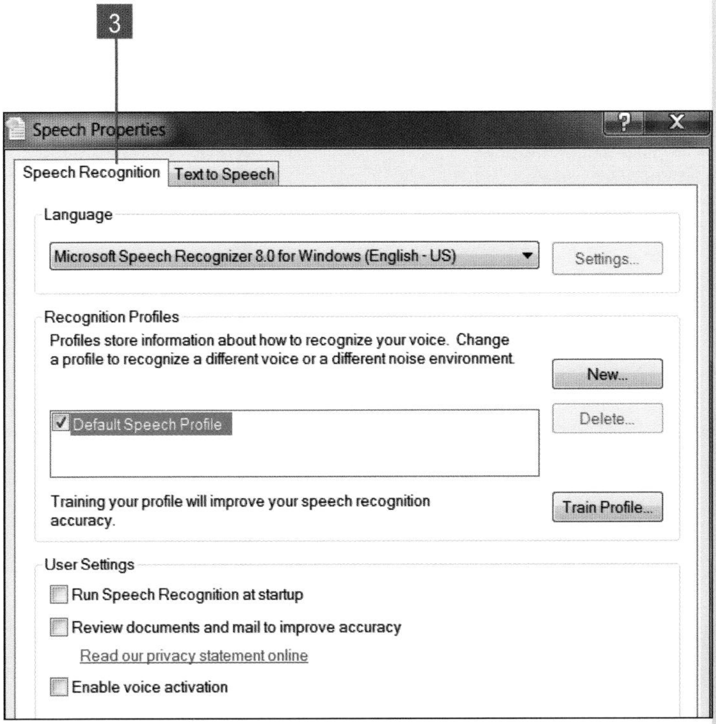
3
Speech Properties
Speech Recognition
Text to Speech
Language
Microsoft Speech Recognizer 8.0 for Windows (English - US)
Settings...
Recognition Profiles
Profiles store information about how to recognize your voice. Change a profile to recognize a different voice or a different noise environment.
New...
Default Speech Profile
Delete...
Training your profile will improve your speech recognition accuracy.
Train Profile...
User Settings
Run Speech Recognition at startup
Review documents and mail to improve accuracy
Read our privacy statement online
Enable voice activation

Did you know?

You can spend the better part of an afternoon working through all of the tutorials. Just keep at it.

Training Windows Speech Recognition

1. Click Start, and in the Start Search window, type Speech.
2. Select Change text to speech settings in the results.
3. Click the Speech Recognition tab. (Note the other option.)
4. Work through the tutorial all the way to the end, or at least as long as you can. Note that you may have to say the command several times for the program to recognise your voice, tone and accent. As you work through the training, the Speech Recognition program will get better and better at recognising the words you speak.

Using Windows Speech Recognition

1. If the Speech Recognition program is not running, click Start, and in the Start Search window type speech. Select Start speech recognition.
2. Say: 'Start speech recognition'. Verify Speech Recognition is 'listening'.
3. Say Start.
4. Say Internet Explorer (Internet Explorer opens).
5. Say Close that (Internet Explorer closes).
6. Say Start.
7. Say Control Panel.
8. Say Close that.

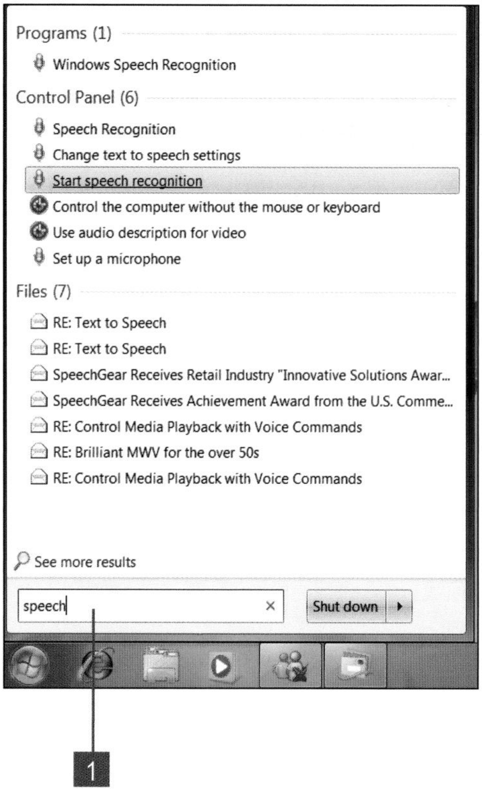
Programs (1)
Windows Speech Recognition
Control Panel (6)
Speech Recognition
Change text to speech settings
Start speech recognition
Control the computer without the mouse or keyboard
Use audio description for video
Set up a microphone
Files (7)
RE: Text to Speech
RE: Text to Speech
SpeechGear Receives Retail Industry "Innovative Solutions Awar...
SpeechGear Receives Achievement Award from the U.S. Comme...
RE: Control Media Playback with Voice Commands
RE: Brilliant MWV for the over 50s
RE: Control Media Playback with Voice Commands
See more results
speech
Shut down
1

8

Safety and security

What you'll do

Add a new user account

Use System Restore

Configure Windows Update

Use Windows Firewall

Use Windows Defender

Resolve Action Center warnings

Set up Parental Controls

Create your first backup

Introduction

Windows 7 comes with a lot of built-in features to keep you and your data safe from Internet ills, nosy children and download-happy grandchildren. Windows 7 also offers help in avoiding email and web criminals whose only purpose in life is to steal your data, get your bank account or credit card numbers, or steal your identity. Mail even informs you if it thinks an email is 'phishing' for information you shouldn't give out.

Now, your reaction to these statements may be that you feel I've exaggerated the actual computer threats you may encounter, or it may make you not want to share your computer, go online or read email ever again. Whatever the case, it's important to understand there are threats out there, and Windows 7 does its best to offer you protection. If you take advantage of the available safeguards, you'll be protected in almost all cases. You just need to be aware of the dangers, heed warnings when they are given, and use all of the available features in Windows 7 to protect yourself and your laptop.

Your laptop was not shipped to you with all of the available safety measures in place. While many measures are enabled by default, which you'll learn about later, some require intervention from you.

Here's an example. If you have grandchildren who use your computer, they can likely access or delete your personal data, download harmful content, install applications, or change settings that will affect the entire computer, all very easily. You can solve all of these problems by creating a computer account just for them. In conjunction, every account you create should be password protected, especially yours. It wouldn't be much good to create accounts and not assign passwords!

Beyond creating user accounts, here are some other ways to protect your laptop, which we'll discuss in depth in this chapter:

- System Restore – if enabled, Windows 7 stores 'restore points' on your laptop's hard drive. If something goes wrong you can run System Restore, choose one of these points and revert to a pre-problem date. Since System Restore only deals with 'system data', none of your personal data will be affected (not even your last email).
- Windows Update – if enabled and configured properly, when you are online Windows 7 will check for security updates automatically and install them. You don't have to do anything, and your laptop is always updated with the latest security patches and features.
- Windows Firewall – if enabled and configured properly, the Firewall will help prevent hackers (people whose job it is to get into your computer and do harm to it) from accessing your laptop and data. The Firewall blocks most programs from communicating outside the network (or outside your laptop). If you want to allow a program to communicate outside your safety zone you can 'allow' a program by adding it to an 'exceptions' list. This is all very easy to do.
- Windows Defender – you don't have to do much to Windows Defender except understand that it offers protection against Internet threats. It's enabled by default and it runs in the background. However, if you ever think your computer has been attacked by an Internet threat (virus, worm, malware, etc.) you can run a manual scan here.
- Action Center Warnings – the Action Center is a talkative application. You can be sure you'll see a pop-up if your anti-virus software is out of date (or not installed), if you don't have the proper security settings configured, or if Windows Update or the Firewall is disabled. You'll learn about warnings and what to do about them in this chapter.
- Parental Controls – if you have grandchildren, children or even a forgetful or scatterbrained spouse who needs

imposed computer limitations, you can apply them using Parental Controls. With these controls you are in charge of the hours a user can access the computer, which games they can play and what programs they can run (among other things).

- Backup and Restore – this feature lets you perform backups and, in the case of a computer failure and restore them (put them back). However, there are other backup options, including copying files to a CD or DVD, copying pictures and media to an external hard drive, USB drive or memory card, or storing them on an Internet server.

8

User accounts and passwords

If every person who accesses your laptop has his or her own standard user account and password, and if every person logs on using that account and then logs off the laptop each time they've finished using it, you'd never have to worry about anyone accessing anyone else's personal data. That's because when a user logs on with his or her own user account, he or she can only access his or her data (and any data other users have specifically elected to share).

Additionally, every user with his or her own user account is provided with a 'user profile' that tells Windows 7 what Desktop background to use, what screensaver, and preferences for mouse settings, sounds and more. Each user also has his or her own Favorites in Internet Explorer 7, and his or her own email settings, address books and personal folders. User accounts help everyone who accesses the computer keep their personal data, well, personal.

Adding a new user account

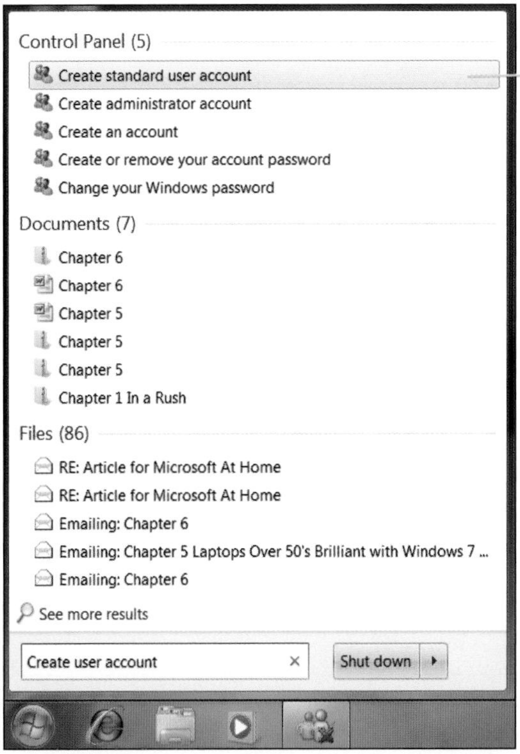
Control Panel (5)
Create standard user account
Create administrator account
Create an account
Create or remove your account password
Change your Windows password
Documents (7)
Chapter 6
Chapter 6
Chapter 5
Chapter 5
Chapter 5
Chapter 1 In a Rush
Files (86)
RE: Article for Microsoft At Home
RE: Article for Microsoft At Home
Emailing: Chapter 6
Emailing: Chapter 5 Laptops Over 50's Brilliant with Windows 7 ...
Emailing: Chapter 6
See more results
Create user account
Shut down
2

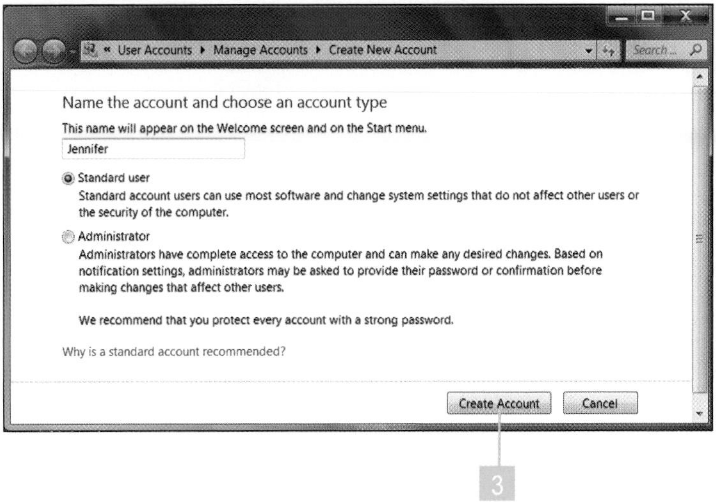
User Accounts ▸ Manage Accounts ▸ Create New Account
Search ...
Name the account and choose an account type
This name will appear on the Welcome screen and on the Start menu.
Jennifer
Standard user
Standard account users can use most software and change system settings that do not affect other users or the security of the computer.
Administrator
Administrators have complete access to the computer and can make any desired changes. Based on notification settings, administrators may be asked to provide their password or confirmation before making changes that affect other users.
We recommend that you protect every account with a strong password.
Why is a standard account recommended?
Create Account
Cancel
3

1. Click Start. In the Start Search window, type Create user account.
2. From the results, click Create standard user account.
3. Type a name for the account, and click Create Account. A new window will open that contains all of the user account names.

8

Adding a new user account (cont.)

4 Click the new account.

5 Click Create a password.

6 Type the new password, type it again to confirm it and then type a password hint.

7 Click Create password.

8 Click the X in the top right corner to close the window.

Important

All user accounts should be password protected. If you see any here that do not have a password, return to this window to create them after completing these steps.

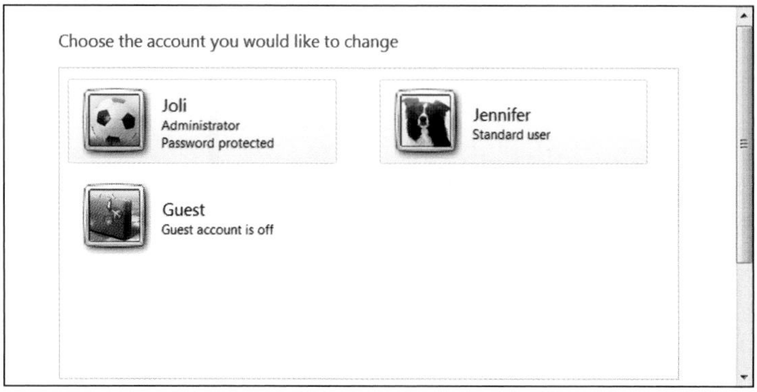

Choose the account you would like to change
Joli
Administrator
Password protected
Jennifer
Standard user
Guest
Guest account is off

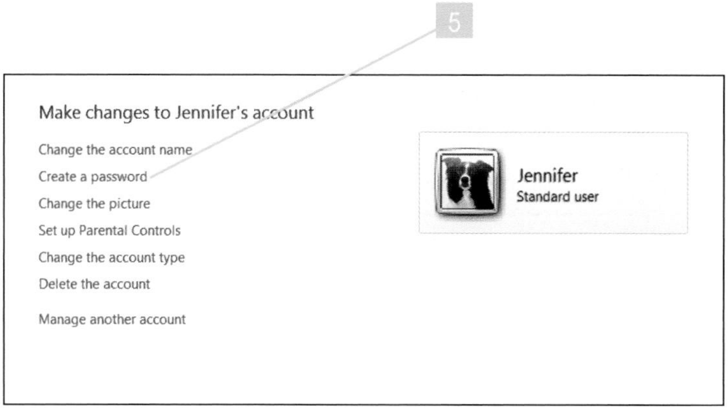

5
Make changes to Jennifer's account
Change the account name
Create a password
Change the picture
Set up Parental Controls
Change the account type
Delete the account
Manage another account
Jennifer
Standard user

Did you know?

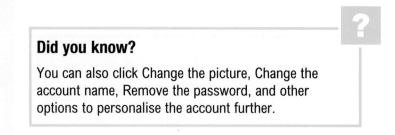

You can also click Change the picture, Change the account name, Remove the password, and other options to personalise the account further.

You learned a little about System Restore, Windows Update, Windows Firewall and Windows Defender in the Introduction, and now it's time to take a look at each of these more closely, and to verify they are set up properly and running as they should be.

Protecting your PC

System Restore

System Restore lets you restore your computer to an earlier time without affecting your personal files, including documents, spreadsheets, email and photos. You'll only use System Restore if and when you install a program or driver that ultimately produces error messages or causes problems for the computer, and uninstalling the problematic application or driver doesn't resolve the issue. System Restore is also appropriate for resolving problems of unknown origin, including blue screens and applications that freeze for no apparent reason.

System Restore, by default, regularly creates and saves restore points that contain information about registry settings and deep-down system information that Windows uses to work properly. Because System Restore works only with its own system files, it can't recover a lost personal file, email or picture. In the same vein, it will not affect this data either.

Did you know?

System Restore can't be enabled unless the computer has at least 300 MB of free space on the hard disk, or if the disk is smaller than 1 GB.

Using Windows Update

1. Click Start.
2. In the Start Search box, type System Restore.
3. Click System Restore under the Programs results.
4. Read the information and click Next.
5. Verify that restore points are available, and select a restore point. You'll want to select a point that was taken prior to the problem's first occurrence.
6. Click Next.
7. Click Finish to run System Restore, otherwise, click Cancel.

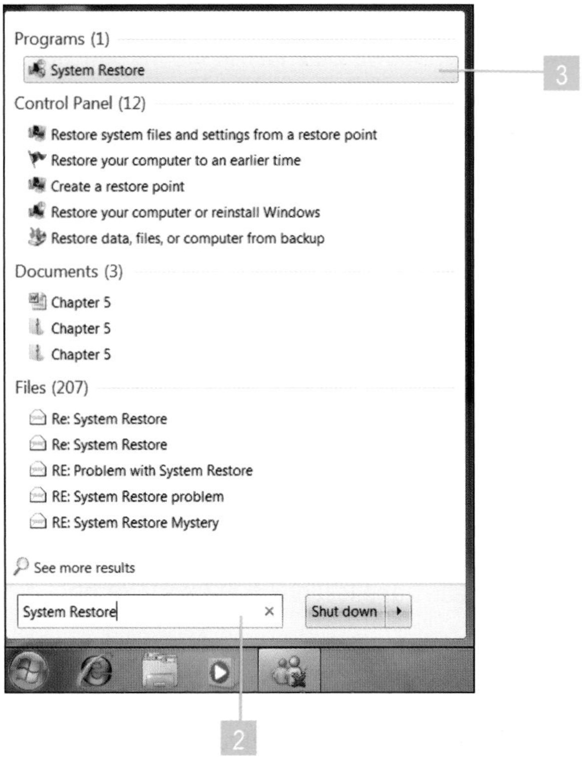

Programs (1)
System Restore
Control Panel (12)
Restore system files and settings from a restore point
Restore your computer to an earlier time
Create a restore point
Restore your computer or reinstall Windows
Restore data, files, or computer from backup
Documents (3)
Chapter 5
Chapter 5
Chapter 5
Files (207)
Re: System Restore
Re: System Restore
RE: Problem with System Restore
RE: System Restore problem
RE: System Restore Mystery
See more results
System Restore
Shut down
3
2

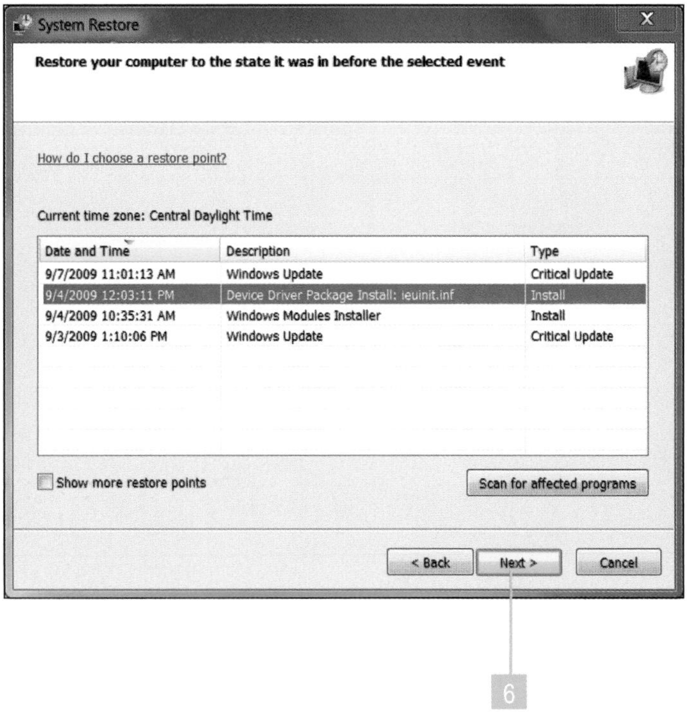

System Restore
Restore your computer to the state it was in before the selected event
How do I choose a restore point?
Current time zone: Central Daylight Time
Date and Time
Description
Type
9/7/2009 11:01:13 AM
Windows Update
Critical Update
9/4/2009 12:03:11 PM
Device Driver Package Install: ieuinit.inf
Install
9/4/2009 10:35:31 AM
Windows Modules Installer
Install
9/3/2009 1:10:06 PM
Windows Update
Critical Update
Show more restore points
Scan for affected programs
< Back
Next >
Cancel
6

Using Windows Update (cont.)

It's very important to configure Windows Update to get and install updates automatically. This is the easiest way to ensure your computer is as up-to-date as possible, at least as far as patching security flaws Microsoft uncovers, having access to the latest features and obtaining updates to the operating system itself. I propose you verify that the recommended settings are enabled as detailed here and occasionally check for optional updates manually.

When Windows Update is configured as recommended in the 'Configuring Windows Update' panel, updates will be downloaded automatically when you are online (on the Internet), installed and, if necessary, your computer will be rebooted automatically. You can configure the time of day you want this to happen.

Timesaver tip

The Windows Help and Support Center offers pages upon pages of information regarding Windows Update, including how to remove them or select updates when more than one is available. I think the above paragraphs state all you need to know as an average 50+ computer user, and that you need not worry about anything else regarding Windows Update.

Configuring Windows Update

1. Click Start. In the Start Search window type Windows Update.
2. Under Programs in the results, click Windows Update.
3. You may see that Windows is up-to-date, or you may see that there are available updates. Anything else means that Windows Update is not configured using recommended settings. Whatever the case, click Change settings. It's in the left pane.
4. Verify that the settings are configured to Install updates automatically (recommended) as shown here. (If you desire, you can choose another setting but I don't recommend it.)
5. Notice the default time of 3:00 AM. Change this to a time when your laptop is connected to the Internet but is not being used. If the computer is not actually online at 3:00 AM, it will check for updates the next time it is.

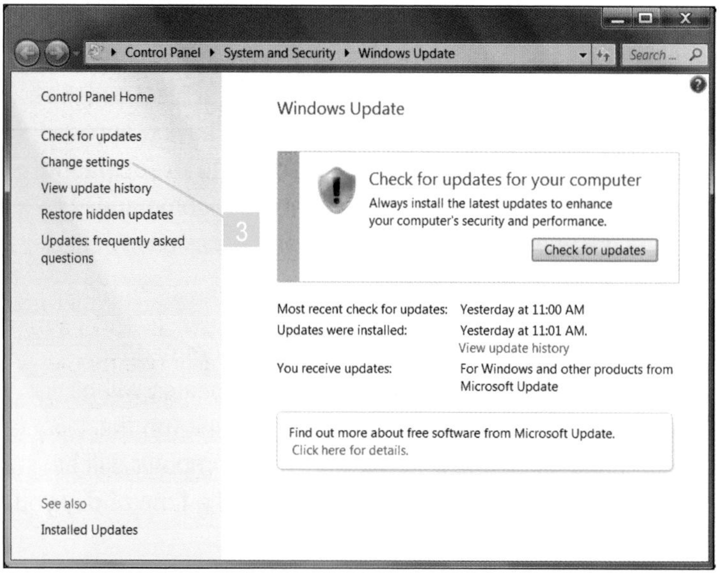

Control Panel ▸ System and Security ▸ Windows Update
Search...
Control Panel Home
Check for updates
Change settings
View update history
Restore hidden updates
Updates: frequently asked questions
3
Windows Update
Check for updates for your computer
Always install the latest updates to enhance your computer's security and performance.
Check for updates
Most recent check for updates: Yesterday at 11:00 AM
Updates were installed: Yesterday at 11:01 AM.
View update history
You receive updates: For Windows and other products from Microsoft Update
Find out more about free software from Microsoft Update.
Click here for details.
See also
Installed Updates

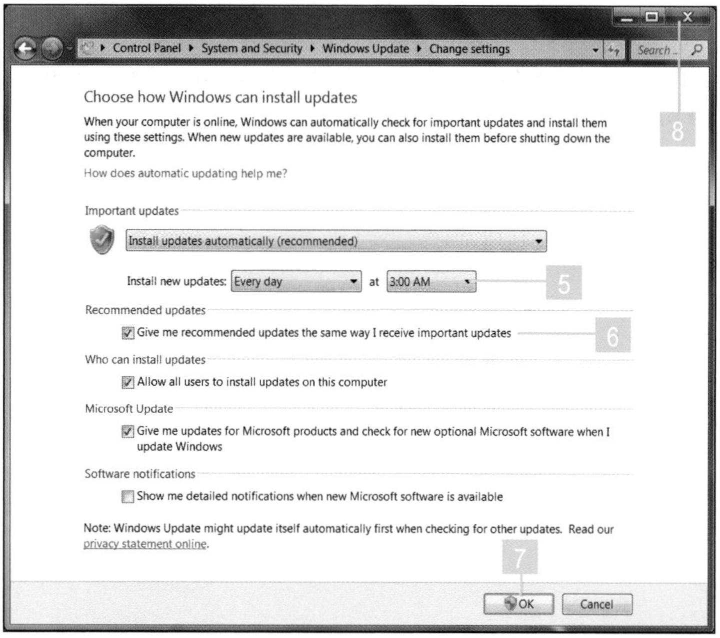

Control Panel ▸ System and Security ▸ Windows Update ▸ Change settings
Search...
8
Choose how Windows can install updates
When your computer is online, Windows can automatically check for important updates and install them using these settings. When new updates are available, you can also install them before shutting down the computer.
How does automatic updating help me?
Important updates
Install updates automatically (recommended)
Install new updates: Every day at 3:00 AM
5
Recommended updates
Give me recommended updates the same way I receive important updates
6
Who can install updates
Allow all users to install updates on this computer
Microsoft Update
Give me updates for Microsoft products and check for new optional Microsoft software when I update Windows
Software notifications
Show me detailed notifications when new Microsoft software is available
Note: Windows Update might update itself automatically first when checking for other updates. Read our privacy statement online.
7
OK
Cancel

Did you know?

If you see that optional components are available (or any other updates for that matter), you can view and install them by clicking the blue link to the updates. Select the items to update and click OK. You do not have to install optional updates.

Windows Security Features

There are two more security features to explore: Windows Firewall and Windows Defender. There isn't much you need to do with these features except to make sure that they are both enabled and are protecting your laptop. By default both are enabled.

Windows Firewall is a software program that checks the data that comes in from the Internet (or a local network) and then decides whether it is good data or bad. If it deems the data harmless, it will allow it to come though the firewall, if not it's blocked. You have to have a firewall to keep hackers from gaining access to your laptop, and to help prevent your computer from sending out malicious code if it is ever attacked by a virus or worm.

Windows Defender protects your laptop against malicious and unwanted software. Generally this is a type of data called spyware, malware or adware. Spyware can install itself on your laptop without your knowledge and can wreak havoc by causing these types of problems:

- Adding toolbars to Internet Explorer.
- Changing Internet Explorer's Home page.
- Taking you to websites you do not want to visit.
- Showing pop-up advertisements.
- Causing the computer to perform slowly.

Windows Defender helps protect this type of data from getting onto your laptop, and thus limits infection.

It's up to you to make sure that the Firewall and Windows Defender are running and configured properly. Additionally, you'll have the option of changing a few of the parameters, such as when scans are completed and what happens when potentially dangerous data is detected.

Configuring Windows Update (cont.)

6. Verify the items checked here are checked on your laptop: include recommended updates when downloading, installing or notifying me about updates, and Use Microsoft Update.
7. Make changes if needed and click OK.
8. Click the X in the top right corner to close the window.

Important

If you work through the steps for using Windows Firewall and it is turned off, it may be turned off because you have a third-party firewall installed. If you aren't sure, go ahead and enable Windows Firewall. If you know you have a third-party firewall, don't enable it. Running two firewalls can cause problems for the PC.

Jargon buster

Adware – Internet advertisements (which are also applications) which often include additional code that can be used to track a user's personal information and pass it on to third parties, without the user's authorisation or knowledge.

Internet server – a computer that stores data off site. Hotmail offers Internet servers to hold email and data, so that you do not have to store them on your PC. Internet servers allow you to access information from any computer that can access the Internet.

Virus – a self-replicating program that infects computers with intent to do harm. Viruses often come in the form of an attachment in an email.

Worm – a self-replicating program that infects computers with intent to do harm. However, unlike a virus, it does not need to attach itself to a running program.

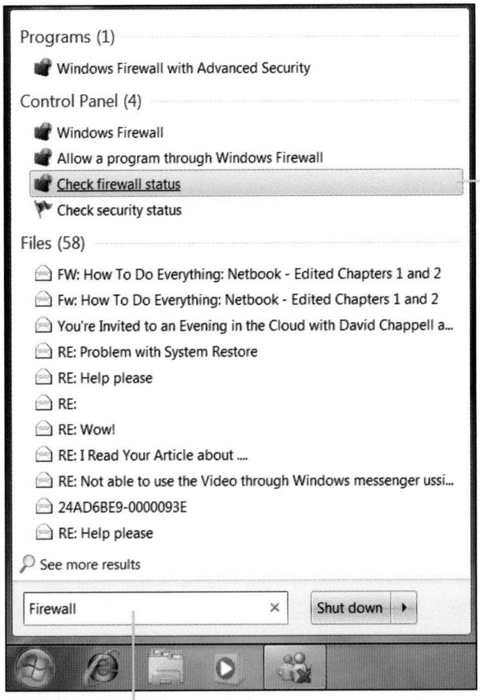
Programs (1)
Windows Firewall with Advanced Security
Control Panel (4)
Windows Firewall
Allow a program through Windows Firewall
Check firewall status
Check security status
Files (58)
FW: How To Do Everything: Netbook - Edited Chapters 1 and 2
Fw: How To Do Everything: Netbook - Edited Chapters 1 and 2
You're Invited to an Evening in the Cloud with David Chappell a...
RE: Problem with System Restore
RE: Help please
RE:
RE: Wow!
RE: I Read Your Article about ....
RE: Not able to use the Video through Windows messenger ussi...
24AD6BE9-0000093E
RE: Help please
See more results
Firewall
Shut down
2
1

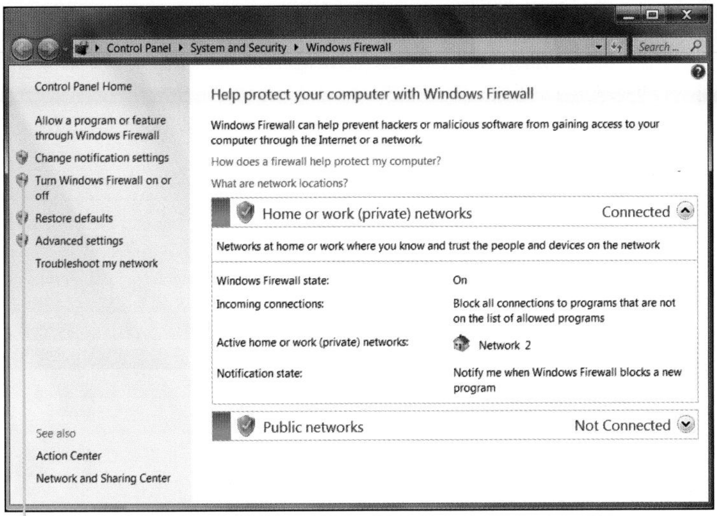
Control Panel ▸ System and Security ▸ Windows Firewall
Search...
Control Panel Home
Allow a program or feature through Windows Firewall
Change notification settings
Turn Windows Firewall on or off
Restore defaults
Advanced settings
Troubleshoot my network
See also
Action Center
Network and Sharing Center
Help protect your computer with Windows Firewall
Windows Firewall can help prevent hackers or malicious software from gaining access to your computer through the Internet or a network.
How does a firewall help protect my computer?
What are network locations?
Home or work (private) networks
Connected
Networks at home or work where you know and trust the people and devices on the network
Windows Firewall state:
On
Incoming connections:
Block all connections to programs that are not on the list of allowed programs
Active home or work (private) networks:
Network 2
Notification state:
Notify me when Windows Firewall blocks a new program
Public networks
Not Connected
4

Using Windows Firewall

1 Click Start, and in the Start Search window type Firewall.

2 Click Check firewall status.

3 Verify that the firewall is turned on. If it is, you can simply close the window.

4 If the firewall is off, and you know you do not have a third-party firewall installed and running, select Turn Windows Firewall on or off.

5 Select Turn on Windows Firewall and accept the default settings. Click OK.

Using Windows Defender

1. Click Start.
2. In the Start Search window, type Windows Defender.
3. Under the results for Control Panel, click Windows Defender.
4. Hopefully, you'll see that no unwanted or harmful software has been detected. If not, you'll be prompted regarding what to do next. (It is highly unlikely you'll see anything wrong.) Click Tools.
5. Click Options. You'll see several choices.
6. Verify that Automatic Scanning is enabled.

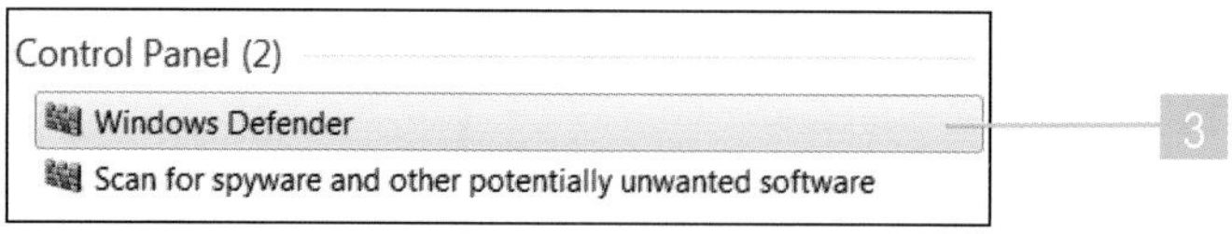

Control Panel (2)
Windows Defender
Scan for spyware and other potentially unwanted software
3

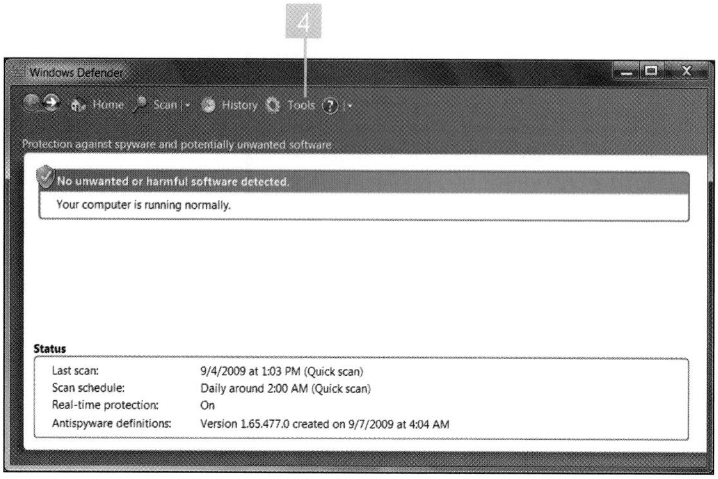

4
Windows Defender
Home
Scan
History
Tools
Protection against spyware and potentially unwanted software
No unwanted or harmful software detected.
Your computer is running normally.
Status
Last scan: 9/4/2009 at 1:03 PM (Quick scan)
Scan schedule: Daily around 2:00 AM (Quick scan)
Real-time protection: On
Antispyware definitions: Version 1.65.477.0 created on 9/7/2009 at 4:04 AM

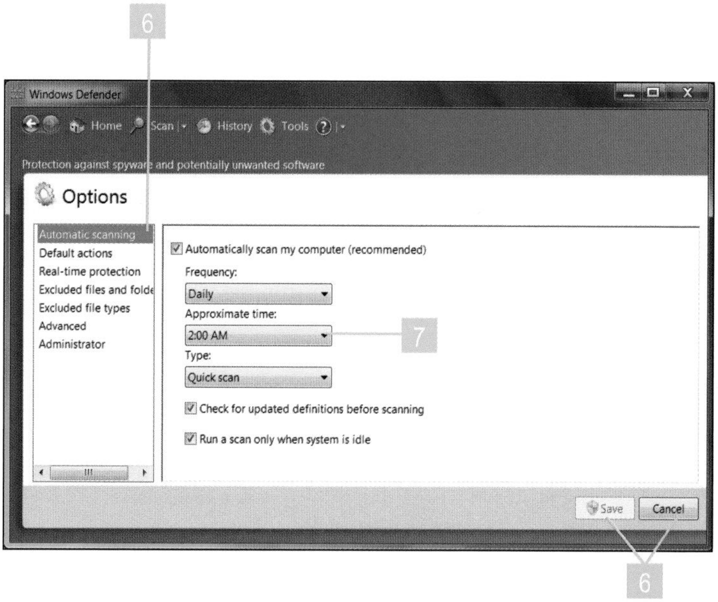

6
Windows Defender
Home
Scan
History
Tools
Protection against spyware and potentially unwanted software
Options
Automatic scanning
Default actions
Real-time protection
Excluded files and folde
Excluded file types
Advanced
Administrator
Automatically scan my computer (recommended)
Frequency:
Daily
Approximate time:
2:00 AM
7
Type:
Quick scan
Check for updated definitions before scanning
Run a scan only when system is idle
Save
Cancel
6

For your information

Check out the additional option in Windows Defender in addition to Automatic Scanning. Click each option to view it.

Using Windows Defender (cont.)

7 If desired, change the approximate time of the scan. It's best to leave the other defaults as-is.

8 Click Save if you've made changes, or Cancel if not.

!

Important

If you think your computer has been infected, open Windows Defender and click Scan. This will cause Windows Defender to scan your PC for problems.

Resolving Action Center warnings

Last but not least, you occasionally need to visit the Action Center to see if any warnings exist. If you see anything in red, the problem needs to be resolved. Anything in yellow means you have a bit of maintenance to do. In this example several things are wrong, and the Action Center has some suggestions.

1. Look at the Notification area of the toolbar; it's at the end to the right.
2. Click the flag icon one time. You'll see something similar to what's shown here.
3. Click Open Action Center.
4. If there's anything in red (or yellow) click the associated button to read about the problem. If there's an option to resolve it, click it.
5. Note the resolution and perform the task.

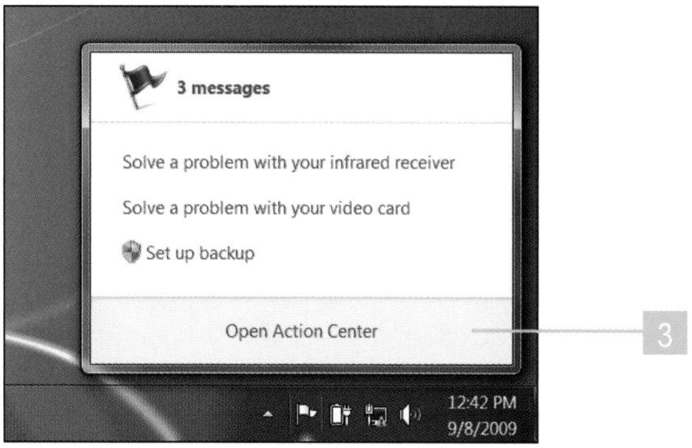

3 messages
Solve a problem with your infrared receiver
Solve a problem with your video card
Set up backup
Open Action Center
3
12:42 PM
9/8/2009

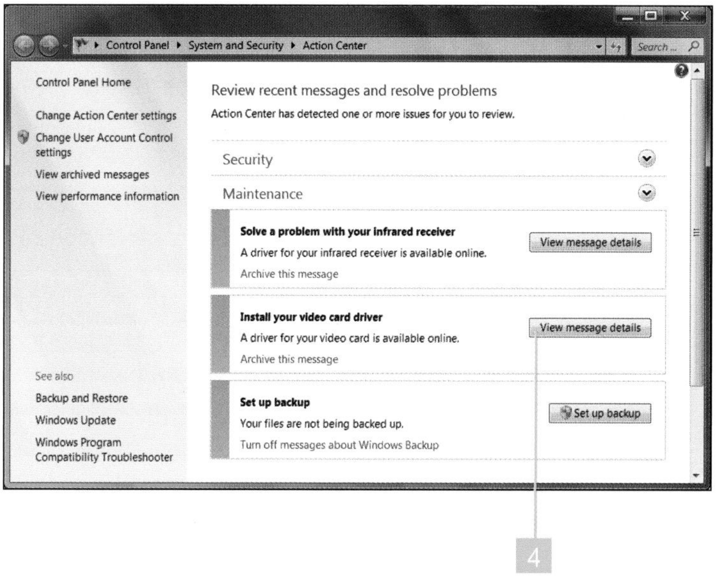

Control Panel ▸ System and Security ▸ Action Center
Search...
Control Panel Home
Change Action Center settings
Change User Account Control settings
View archived messages
View performance information
See also
Backup and Restore
Windows Update
Windows Program Compatibility Troubleshooter
Review recent messages and resolve problems
Action Center has detected one or more issues for you to review.
Security
Maintenance
Solve a problem with your infrared receiver
A driver for your infrared receiver is available online.
Archive this message
View message details
Install your video card driver
A driver for your video card is available online.
Archive this message
View message details
Set up backup
Your files are not being backed up.
Turn off messages about Windows Backup
Set up backup
4

Did you know?

To change how often you're notified about changes made to your computer, click User Account Control Settings in the Action Center window.

There are two other things you can do to protect your family and data. First, protect the children and grandchildren with Parental Controls. Parental Controls isn't a cure-all, but it does help. You still have to find a way to protect your children from Internet bad guys when they're away from home, but at least while they're under your roof you can look after them. Second, learn how to create backups of your data and settings. Although it's unlikely something will happen in the immediate future that is so bad it would destroy your PC and all of your data, it could happen (and it does). It's best to be prepared.

Protecting your family and your data

Parental Controls

As noted above, Parental Controls can be applied to children, grandchildren, guests and even spouses. You can configure Parental Controls to set limits on when people can use the computer (and for how long), what games they can play, what websites that they can visit, and what programs they can run. Once you've configured Parental Controls, you can review 'activity reports' that let you see what each person has been doing with their computer time. You can also view what content has been blocked, which will allow you to see how far the user has been testing the limits of the controls you've set.

Important

You can only apply Parental Controls to users with a Standard user account. Additionally, all other user accounts should have passwords so that standard users cannot log on with another account when they are not allowed on the PC.

With Parental Controls, there are options to set time limits, games and access to programs. There is also an option to enable web filtering and activity reporting using an additional service you purchase and/or configure.

Setting up Parental Controls

1. Click Start. In the Start Search window, type Parental.
2. In the results under Control Panel, click Set up parental controls for any user.
3. Click the user account for which you want to set Parental Controls. Remember, it has to be a standard account.
4. Under Parental Controls, click On.
5. Click Time limits.
6. Click and drag to set times to block and allow. Blue is blocked.
7. Click OK.
8. Click Games and then Allow and block specific programs to configure additional controls.
9. Click OK when finished.

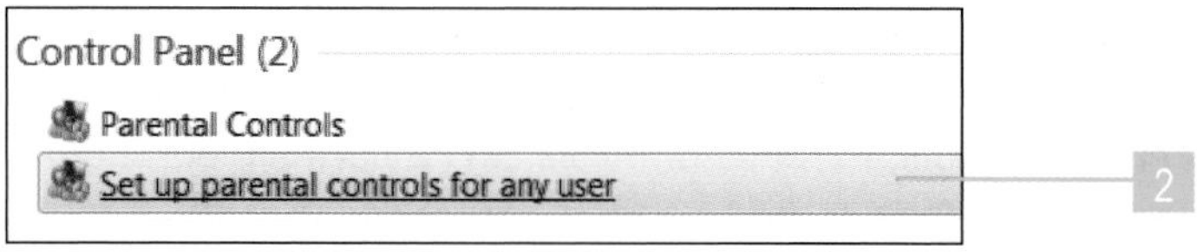

Control Panel (2)
Parental Controls
Set up parental controls for any user
2

Important

If you see a warning stating that one or more accounts do not have passwords, click to apply them.

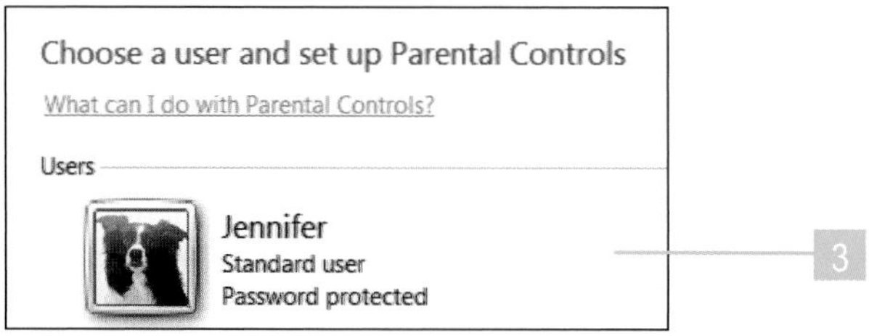

Choose a user and set up Parental Controls
What can I do with Parental Controls?
Users
Jennifer
Standard user
Password protected
3

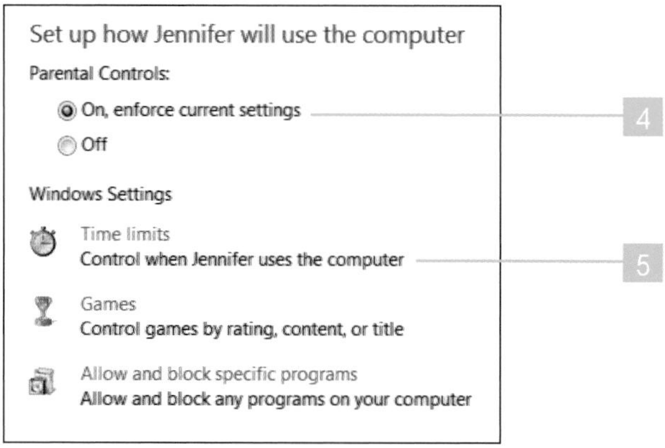

Set up how Jennifer will use the computer
Parental Controls:
On, enforce current settings
Off
Windows Settings
Time limits
Control when Jennifer uses the computer
Games
Control games by rating, content, or title
Allow and block specific programs
Allow and block any programs on your computer
4
5

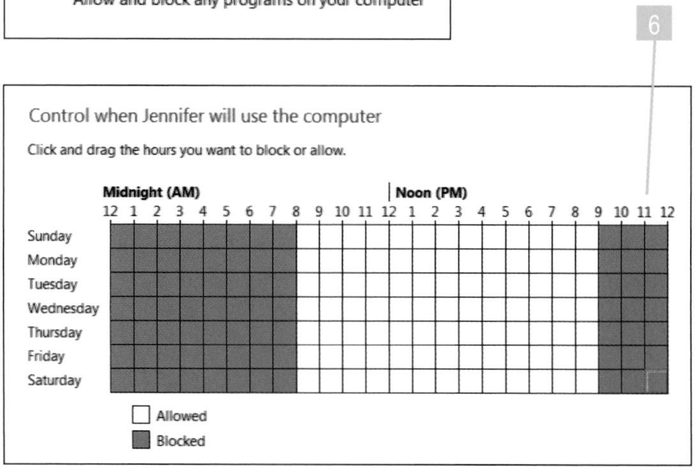

6
Control when Jennifer will use the computer
Click and drag the hours you want to block or allow.
Midnight (AM)
Noon (PM)
12 1 2 3 4 5 6 7 8 9 10 11 12 1 2 3 4 5 6 7 8 9 10 11 12
Sunday
Monday
Tuesday
Wednesday
Thursday
Friday
Saturday
Allowed
Blocked

Backing up data

Windows 7 comes with a backup program you can use to backup your personal data. The backup program is called Backup and Restore.

Creating your first backup

1 Click Start. In the Start Search window, type Backup.

2 In the results, under Programs, click Backup and Restore.

3 Click Set up backup.

4 When prompted, choose a place to save your backup. Since backups can be large, consider a USB drive, external hard drive or DVD. You can also choose a network location. For the first backup, if possible select a location that has lots of GBs of space, such as an external hard drive or network location, just to be safe.

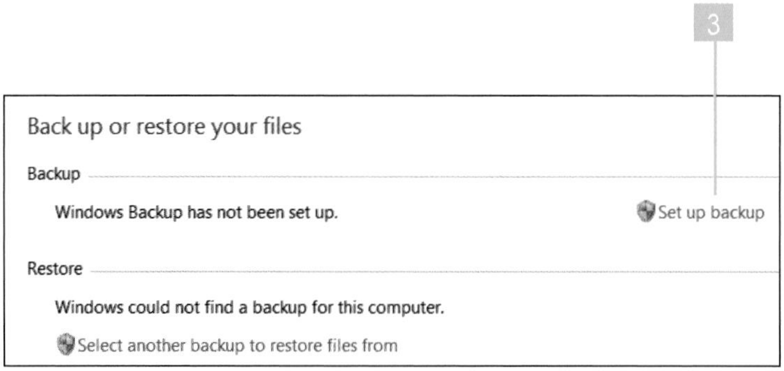

3
Back up or restore your files
Backup
Windows Backup has not been set up.
Set up backup
Restore
Windows could not find a backup for this computer.
Select another backup to restore files from

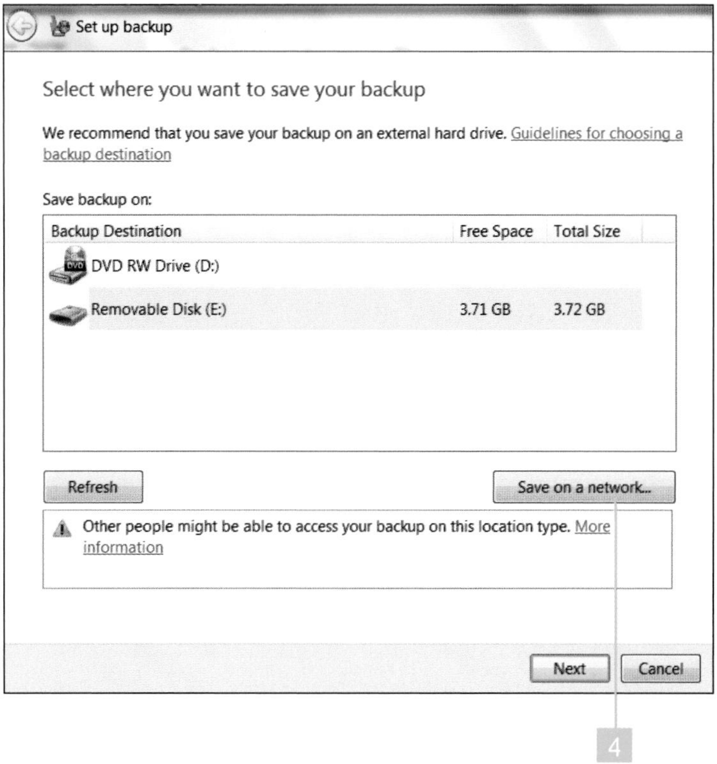

Set up backup
Select where you want to save your backup
We recommend that you save your backup on an external hard drive. Guidelines for choosing a backup destination
Save backup on:
Backup Destination
Free Space
Total Size
DVD RW Drive (D:)
Removable Disk (E:)
3.71 GB
3.72 GB
Refresh
Save on a network...
Other people might be able to access your backup on this location type. More information
Next
Cancel
4

Did you know?

You can't create a backup on the hard disk of the computer you are backing up.

Timesaver tip

To choose a network location, such as another computer on your home network, click Save on a network. Locate the folder and input credentials to access the computer (your administrator name and password will do). Click OK to apply the changes.

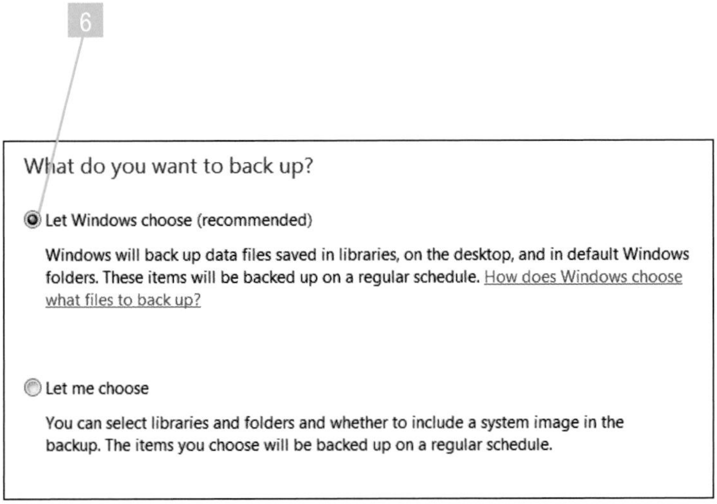
6
What do you want to back up?
Let Windows choose (recommended)
Windows will back up data files saved in libraries, on the desktop, and in default Windows folders. These items will be backed up on a regular schedule. How does Windows choose what files to back up?
Let me choose
You can select libraries and folders and whether to include a system image in the backup. The items you choose will be backed up on a regular schedule.

Creating your first backup (cont.)

5 Click Next. (If prompted for any other information, such as a hard drive partition, to insert a blank DVD or insert a USB drive, do so.)

6 Select what to backup. First timers should select Let Windows choose (recommended). Click Next.

7 Note the time and date for the backups to occur. If you want to, click Change schedule and choose settings for how often, what day and what time future backups should occur.

8 Click Save settings and start backup.

9 Follow the same procedure to restore data from a backup if and when necessary.

9

Connecting to the Internet

Introduction

If you aren't online already, now's the time to take the plunge. There are a few things you'll need to do before you can start surfing the web including selecting an ISP, subscribing to it, installing the necessary hardware and software, and obtaining the required configuration settings. You may also need to choose a user name, password and email address. Once you have all of that, you'll be ready to go.

If you do not want to pay a monthly fee for Internet access, you can visit free or minimal cost 'hotspots' where you can access the Internet, provided you have a wireless network adapter installed in your laptop. If you have a new laptop, you probably do. If you want to try free Internet service, take your laptop to a posh hotel or a Starbucks, and ask if they have free Wi-Fi. If you have the required hardware, you can connect easily.

In this chapter we need to talk about two specific scenarios. The first scenario is that you are a home user and you happen to be using a laptop. If this is the case, you can choose dial-up, DSL or broadband. You can even use satellite if you like. But in this scenario, the laptop is your main PC and you use it at home.

The second scenario is that you purchased and will use your laptop for travel and would like to have Internet access wherever you are. For this type of connection, you'll use wireless hardware such as a wireless card to connect to the Internet.

What you'll do

Create a connection to the Internet

Find out if you have wireless hardware

Connect at a free hotspot

Choose from dial-up, broadband, mobile, wireless, satellite

Did you know?

Even if your laptop does not come with a wireless card or wireless capability, you can still sign up for wireless Internet. Wireless Internet providers offer hardware that connects to an available USB port that can be used to acquire a wireless signal.

There are a number of options for connecting to the Internet. If you use your laptop at home and rarely travel, you will likely want to connect using your phone line (dial-up) or cable modem (broadband or DSL). These options are less expensive than wireless options, but you must remain physically connected to the signal.

If you are a laptop user who travels, the most common type of network is one you do not physically have to connect to. It would not make sense to pay for a dial-up connection if you travel with your laptop, because locating a phone line to plug your laptop into to connect to the Internet would be difficult. You might also have to pay long distance fees if there's no dial-up server close to where you are. Cable and DSL offer the same problem. With cable and DSL connections you have to connect physically to a modem, which in turn is physically connected to a wall outlet and, since a laptop is best used for travel and mobility, this will inhibit its usefulness. So, if you use your laptop for travel, you'll want to choose a provider that allows you to connect wirelessly (via satellite) from anywhere.

All Internet options offer varying rate plans that can be calculated based on how often you go online, whether or not you have an existing service with the provider such as mobile phone service, cable TV or digital phone, and/or how much 'bandwidth' you use, which has to do with the amount of data you send and receive. To make the best choice, read on.

Call your cable, satellite and/or mobile phone providers

If you already have service with a land-line phone company, mobile phone provider and/or a cable or satellite company (for television service), give those companies a call. Most offer bundled services, and offer discounts if you sign up for their Internet service. Right now, mobile phone companies don't offer much in the way of discounts, but cable and satellite companies do. To make sure you explore all possibilities, call anyway.

Note: If you don't have any existing services or are unhappy with your current television or mobile phone provider, start cold calling ISP providers. You might try Sky, BT, Virgin or Tesco, among others. Ask friends and neighbours what they use too.

Consider speed and connectivity limits

While you're researching, consider how fast you want to be able to surf the Internet and how often. If you don't travel with your laptop, only want to get online once a week to check email from your grandchildren and really don't care if that process is fast or slow, consider dial-up. Dial-up is inexpensive and you can opt for a pay-as-you-go plan with several companies. If you would like unlimited access to the Internet, and you want a fast connection, consider broadband through a cable company. Finally, if you want to be online wherever you are, get a satellite connection. If you go wireless, you can get a USB adapter or a wireless network card that goes where you go. Satellite connections are great if you have a laptop and you travel. No matter where you are, you can get online.

Decide on a monthly budget

After you've decided what your ISP options are and have done a little research into cost and speed, decide on a monthly budget. Go to a friend's house if necessary and visit a website such as www.broadband-finder.co.uk to compare prices and services.

Choose from dial-up, broadband, mobile, wireless, satellite (cont.)

Important !

Don't pay a set-up cost. There are too many companies that will set up your connection for free, making this an unnecessary expense. Note that you may have to purchase hardware, though.

Configuring your home Internet connection

For your information

This section is only for readers who use a laptop at home as their main PC and want to connect to the Internet using cable, satellite, dial-up or DSL.

With hardware (and possibly software) at hand, it's time to configure your home Internet connection. You'll first need to install any hardware you received. If you're setting up a connection in your home using a physical connection, this may mean connecting a cable modem, wireless access point or DSL modem. If you've selected satellite, you will likely only need to insert a wireless network card or other hardware. Additionally, there may be a router or driver software involved. You'll have to follow the directions that came with the hardware and software to set it up, but don't panic. If you get in a bind, call the ISP. They are there to help; it's their job. They will walk you through the set-up process and will stay on the phone with you until it's set up properly.

Did you know?

If you're unsure about installing the hardware yourself, ask if there's an extra fee for having someone come to your home to set it up. If there is, and you would rather pay someone than do it yourself, by all means treat yourself to the luxury. Keep in mind that people of all ages, nationalities and experience levels install their own hardware, and you can too; you'll just need to set aside a little time for the task.

Once the hardware is configured, and if the ISP does not walk you through the process of configuring the connection in Windows 7, you'll need to access the Network and Sharing Center to create the connection yourself. Once inside the Network and Sharing Center, you'll select Set up a connection or network. Here's the Network and Sharing Center in Windows 7. Note that there is not yet a working connection to the Internet.

Configuring your home Internet connection (cont.)

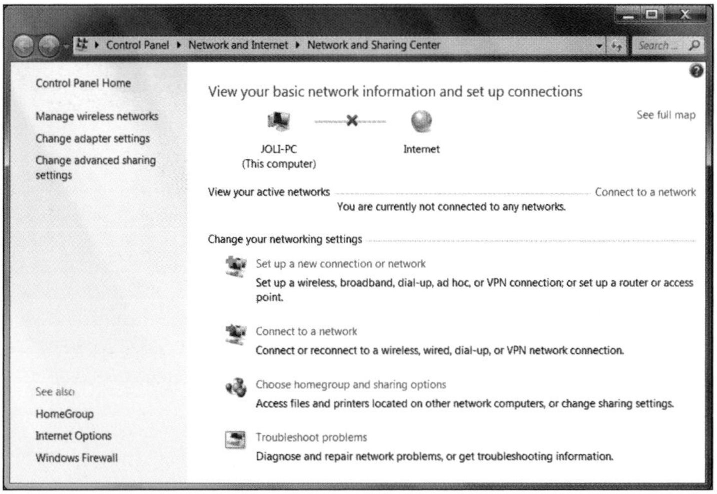
Control Panel ▸ Network and Internet ▸ Network and Sharing Center
Search...
Control Panel Home
Manage wireless networks
Change adapter settings
Change advanced sharing settings
View your basic network information and set up connections
See full map
JOLI-PC
(This computer)
Internet
View your active networks
Connect to a network
You are currently not connected to any networks.
Change your networking settings
Set up a new connection or network
Set up a wireless, broadband, dial-up, ad hoc, or VPN connection; or set up a router or access point.
Connect to a network
Connect or reconnect to a wireless, wired, dial-up, or VPN network connection.
Choose homegroup and sharing options
Access files and printers located on other network computers, or change sharing settings.
Troubleshoot problems
Diagnose and repair network problems, or get troubleshooting information.
See also
HomeGroup
Internet Options
Windows Firewall

During the set-up process you'll need to input the following information, which you can acquire from your ISP. If you don't have it, call them. Write this information down and keep it in a safe place:

- user name
- email address
- password
- incoming POP3 server name
- outgoing SMTP server name
- account name (may be the same as user name).

!

Important

You only need to perform the following steps if you just installed hardware for a new Internet connection in your home, and you want to connect your laptop to it to access the Internet using a physical connection such as broadband, satellite or DSL. If you are installing a wireless network card into a laptop, the software included with your hardware will likely get you connected, or at the very least walk you through the process.

Creating a connection to the Internet

1 Click Start.

2 Type Network and Sharing.

3 Under Control Panel, select Network and Sharing Center.

4 Under Tasks, click Set up a new connection or network. This screen was shown on page 135.

5 Click Connect to the Internet – Set up a wireless, broadband, or dial-up connection to the Internet.

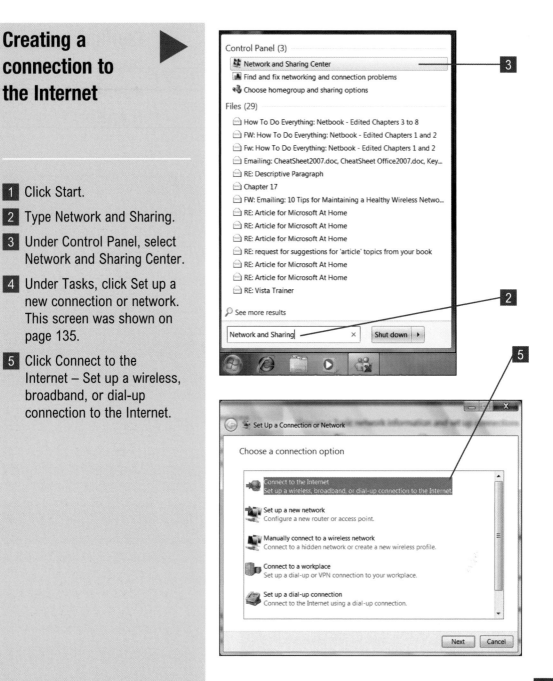

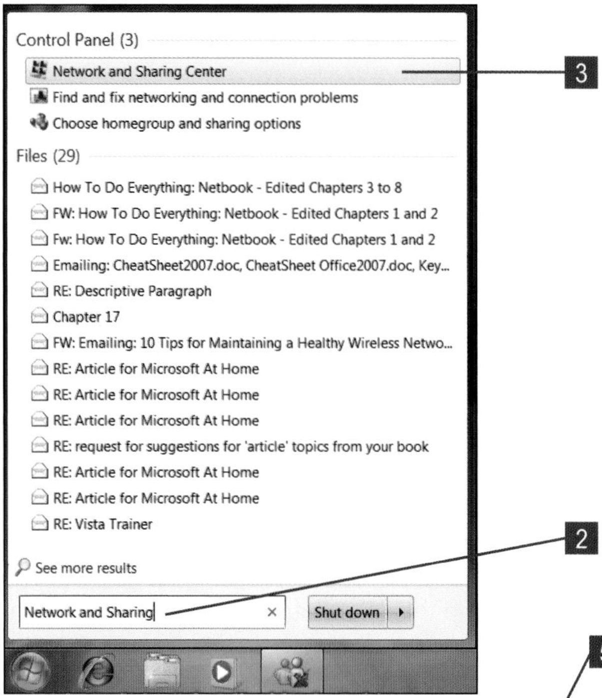
Control Panel (3)
Network and Sharing Center
Find and fix networking and connection problems
Choose homegroup and sharing options
Files (29)
How To Do Everything: Netbook - Edited Chapters 3 to 8
FW: How To Do Everything: Netbook - Edited Chapters 1 and 2
Fw: How To Do Everything: Netbook - Edited Chapters 1 and 2
Emailing: CheatSheet2007.doc, CheatSheet Office2007.doc, Key...
RE: Descriptive Paragraph
Chapter 17
FW: Emailing: 10 Tips for Maintaining a Healthy Wireless Netwo...
RE: Article for Microsoft At Home
RE: Article for Microsoft At Home
RE: Article for Microsoft At Home
RE: request for suggestions for 'article' topics from your book
RE: Article for Microsoft At Home
RE: Article for Microsoft At Home
RE: Vista Trainer
See more results
Network and Sharing
Shut down
3
2

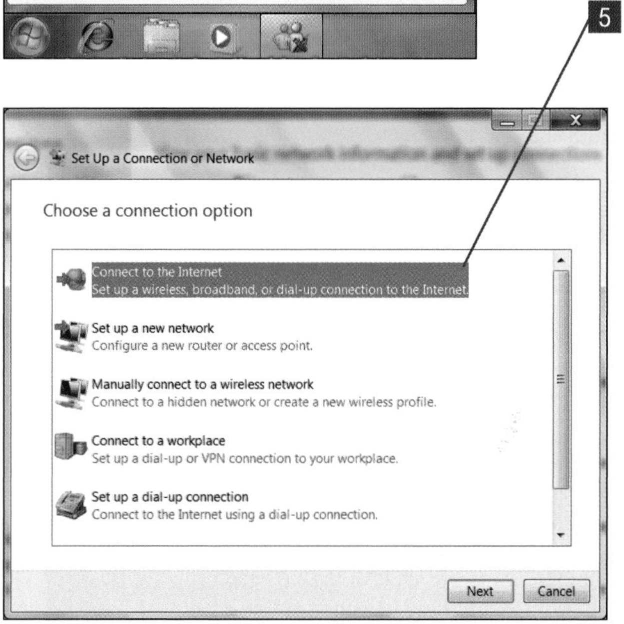
5
Set Up a Connection or Network
Choose a connection option
Connect to the Internet
Set up a wireless, broadband, or dial-up connection to the Internet.
Set up a new network
Configure a new router or access point.
Manually connect to a wireless network
Connect to a hidden network or create a new wireless profile.
Connect to a workplace
Set up a dial-up or VPN connection to your workplace.
Set up a dial-up connection
Connect to the Internet using a dial-up connection.
Next
Cancel

Timesaver tip

As noted earlier, if you choose to set up a wireless Internet connection, use the software that came from the ISP and with the wireless hardware.

Creating a connection to the Internet (cont.)

Did you know?

Passwords are case-sensitive.

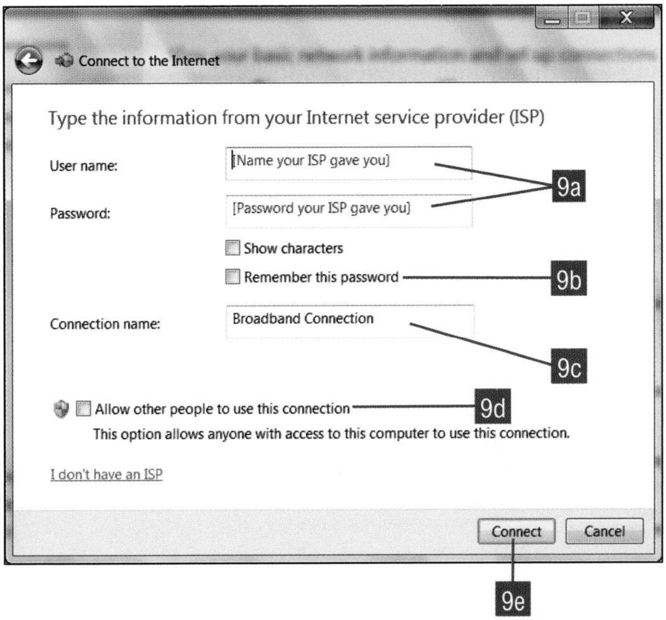
Connect to the Internet
Type the information from your Internet service provider (ISP)
User name:
[Name your ISP gave you]
Password:
[Password your ISP gave you]
Show characters
Remember this password
Connection name:
Broadband Connection
Allow other people to use this connection
This option allows anyone with access to this computer to use this connection.
I don't have an ISP
Connect
Cancel
9a
9b
9c
9d
9e

6 Click Next.

7 Select either broadband or Dial-up, based on the ISP's connection option.

8 Click Next (it will appear after you make a selection in Step 7).

9 For broadband:

a Type your user name and password.

b Select Remember this password (otherwise you'll have to type the password each time you use the connection).

c If desired, type a new connection name.

d If you have a home network and would like to share this computer with others on the network, check Allow other people to use this connection.

e Click Connect.

Creating a wireless satellite connection

If you've chosen satellite Internet, you'll need to install the wireless hardware and software your ISP sent you (or that you purchased). For the most part, when you connect the hardware, you'll be prompted to install the program. Most installations of this type only require you to click Next when prompted, and wait for the process to complete. Once the hardware and software has been installed, click Connect.

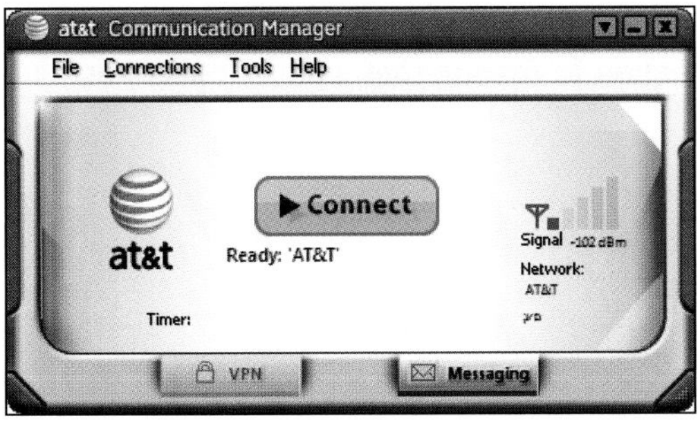
at&t Communication Manager
File Connections Tools Help
Connect
at&t
Ready: 'AT&T'
Signal -102 dBm
Network:
AT&T
Timer:
VPN
Messaging

Creating a connection to the Internet (cont.)

10 For dial-up:

a. Type the phone number. It should be a local number, otherwise you'll incur dial-up charges. If it is not a local number, call your ISP and ask for one.
b. Click Dialing Rules. Input the proper information and click OK.
c. Type your user name and password.
d. Select Remember this password (otherwise you'll have to type the password each time you use the connection).
e. If desired, type a new connection name.
f. If you have a home network and would like to share this computer with others on the network, check Allow other people to use this connection.
g. Click Connect.

> **Important**
>
> If prompted regarding the network type, choose Work or Home, not Public.

Viewing and managing network connections

Once your Internet connection is set up, you can view its status in the Network and Sharing Center. You can also view and access your networked computers (if you have any), and the hardware you've installed to connect to the Internet, by clicking Network Map. You can also diagnose and repair connectivity problems or manage your Internet connection. As you can see here, a connection to the Internet is not working properly. To resolve the problem, simply click the red X.

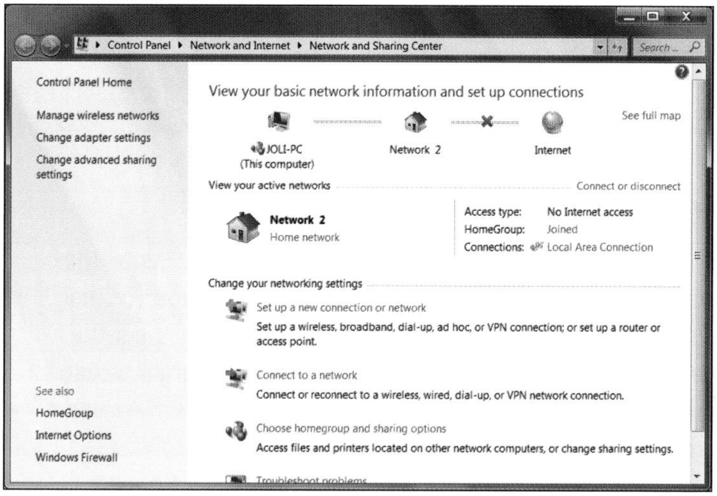

Control Panel ▸ Network and Internet ▸ Network and Sharing Center
Search...
Control Panel Home
Manage wireless networks
Change adapter settings
Change advanced sharing settings
View your basic network information and set up connections
See full map
JOLI-PC
(This computer)
Network 2
Internet
View your active networks
Connect or disconnect
Network 2
Home network
Access type: No Internet access
HomeGroup: Joined
Connections: Local Area Connection
Change your networking settings
Set up a new connection or network
Set up a wireless, broadband, dial-up, ad hoc, or VPN connection; or set up a router or access point.
Connect to a network
Connect or reconnect to a wireless, wired, dial-up, or VPN network connection.
Choose homegroup and sharing options
Access files and printers located on other network computers, or change sharing settings.
See also
HomeGroup
Internet Options
Windows Firewall

You can also manage connections. On the next page you can see a wireless connection to the Internet, and that also has a strong signal.

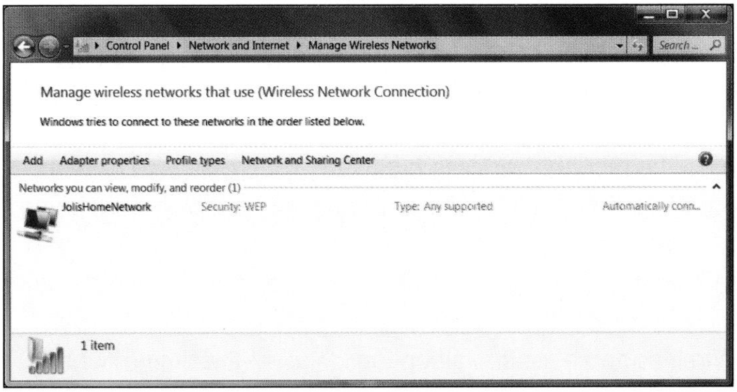
Control Panel ▸ Network and Internet ▸ Manage Wireless Networks
Search...
Manage wireless networks that use (Wireless Network Connection)
Windows tries to connect to these networks in the order listed below.
Add
Adapter properties
Profile types
Network and Sharing Center
Networks you can view, modify, and reorder (1)
JolisHomeNetwork
Security: WEP
Type: Any supported
Automatically conn...
1 item

Creating a connection to the Internet (cont.)

Using free Wi-Fi hotspots

Wi-Fi hotspots are popping up all over the country. Wi-Fi hotspots let you connect to the Internet without having to be tethered to an Ethernet cable or tied down with a high monthly wireless bill. Sometimes this service is free, provided you have the required wireless hardware. (You may also have to buy a cup of coffee for the privilege, but, hey, you were going to anyway, right?) More often than not, though, you'll need to have some sort of subscription or membership, which can include a monthly or a pay-as-you-go fee. The Cloud, Divine Wireless and iPass are all options, and, at the time of writing, you can get started from around £6.99 a month for a single device.

To find a Wi-Fi hotspot close to you, go to www.maps.google.com and search for Wi-Fi hotspots, or go to a website such as www.totalhotspots.com. Your search should provide results that include airports, hotels, bars, cafes, restaurants and more.

Because almost all newer laptops now come with wireless capabilities, it's worth trying out. First, you need to find out if your laptop has wireless hardware before you take a trek to the local coffee shop or hotel reception.

Network adapters
Atheros AR5007EG Wireless Network Adapter
NVIDIA nForce Networking Controller
5

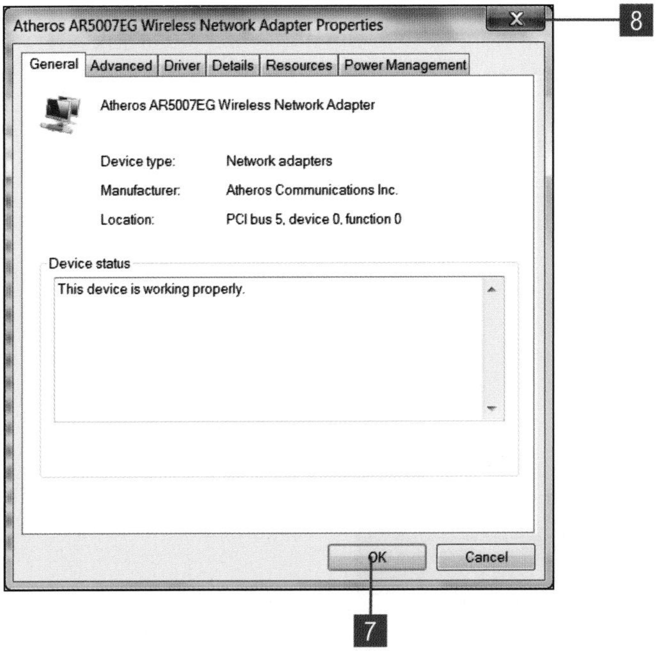
Atheros AR5007EG Wireless Network Adapter Properties
8
General
Advanced
Driver
Details
Resources
Power Management
Atheros AR5007EG Wireless Network Adapter
Device type: Network adapters
Manufacturer: Atheros Communications Inc.
Location: PCI bus 5, device 0, function 0
Device status
This device is working properly.
OK
Cancel
7

Find out if you have wireless hardware

1. Click Start.
2. In the Start Search dialogue box, type Device Manager.
3. Locate Network Adapters.
4. Click the triangle to expand it – it will turn sideways as shown here.
5. Locate a device with the word ‘wireless’ in it.
6. If you see a wireless adapter listed, double-click it to verify it is working properly. You’ll see the window shown here.
7. Click OK to close this dialogue box.
8. Click the X in the top right corner of Device Manager to close it.

Connecting at a free hotspot

1. Turn on your wireless laptop within range of a wireless network. Generally, this will mean going into the building that offers the wireless connection, or sitting right outside, perhaps in a patio area.
2. You'll be prompted from the Notification area that wireless networks are available.
3. Click Connect to a network, if you see a pop-up.
4. If you do not see a pop-up, and sometimes you won't, click the network icon in the Notification area of the Taskbar. You can see it in this figure; it is to the left of the speaker icon in the bottom right corner. When you click the icon, you'll see the available wireless networks. Click the network to connect to it. There are two here.
5. Click Connect.
6. You should be connected automatically but, if you aren't, type the required credentials. You'll need to ask an employee for the credentials if it's a free hotspot, or you'll need to type in your own credentials, offered by your wireless provider.

For your information

If more than one wireless network is available, locate the one that you want to use. Often this is the one with the most green bars. If you aren't sure, ask someone who is already connected or who is an employee.

Wireless Network Connection
O1NYO
6HGE5
Open Network and Sharing Center
1:49 PM
4

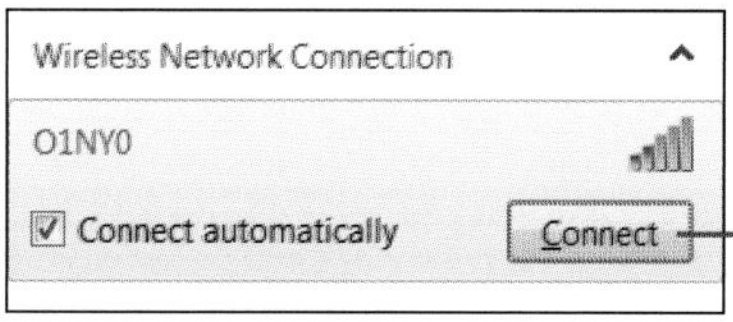

Wireless Network Connection
O1NYO
Connect automatically
Connect
5

Jargon buster

Network adapter – a piece of hardware that lets your computer connect to a network, such as the Internet or a local network.

Media applications

10

Introduction

Windows 7 comes with several media applications including Windows Media Player and Windows Media Center. You'll also need Windows Live Essentials, which includes programs you'll need to round out your media requirements including (but not limited to) Windows Live Photo Gallery and Windows Movie Maker. You'll need to download Live Essentials from the Internet but, don't worry, it's free and easy. When you're ready, you will use these applications to watch DVDs, watch, pause and record live TV, listen to and download music, movies and video, create your own movies from your own video footage, and manage your digital pictures.

In this chapter you'll learn just enough about many of these applications to get started. There's a lot more to them than what you'll see here though, so you'll want to experiment on your own. Remember, you can't hurt anything; and, even if you did, you could use System Restore to fix it!

What you'll do

Listen to Sample Music

Rip your CD collection

Burn a CD

Windows Live Download

Import pictures from a digital camera, media card or USB drive

Fix pictures

Email pictures

Watch a DVD

Watch live TV

Record a TV show or series

Using Windows Media Player

Windows Media Player offers all you'll need to manage your music library, get music online and copy the CDs from your own music collection to your laptop. You can also use it to burn music CDs you can listen to in your car, share music using your local network, and more.

Windows Media Player stands apart from other applications because it's used to acquire, play, share and listen to music. You can also work with video and pictures but, for the most part, you'll use Media Player for music management. That said, if you've never used a music application on a laptop or mobile device, there are a few things you'll need to know beforehand. So, before we get started, let's review some terms you'll see throughout this part of the chapter:

- Playlist – a group of songs that you can save and then listen to as a group, burn to a CD, copy to a portable music player and more.
- Rip – a term used to describe the process of copying files from a physical CD to your hard drive and thus your music library.
- Burn – a term used to describe the process of copying music from a computer to a CD or DVD. Generally, music is burned to a CD, since CDs can be played in cars and generic CD players, and videos are burned to DVDs since they require much more space and can be played on DVD players.

If you've never used Windows Media Player, the first time you open it you'll have to work through a wizard to tell Windows Media Player how you would like it to perform. You'll have two options: Express or Custom. If you're new to Media Player it's OK to select Express and accept the defaults. You can always change any options you decide you don't like after you've worked with it for a while.

After completing set-up, you'll probably see something like what's shown here. You'll see familiar attributes, like the Back and Forward buttons, and menus. You'll also see tab titles: Play, Burn and Sync, on the right side of the menu bar. Look deeper and you'll also see Media Guide (bottom left).

Using Windows Media Player (cont.)

10

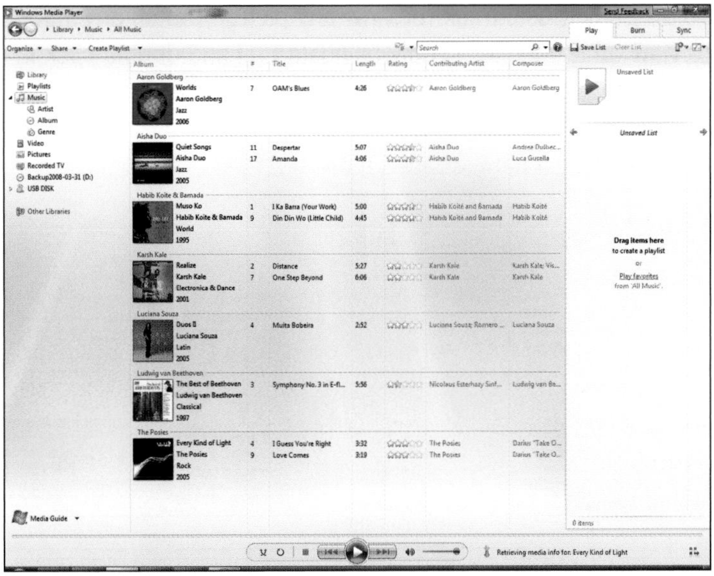
Windows Media Player
Library
Music
All Music
Organize
Share
Create Playlist
Album
Title
Length
Rating
Contributing Artist
Composer
Library
Playlists
Music
Artist
Album
Genre
Video
Pictures
Recorded TV
USB DISK
Other Libraries
Media Guide
Play
Burn
Sync
Save List
Unsaved List
Drag items here
to create a playlist
Play favorites
from 'All Music'.
0 items
Retrieving media info for: Every Kind of Light

On the left pane you can access playlists, which you can create, and everything in your music library. You can sort by artist, album and genre, by default, but you can right-click Music to access the command Customize Navigation Pane where you can then add additional categories such as year, rating, composer and more. To play any song, double-click it.

Playing media

To play any music track (or view any picture, watch any video or view other media), simply navigate to it and double-click it.

Listening to sample music

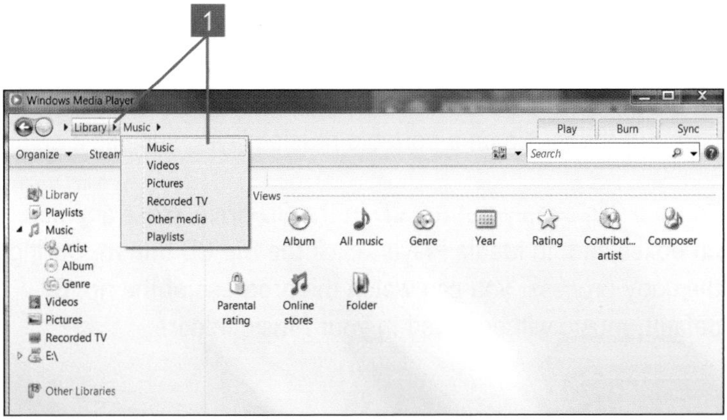
1
Windows Media Player
Library
Music
Play
Burn
Sync
Organize
Stream
Search
Music
Videos
Pictures
Recorded TV
Other media
Playlists
Library
Playlists
Music
Artist
Album
Genre
Videos
Pictures
Recorded TV
E:\
Other Libraries
Views
Album
All music
Genre
Year
Rating
Contribut... artist
Composer
Parental rating
Online stores
Folder

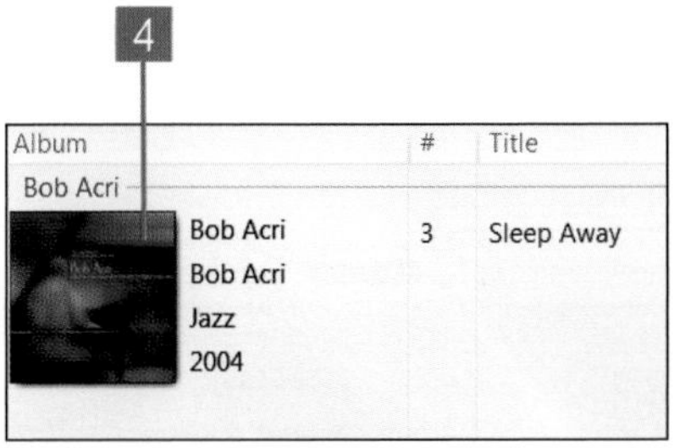
4
Album
#
Title
Bob Acri
Bob Acri
3
Sleep Away
Bob Acri
Jazz
2004

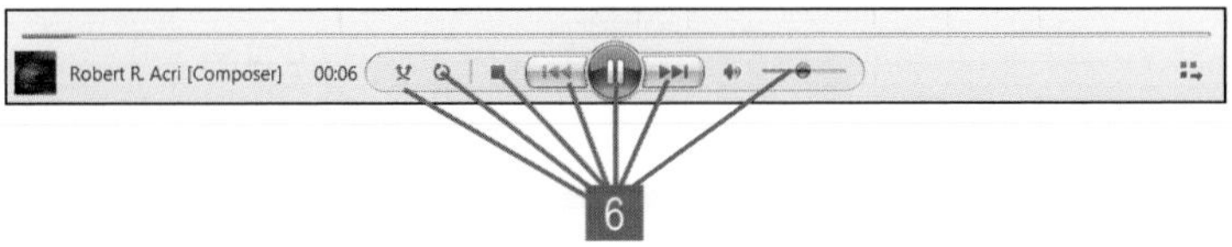
Robert R. Acri [Composer]
00:06
6

1 Open Media Player. Music should be selected. If it isn't, just click the arrow by Library, and select Music from the list.

2 Click Album.

3 Double-click any album to play it.

4 Double-click the album icon when it appears to play the album from the beginning, otherwise click any song on the album to play it.

5 Note the controls at the bottom of the interface. From left to right: Shuffle (to play songs in random order), Repeat, Stop, Previous, Play/ Pause, Next, Mute and a volume slider. Use these controls to manage the song and to move from one song to the next.

6 Continue experimenting with the controls until you are comfortable playing music.

Rip a CD

To rip means to copy in media-speak. When you rip a CD, you copy the CD to your laptop's hard drive. If you have a large CD collection, this could take some time, but it will ultimately be worth it. Once music is on your laptop, you can listen to it in Media Player, burn compilations of music to other CDs and even put the music on a portable music player, such as a Zen.

To rip a CD, simply put the CD in the CD drive, close any pop-up boxes and, in Media Player, click the Rip CD button. During the copy process, you can watch the progress of the rip. By default, music will be saved in your Music folder.

Ripping your CD collection

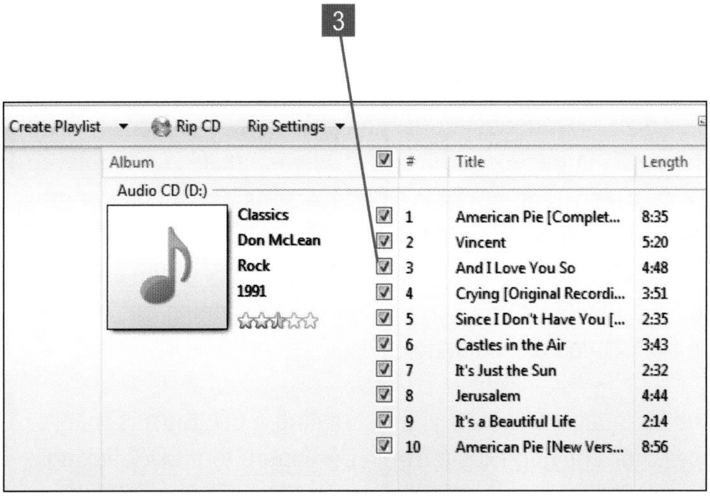
3
Create Playlist
Rip CD
Rip Settings
Album
#
Title
Length
Audio CD (D:)
Classics
Don McLean
Rock
1991
1 American Pie [Complet... 8:35
2 Vincent 5:20
3 And I Love You So 4:48
4 Crying [Original Recordi... 3:51
5 Since I Don't Have You [... 2:35
6 Castles in the Air 3:43
7 It's Just the Sun 2:32
8 Jerusalem 4:44
9 It's a Beautiful Life 2:14
10 American Pie [New Vers... 8:56

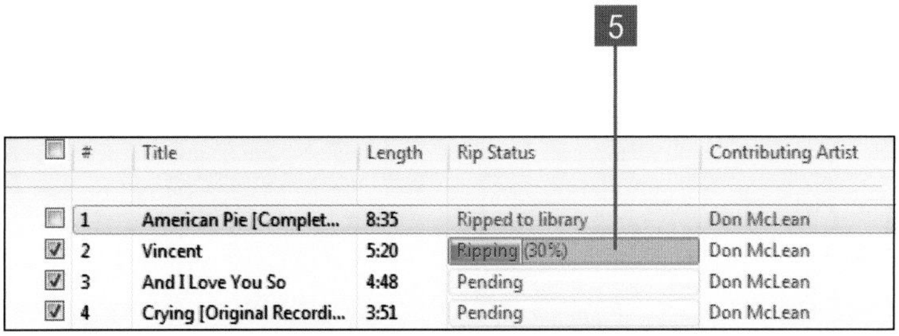
5
#
Title
Length
Rip Status
Contributing Artist
1 American Pie [Complet... 8:35 Ripped to library Don McLean
2 Vincent 5:20 Ripping (30%) Don McLean
3 And I Love You So 4:48 Pending Don McLean
4 Crying [Original Recordi... 3:51 Pending Don McLean

1. Insert the CD to copy into the CD drive.
2. If any pop-up boxes appear, click the X to close them. This step isn't actually necessary, as you can select Rip CD in Windows Media Player from the dialogue box that appears, but I'd like to introduce ripping from Media Player, not from a dialogue box, so that you can access all available options.
3. Deselect any songs you do not want to copy to your Laptop. (All songs are selected by default.)
4. In Windows Media Player, click the Rip CD button.
5. Watch as the CD is copied; you can view the Rip Status as shown here.
6. The ripped music will now appear in your music library under Recently Added, as well as Artist, Album and Genre.

Did you know?

You can deselect songs during the rip process if you decide you don't want to wait for them to be copied.

Burning a CD

There are two ways to take music with you when you are on the road or on the go. You can copy the music to a portable device such as a mobile phone, Zen or other music player (and keep it synchronised using Media Player), or you can create your own CDs, choosing the songs to copy and placing them on the CD in the desired order. CDs you create can be played in car stereos and portable CD players, as well as lots of other CD devices. A typical CD can hold about 80 minutes of music, but, don't worry, Media Player will keep track of the songs you select and will let you know when you're running out of space on the CD you are creating.

The Burn tab can assist you in creating a CD. Burn is media-speak for copying music from your laptop to a CD. Clicking Burn brings up the List pane, where Media Player will tell you to insert a blank CD if one is not in the drive already, and allow you to drag and drop songs into the List pane to create a burn list. As music is added, the progress bar at the top of the List pane shows how much available space you've used.

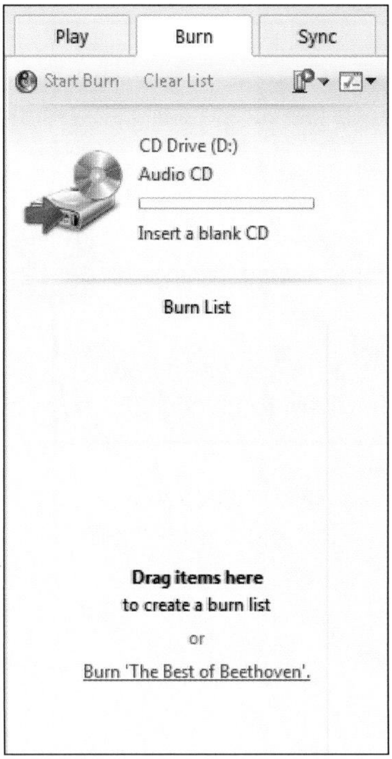
Play
Burn
Sync
Start Burn
Clear List
CD Drive (D:)
Audio CD
Insert a blank CD
Burn List
Drag items here
to create a burn list
or
Burn 'The Best of Beethoven'.

For your information

Once you've added music, the Start Burn button becomes active.

Did you know?

You can right-click any song in the Burn list to access additional options, including the option to delete the song from the list (not the Laptop), or to move up or move down in the list order.

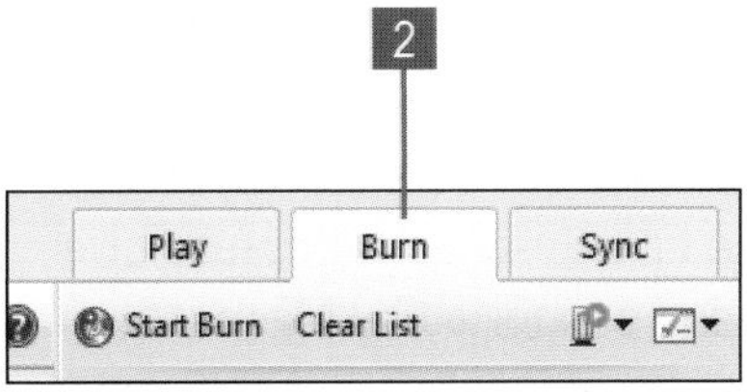
2
Play
Burn
Sync
Start Burn
Clear List

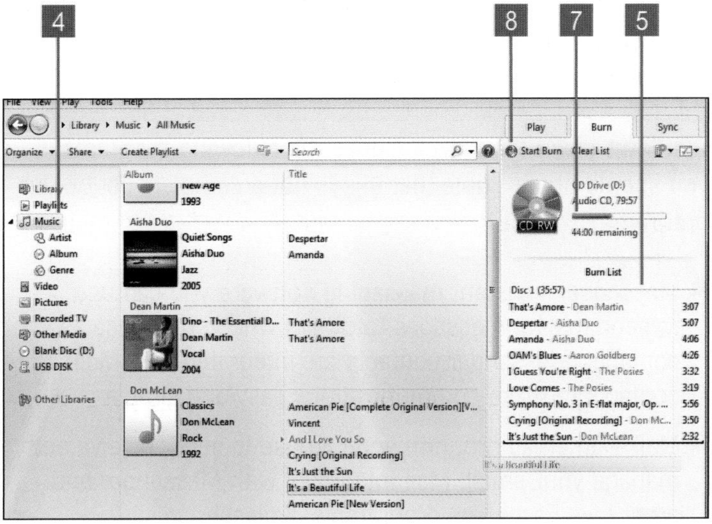
4
8
7
5
Library ▸ Music ▸ All Music
Play
Burn
Sync
Organize
Share
Create Playlist
Search
Start Burn
Clear List
Album
Title
Library
Playlists
Music
Artist
Album
Genre
Video
Pictures
Recorded TV
Other Media
Blank Disc (D:)
USB DISK
Other Libraries
New Age
1993
Aisha Duo
Quiet Songs
Aisha Duo
Jazz
2005
Despertar
Amanda
Dean Martin
Dino - The Essential D...
Dean Martin
Vocal
2004
That's Amore
That's Amore
Don McLean
Classics
Don McLean
Rock
1992
American Pie [Complete Original Version][V...
Vincent
And I Love You So
Crying [Original Recording]
It's Just the Sun
It's a Beautiful Life
American Pie [New Version]
CD Drive (D:)
Audio CD, 79:57
CD RW
44:00 remaining
Burn List
Disc 1 (35:57)
That's Amore - Dean Martin 3:07
Despertar - Aisha Duo 5:07
Amanda - Aisha Duo 4:06
OAM's Blues - Aaron Goldberg 4:26
I Guess You're Right - The Posies 3:32
Love Comes - The Posies 3:19
Symphony No. 3 in E-flat major, Op. ... 5:56
Crying [Original Recording] - Don Mc... 3:50
It's Just the Sun - Don McLean 2:32

For your information

You do not need to fill the entire CD with songs if you don't want to.

Did you know?

Click the blue question mark next to the Search box for more information on how to use Windows Media Player.

Burning a CD

1. Open Media Player.
2. Click the Burn tab.
3. Insert a blank, recordable, CD into the CD drive.
4. Under Library, click Music, if Music is not already selected.
5. Click any song title to add, and drag it to the Burn List pane.
6. Drop the song in the Burn List pane to add it to the Burn List. Continue as desired.
7. Look at the slider in the List pane to verify there is room left on the CD. Continue to add songs until the CD is full or until desired.
8. When you've added the songs you want, click Start Burn.

Download and install Windows Live Essentials

Windows 7 is missing a few things. Notably, it's missing a photo-editing program, an email program and a messaging program. You can get all of this and more free, when you download and install Windows Live Essentials. Because Live Essentials is created, offered and supported by Microsoft, each program in Windows Live Essentials is compatible and/or accessible from the others. This makes obtaining this suite of applications even more desirable, and a must-have addition to Windows 7.

Windows Live Essentials includes the following programs you should obtain (note that this is not a complete list of Live programs):

- Messenger – instant messaging software you can use to send instant messages to others who you choose as contacts. Messenger contacts are integrated with Mail contacts to make communications easy and simple.
- Mail – an email program you can use to send, receive and manage your email. Mail integrates with Messenger and other Live Essentials programs seamlessly.
- Writer – a program that lets you share your photos and videos on blog services such as Windows Live, Wordpress, Blogger, Live Journal and more. A 'blog' is a 'web-log', and is generally used to share one's opinions, thoughts and personal information.
- Photo Gallery – a web-based photo editing and management program that lets you move pictures from your camera to your laptop. With Photo Gallery you can edit, share and create panoramic photos.
- Movie Maker – this program lets you create movies from video clips taken from your digital camera or other sources, and share them with friends and family via CD, DVD or even the web.
- Toolbar – this is a toolbar that, after installation, appears in Internet Explorer. The toolbar integrates access to Mail, Messenger, Photos, Calendar and more, all from a single place.

- Family Safety – this program helps you keep your family safe from Internet sites that could harm your laptop or be inappropriate for viewing. You can configure Family Safety to block websites when your grandchildren log on, allow them (or not) to speak with contacts, and even monitor where your grandchildren are going when they are online. Family Safety has to be installed on all laptops your grandchildren use, though, so if you have more than one laptop that is something to consider. Unless you have grandchildren to protect, I suggest you do not install this program.

Download and install Windows Live Essentials (cont.)

Downloading Windows Live

1. Open Internet Explorer and go to http://download.live.com.
2. Click Download.
3. Click Run.
4. Select the programs to install. I suggest you install Messenger, Mail, Photo Gallery and Toolbar, at the very least. You may find you already have these programs installed, as shown here.

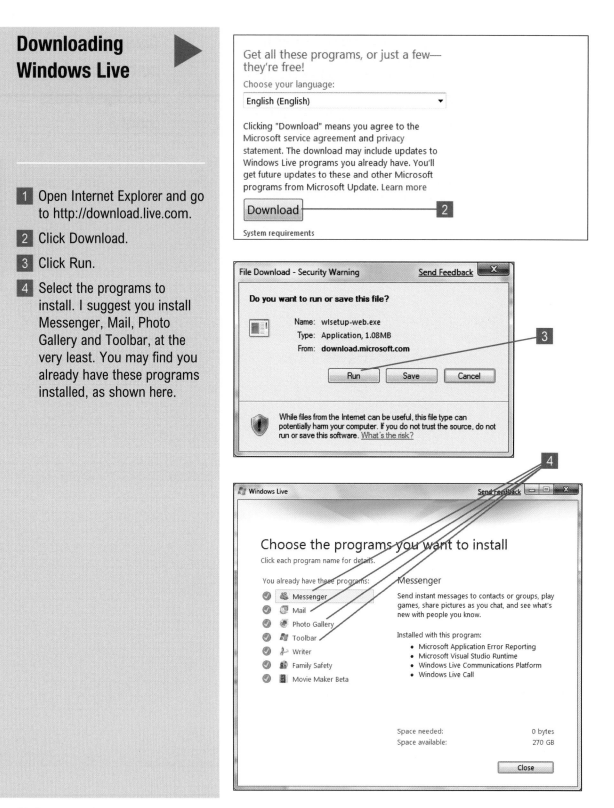

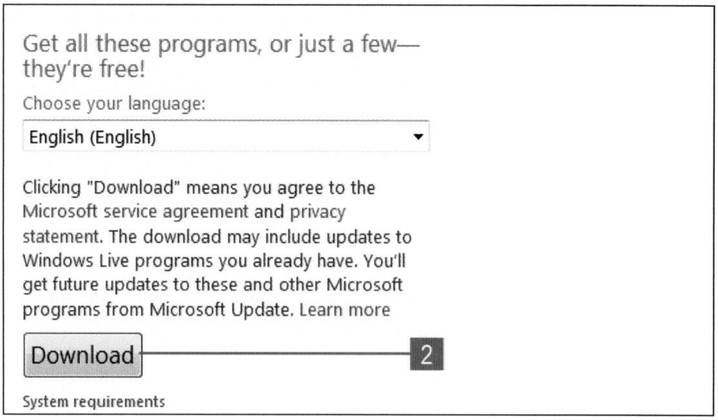
Get all these programs, or just a few—they're free!
Choose your language:
English (English)
Clicking "Download" means you agree to the Microsoft service agreement and privacy statement. The download may include updates to Windows Live programs you already have. You'll get future updates to these and other Microsoft programs from Microsoft Update. Learn more
Download
2
System requirements

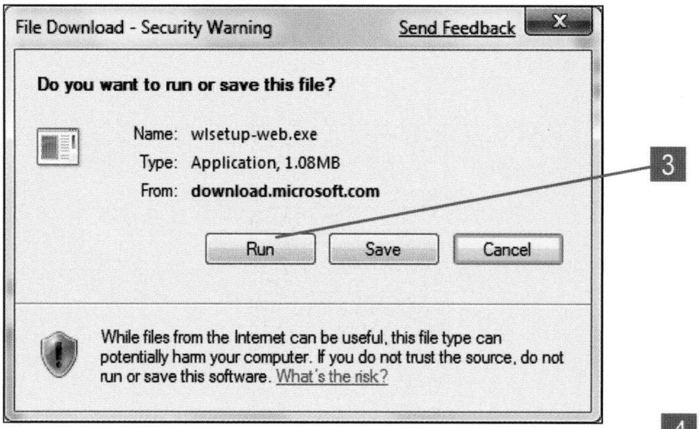
File Download - Security Warning
Send Feedback
Do you want to run or save this file?
Name: wlsetup-web.exe
Type: Application, 1.08MB
From: download.microsoft.com
Run
Save
Cancel
3
While files from the Internet can be useful, this file type can potentially harm your computer. If you do not trust the source, do not run or save this software. What's the risk?

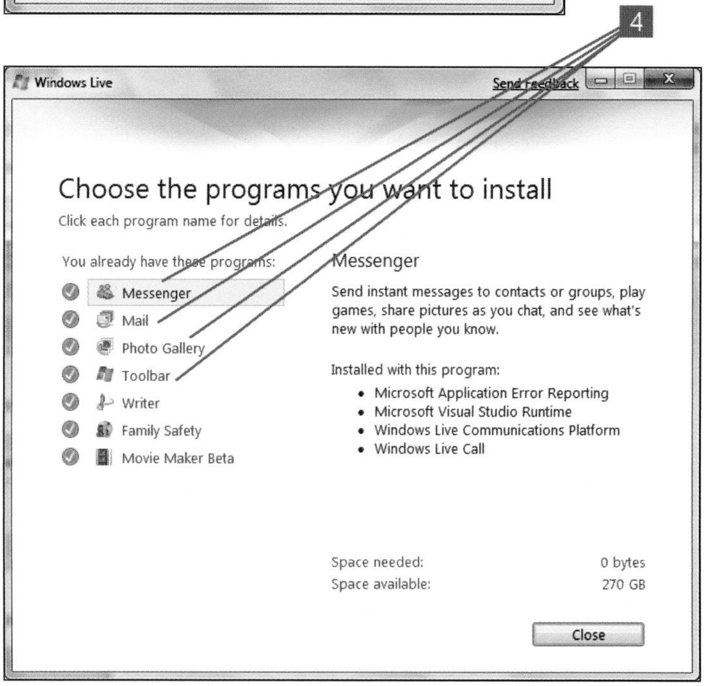
4
Windows Live
Send Feedback
Choose the programs you want to install
Click each program name for details.
You already have these programs:
Messenger
Mail
Photo Gallery
Toolbar
Writer
Family Safety
Movie Maker Beta
Messenger
Send instant messages to contacts or groups, play games, share pictures as you chat, and see what's new with people you know.
Installed with this program:
Microsoft Application Error Reporting
Microsoft Visual Studio Runtime
Windows Live Communications Platform
Windows Live Call
Space needed: 0 bytes
Space available: 270 GB
Close

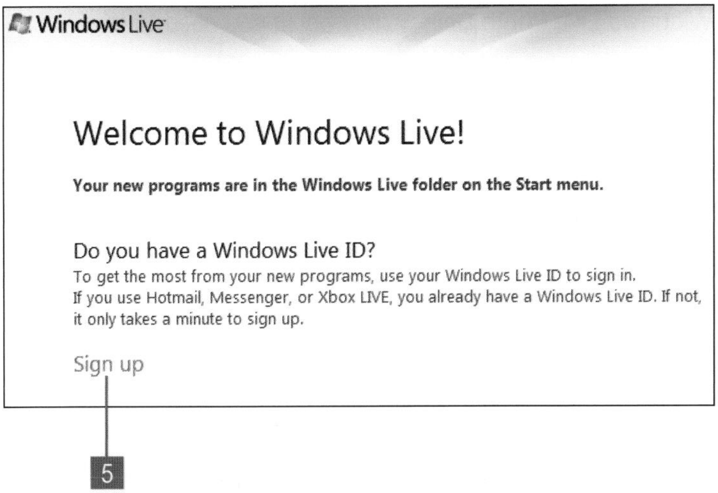
Windows Live
Welcome to Windows Live!
Your new programs are in the Windows Live folder on the Start menu.
Do you have a Windows Live ID?
To get the most from your new programs, use your Windows Live ID to sign in.
If you use Hotmail, Messenger, or Xbox LIVE, you already have a Windows Live ID. If not, it only takes a minute to sign up.
Sign up
5

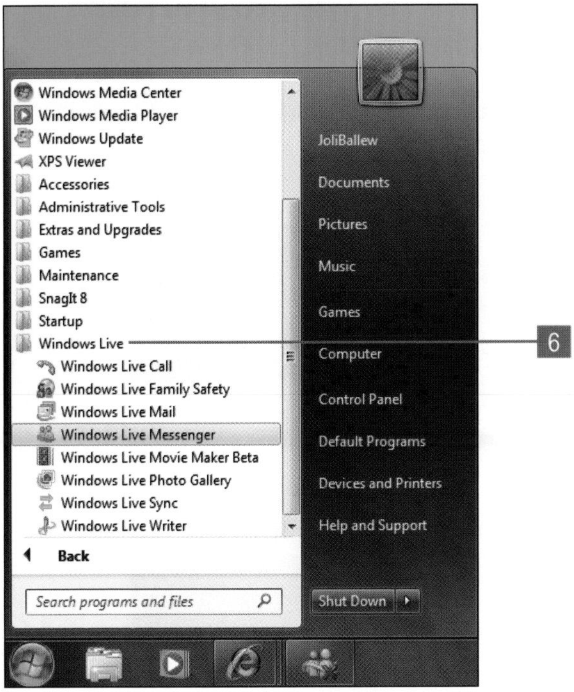
Windows Media Center
Windows Media Player
Windows Update
XPS Viewer
Accessories
Administrative Tools
Extras and Upgrades
Games
Maintenance
SnagIt 8
Startup
Windows Live
Windows Live Call
Windows Live Family Safety
Windows Live Mail
Windows Live Messenger
Windows Live Movie Maker Beta
Windows Live Photo Gallery
Windows Live Sync
Windows Live Writer
Back
Search programs and files
JoliBallew
Documents
Pictures
Music
Games
Computer
Control Panel
Default Programs
Devices and Printers
Help and Support
Shut Down
6

Timesaver tip

Because all Windows Live programs are integrated, you only have to log in one time to access all of the programs. And because you log in, each program is tailored to meet your specific needs.

Downloading Windows Live (cont.)

5 When installation is complete, click Sign up if you do not have a Windows Live ID, and fill out the required information. Otherwise, log in.

6 Click Start, click All Programs and click Windows Live. Note the available programs. Click any program to open it.

Windows Live Photo Gallery

Windows Live Photo Gallery may be all you need to manage, manipulate, view and share your digital photos. Before you install additional software, including software that was included on the CD that was shipped with your digital camera or printer, try this program. It's not included with Windows 7, though; it requires you to download and install it. If you haven't done that yet, refer to the previous section.

The first time you open Windows Live Photo Gallery, you'll note that it has two default panes, and each offers specific functionality. The pane to the left is the View pane, where you'll select the folder or subfolder that contains the pictures you want to view, manage, edit or share. The Thumbnail pane is on the right, and this is where you preview the pictures in the folder selected in the View pane.

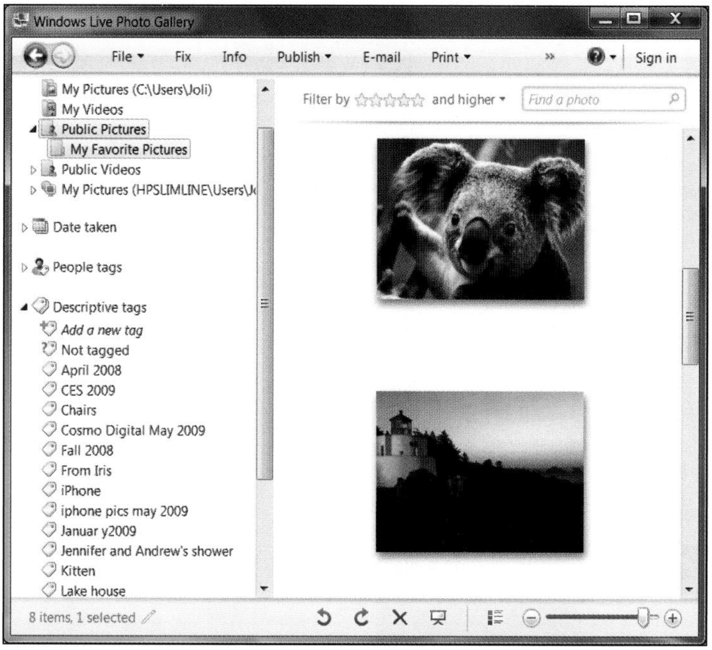
Windows Live Photo Gallery
File
Fix
Info
Publish
E-mail
Print
Sign in
My Pictures (C:\Users\Joli)
My Videos
Public Pictures
My Favorite Pictures
Public Videos
My Pictures (HPSLIMLINE\Users\J
Date taken
People tags
Descriptive tags
Add a new tag
Not tagged
April 2008
CES 2009
Chairs
Cosmo Digital May 2009
Fall 2008
From Iris
iPhone
iphone pics may 2009
Januar y2009
Jennifer and Andrew's shower
Kitten
Lake house
Filter by
and higher
Find a photo
8 items, 1 selected

When you double-click a picture in the Thumbnail pane, it opens in a new pane where you can then edit, share, add tags and perform other image-related tasks. Note that, when you double-click an image, the View pane disappears and a new pane appears on the right. From that new pane, called the Info pane, you can rate the image and add tags easily.

Windows Live Photo Gallery (cont.)

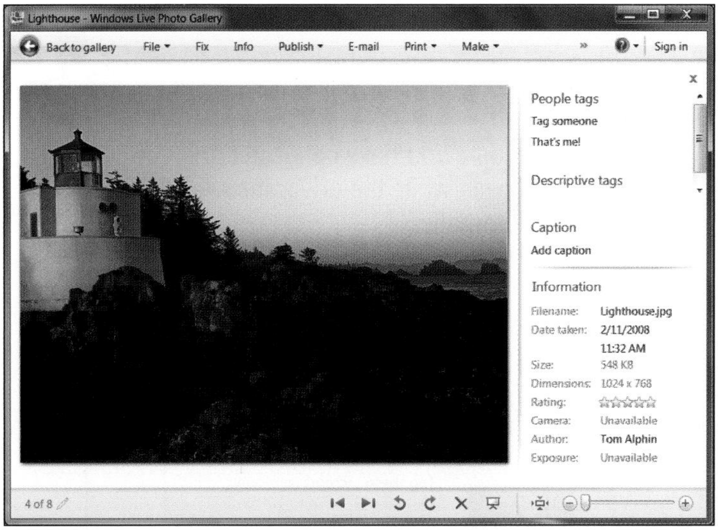
Lighthouse - Windows Live Photo Gallery
Back to gallery
File
Fix
Info
Publish
E-mail
Print
Make
Sign in
People tags
Tag someone
That's me!
Descriptive tags
Caption
Add caption
Information
Filename: Lighthouse.jpg
Date taken: 2/11/2008 11:32 AM
Size: 548 KB
Dimensions: 1024 x 768
Rating:
Camera: Unavailable
Author: Tom Alphin
Exposure: Unavailable
4 of 8

You can also click Fix to access additional tools. You can adjust the exposure and colour for instance, or crop or straighten the photo, among other things. You'll notice at the bottom of the Photo Gallery window that there are navigational controls. The slider that allows you to zoom is quite helpful. Zooming is a great way to get to an area of an image to fix, especially if it's a small area, like red-eye. There are other navigational controls including a toggle switch to move from the image's actual size to fit to screen, arrows for Previous (to move to the previous picture in the folder), Play Slide Show (to play a slide show of the folder's pictures), Next (to move to the next picture in the folder), Rotate Counterclockwise, Rotate Clockwise and Delete.

Before you can do much, you'll need to import some digital photos. If you have a digital camera, mobile phone, SD card with images on it or some other device that contains photos, you can import the photos from it into Photo Gallery.

Importing pictures from a digital camera, media card or USB drive (and even an iPhone)

1. Connect the device. If applicable, turn it on.
2. When prompted, choose Import Pictures using Windows Live Photo Gallery.
3. Click Import all new items now, and type a descriptive name for the group of pictures you're importing.
4. Click Import.
5. If desired, check Erase after importing. This will cause Windows 7 to erase the images from the device after the import is complete.
6. Windows Live Photo Gallery will open and you can view the pictures.

Windows 7 won't recognise all devices, but it does a pretty good job. In fact, it will import pictures from many kinds of mobile phones, including the iPhone. However, on the slim chance your device isn't immediately recognised, you can click File, and click Import from Camera or Scanner, and you'll be given access to additional devices attached to your laptop, even scanners.

For your information

If this is the first time you have connected the device you may have to wait while the driver installs. This is almost always automatic.

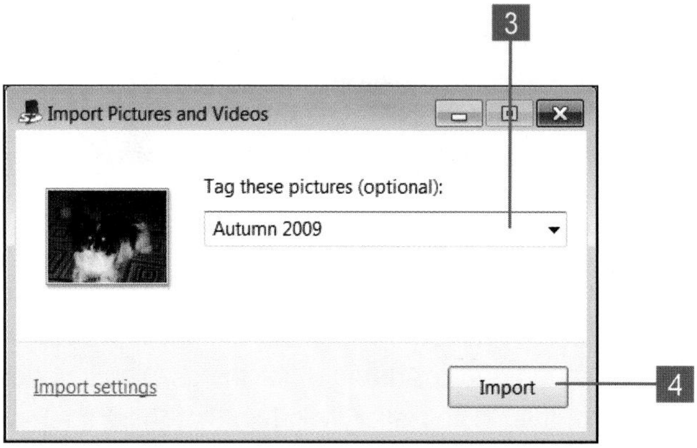

3
Import Pictures and Videos
Tag these pictures (optional):
Autumn 2009
Import settings
Import
4

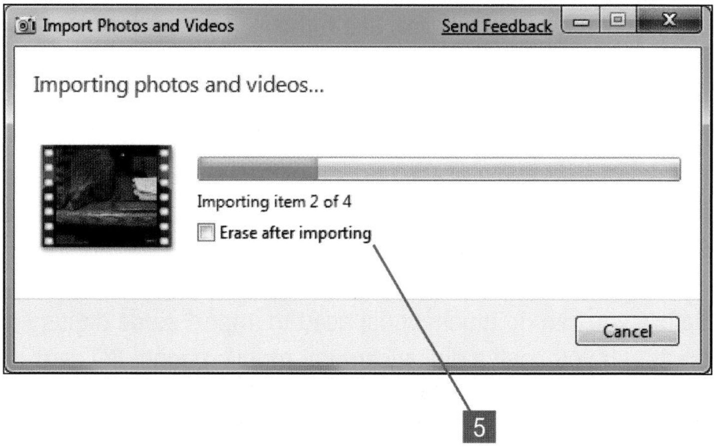

Import Photos and Videos
Send Feedback
Importing photos and videos...
Importing item 2 of 4
Erase after importing
Cancel
5

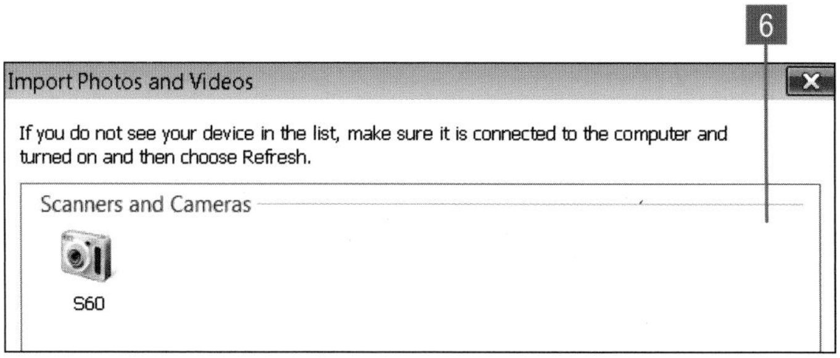

6
Import Photos and Videos
If you do not see your device in the list, make sure it is connected to the computer and turned on and then choose Refresh.
Scanners and Cameras
S60

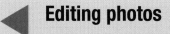

Editing photos

With pictures now on your laptop and available in Windows Photo Gallery, your next step is likely to perform some editing. As noted earlier, Photo Gallery offers many editing options. These include the ability to correct brightness and contrast, colour temperature, tint and saturation, as well as crop images and fix red-eye. You may find, after a bit of time with Photo Gallery, that you need more editing options. If that turns out to be the case, consider Photoshop Elements. It's a great program for beginners and offers all you'll probably ever need.

To begin editing a picture, first double-click it. From the Menu bar, click Fix. In the new pane that appears, choose from the following:

- Auto Adjust – this tool automatically assesses the image and alters it, which most of the time results in a better image. However, there's always the Undo button, and you'll likely use it on occasion.
- Adjust Exposure – this tool offers slider controls for Brightness and Contrast. You move these sliders to the left and right to adjust as desired.
- Adjust Color – this tool offers slider controls to adjust the temperature, tint and saturation of the photo. Temperature runs from blue to yellow, allowing you to change the 'atmosphere' of the image. Tint runs from green to red, and saturation moves from black and white to colour.
- Straighten Photo – this tool automatically straightens photos and offers a slider you can use as well.
- Crop Picture – this tool removes parts of a picture you don't want.
- Adjust Detail – this tool allows you to sharpen the image and reduce 'noise'. This can help bring a fuzzy or blurry picture into focus. You can apply changes automatically or manually.
- Fix Red Eye – this lets you draw a rectangle around any eye that has a red dot in it, and the red dot is automatically removed.
- Black and White Effects – this tool lets you apply effects to the image, to change the 'tone' (colour) of the image.

Fixing pictures

1. Open Windows Live Photo Gallery.
2. In the View pane, select any folder that contains pictures.
3. Position the Zoom slider so you can see several images at once.
4. Double-click a picture to edit. (It's best not to use the Sample Pictures; they're already optimised.)
5. Click Fix.
6. Click Auto Adjust.
7. If you like the result, jump to Step 8. If not, click Undo.
8. Adjust Exposure should be open; if not, click it to view the options.
9. Move the sliders for Brightness and Contrast. Click Undo to return to the original image settings. You may need to click Undo more than once.

Timesaver tip

If you click Fix and don't see the editing options, click it again. It toggles the options on and off.

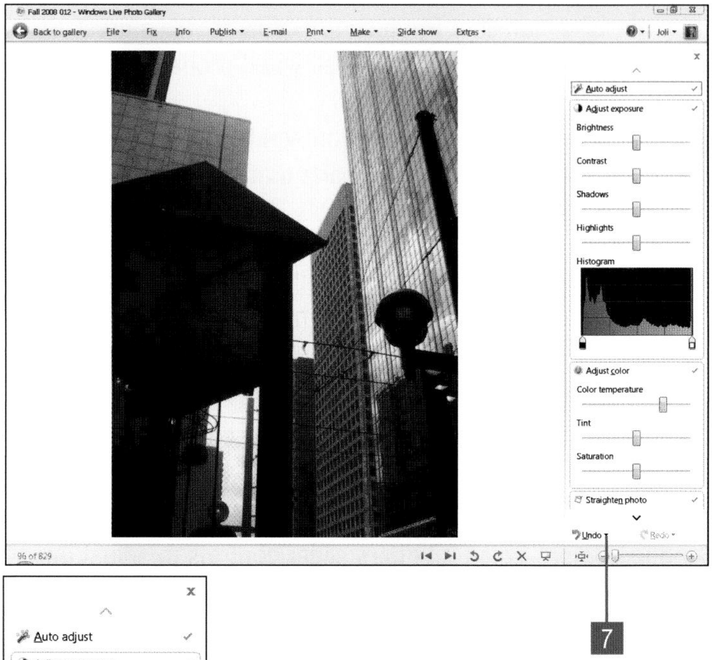

Fall 2008 012 - Windows Live Photo Gallery
Back to gallery
File
Fix
Info
Publish
E-mail
Print
Make
Slide show
Extras
Joli
Auto adjust
Adjust exposure
Brightness
Contrast
Shadows
Highlights
Histogram
Adjust color
Color temperature
Tint
Saturation
Straighten photo
Undo
Redo
96 of 829
7

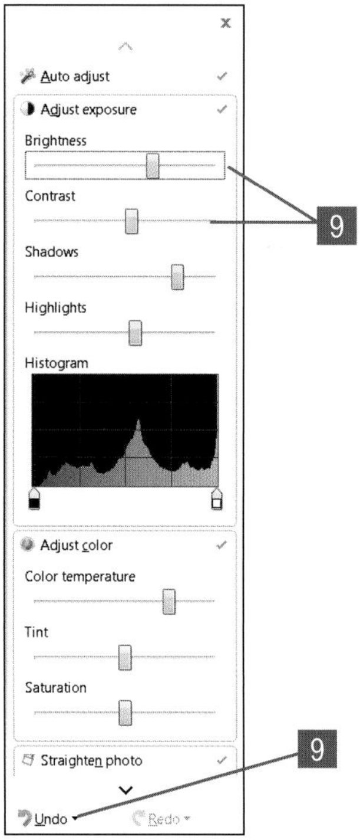

Auto adjust
Adjust exposure
Brightness
Contrast
Shadows
Highlights
Histogram
Adjust color
Color temperature
Tint
Saturation
Straighten photo
Undo
Redo
9
9

Timesaver tip

If the picture looks crooked, click Straighten Picture.

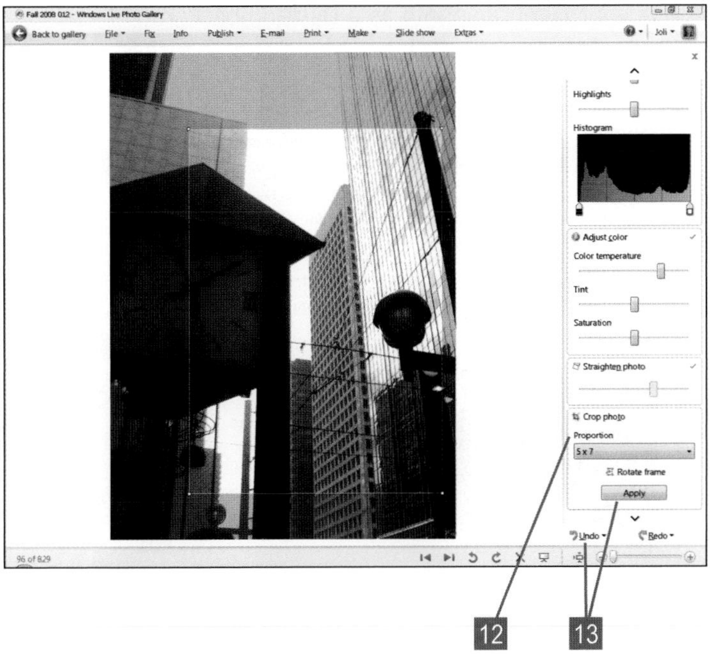
Fall 2008 012 - Windows Live Photo Gallery
Back to gallery
File
Fix
Info
Publish
E-mail
Print
Make
Slide show
Extras
Highlights
Histogram
Adjust color
Color temperature
Tint
Saturation
Straighten photo
Crop photo
Proportion
5 x 7
Rotate frame
Apply
Undo
Redo
96 of 829
12
13

For your information

If the image seems blurry or out of focus, click Adjust Detail and then click Analyze. You may be able to sharpen the image a little.

Fixing pictures (cont.)

10 Continue to experiment with the adjustment options.

11 Click Crop Picture. If you can't see the Crop Picture option, either close the open editing options or use the down arrow key to access additional options.

12 Drag the corners of the box to resize it, and drag the entire box to move it around in the picture. If desired, under Proportion, select any option. (Note you can also rotate the frame.)

13 Click Apply or Undo.

14 If there's red-eye in the picture, click Fix Red Eye.

15 Drag the mouse over the red part of the eye. When you let go, the red-eye in the picture will be removed.

16 Click Undo if desired.

17 To save the changes to the original file, i.e. write over the existing file, click Back to Gallery.

18 If you later decide you do not like the changes applied to the picture, double-click it, and choose Revert.

Sharing photos

There are a number of ways to share your photos. You can view them on your laptop, email them to others, and burn them to CDs and DVDs, just to name a few. And you know (if you've worked through this book from the beginning) how to do most of this already. Here are a few ideas for sharing photos:

- Use your favourite photo as a Desktop background – in Photo Gallery, right-click any photo and choose Set as desktop background.

2576 x 1932
Preview photo
Open with
Open file location
Set as desktop background
Rotate clockwise
Rotate counterclockwise
Change time taken...
Copy
Delete
Rename...
Resize...
Properties
2576 x 1932
2576 x 1932

- Use a slideshow of your photos as a screensaver – open Personalization, and choose Screensaver. For Screensaver, select Photos. Click Settings to choose the folder to use.
- Print pictures using a photo printer – click Print in Windows Photo Gallery. Note you can also order prints online.
- Email photos – in Photo Gallery, select the files to email, click Email and, when prompted, choose either Small or Smaller (for best results). Click Attach.

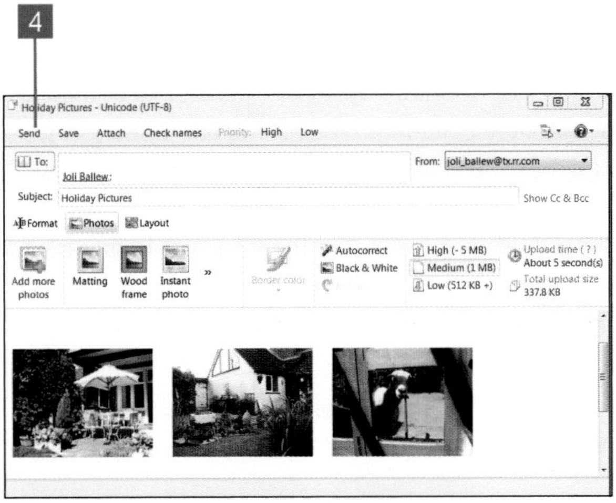

4
Holiday Pictures - Unicode (UTF-8)
Send
Save
Attach
Check names
Priority:
High
Low
To:
Joli Ballew;
From:
joli_ballew@tx.rr.com
Subject:
Holiday Pictures
Show Cc & Bcc
Format
Photos
Layout
Add more photos
Matting
Wood frame
Instant photo
Border color
Autocorrect
Black & White
High (~ 5 MB)
Medium (1 MB)
Low (512 KB +)
Upload time (?)
About 5 second(s)
Total upload size
337.8 KB

Emailing pictures

10

1. Open Windows Photo Gallery.
2. Select pictures to email.
3. Click Email. If Windows Live Mail is your default mail program, jump to Step 4. Otherwise, you may be prompted to select a picture size and attach the image(s).
4. Complete the email and click Send.

Watch DVDs

You can watch a DVD on your computer just as you would on your home entertainment centre. In fact, some people are now getting rid of their home theatre systems in favour of a 'media centre laptop' that they connect to their large flat-screen TVs. New laptops built as media computers have television, DVRs, DVD players, music players, speakers, surround sound and more, installed and ready to use. And the best part is that it's often a more compact option than a combination of television, DVD player, cable box, DVR, stereo system, speakers and stacks of DVDs and CDs. That said, it's certainly possible to watch a DVD on your laptop; it's one of the most basic entertainment options.

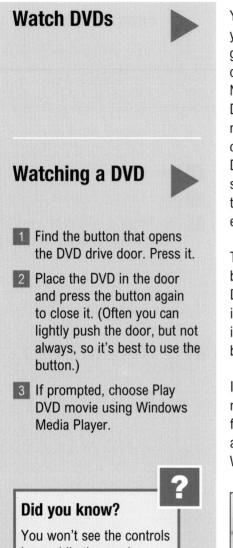

Watching a DVD

1. Find the button that opens the DVD drive door. Press it.
2. Place the DVD in the door and press the button again to close it. (Often you can lightly push the door, but not always, so it's best to use the button.)
3. If prompted, choose Play DVD movie using Windows Media Player.

The first time you insert a DVD into the DVD drive, you may be prompted regarding what program to use when playing DVDs. You may not. The DVD may begin to play automatically in Windows Media Player. If you have third-party software installed on the laptop that can also play DVDs, the DVD may begin to play in that program.

If prompted, to watch a DVD, simply make a choice. Once the movie has started, you'll have access to controls, including fast forward, pause, rewind, stop, resume, volume and more. Here's a DVD that's just about to start in Windows Media Player. Windows Media Player was covered earlier in this chapter.

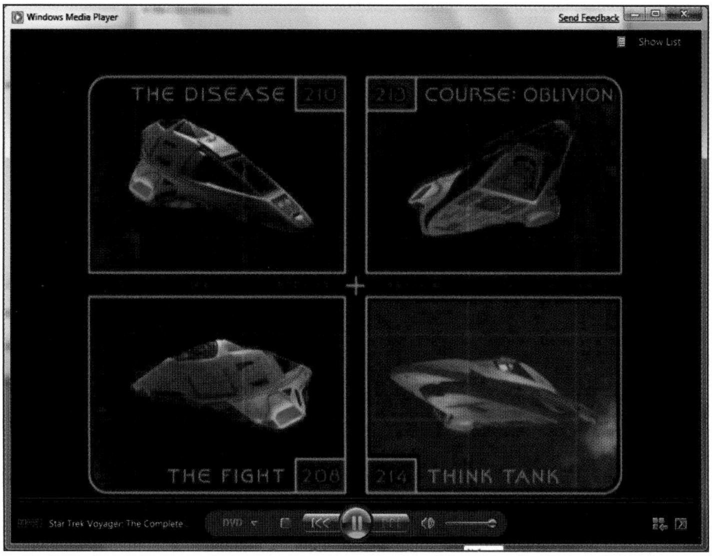
Windows Media Player
Send Feedback
Show List
THE DISEASE 210
213 COURSE: OBLIVION
THE FIGHT 208
214 THINK TANK
Star Trek Voyager: The Complete

Did you know?

You won't see the controls here while the movie is playing unless you position your mouse there or access the proper buttons on a remote control.

Watch TV using Windows Media Center

Windows Media Center is a one-stop media application that lets you access and manage pictures, videos, movies, music, online media, television, DVDs and CDs, and radio. As you already know, though, you can do much of this elsewhere. You can manage pictures in Windows Live Photo Gallery; and you can manage music, online media, radio stations and portable devices in Media Player. So where does Media Center shine then, and how should you use it?

Media Center, although it can be used to listen to music, really stands out for viewing, recording, watching and managing cable and Internet TV, obtaining and viewing online media, or watching DVDs you own or rent. It's a 'media centre', if you will, a place to enjoy the media you already have access to and have already 'managed'. Media Center has an online guide to help you find out what's available to watch and when, and you can record television programmes, pause live TV, and then fast forward or rewind through what you've paused.

You should start with Media Center by watching and recording TV, and then move on to watching online media. As time passes and you get more comfortable with Media Center, you may find you prefer it over Media Player and Windows Live Photo Gallery. How far to take it is up to you!

Once Media Center is set up and you know how to navigate through it, it's simple to watch TV. Just browse to TV, and click Live TV. If everything is set up and installed as it should be, you'll get a live TV signal. And once you have a live TV signal, it's almost as easy to get started recording TV.

Watching live TV

When you're watching live TV, you'll see the broadcast, of course, but other items will appear and disappear, seemingly at will. By moving the mouse around various areas of the screen you can see the channel number as well as the show's name (among other things), as do familiar-looking controls. The show's broadcast information appears when you change to the channel, and you can also bring it up by right-clicking in that area of the screen.

Important

In order to watch live TV on your laptop you must have a TV tuner installed or an external TV tuner connected.

Watch TV using Windows Media Center (cont.)

There are also TV controls. These controls appear when you move your mouse to the bottom of the screen, if you press specific buttons on a remote control or keyboard, and in a few other instances. With these controls you can:

- Record the show you're watching by pressing the Record button.
- Change the channel using the Channel Up and Channel Down buttons.
- Stop watching TV using the Stop button.
- Rewind quickly or more slowly using the two Rewind buttons.
- Pause (and then Play) live TV using the Pause/Play button.
- Fast forward slowly or more quickly using the two Fast Forward buttons.
- Mute the TV by clicking the Mute button. (The X here means the volume is currently muted.)
- Decrease or increase the volume using the Volume Down and Volume Up buttons.

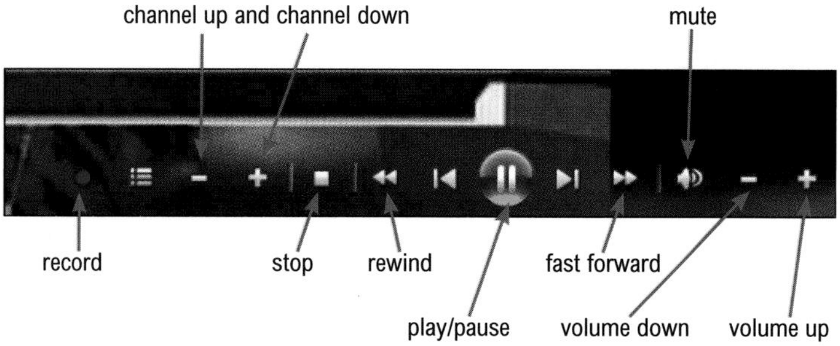

channel up and channel down
mute
record
stop
rewind
fast forward
play/pause
volume down
volume up

You can pause up to 30 minutes of live TV. After 30 minutes, the broadcast becomes unpaused and starts playing again – from where you paused it. When you close Media Center or change the television channel, the 30 minutes of saved television is automatically deleted. Pausing is great for skipping through commercials. Just pause the TV for a while at any point, and when commercials come on, simply fast-forward through it.

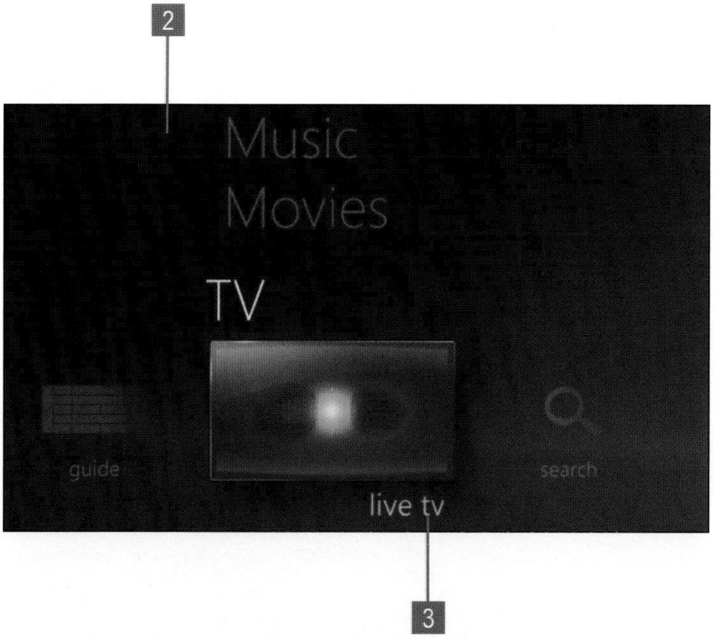
2
Music
Movies
TV
guide
search
live tv
3

Watching live TV

1. Open Media Center.
2. Click TV.
3. Click live tv.
4. Experiment with the Channel Up and Channel Down buttons.
5. Click Pause. Wait a few minutes.
6. Click Play.
7. Mute and unmute the sounds.
8. Change the volume using the Volume Up and Volume Down buttons.
9. Fast forward and rewind using the Fast forward and Rewind buttons.

Record television

Important

Important

Remember, you can always click the Back arrow (it will appear when you hover the mouse over the top left corner) to return to the previous screen.

There are a lot of ways to access the commands to Record and Record Series. As you learned in the previous section, you can right-click on the bottom part of the screen while watching a live TV show to access these commands. You won't always want to record what you're watching, though; you will more likely want to record something that is coming on later in the week. That's what the guide is for. And while there are multiple ways to access the guide, the most straightforward is from the TV menu you're already familiar with. (You can also open the guide using a remote control or media keyboard if you have one.)

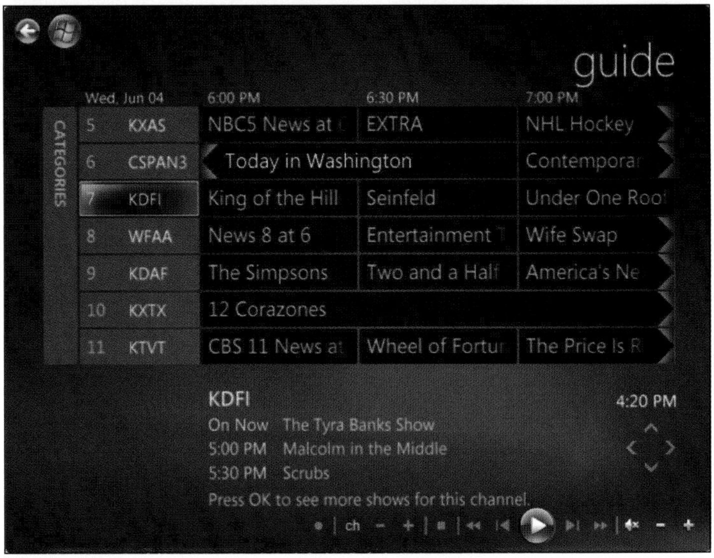

guide
Wed, Jun 04
6:00 PM
6:30 PM
7:00 PM
CATEGORIES
5 KXAS
NBC5 News at
EXTRA
NHL Hockey
6 CSPAN3
Today in Washington
Contempora
7 KDFI
King of the Hill
Seinfeld
Under One Roo
8 WFAA
News 8 at 6
Entertainment
Wife Swap
9 KDAF
The Simpsons
Two and a Half
America's Ne
10 KXTX
12 Corazones
11 KTVT
CBS 11 News at
Wheel of Fortun
The Price Is R
KDFI
4:20 PM
On Now The Tyra Banks Show
5:00 PM Malcolm in the Middle
5:30 PM Scrubs
Press OK to see more shows for this channel.

Program Details
Record
Series Info
Search
View Categories
Edit Channel
Settings

Record television (cont.)

You move through the guide using the arrow keys on your keyboard, using a scroll wheel on a mouse or using a remote control. You can click with the mouse on these arrows to move through the guide as well. The arrow will appear when you hover the mouse over that particular area of the screen.

You can access more options for a program by clicking it. Clicking a program offers the options shown here, including the option to record. (You'll see Record Series if the program is part of a series.)

Recording a TV show or series

1. Click TV and locate guide.
2. Use your mouse, arrows on the keyboard or another method to locate the show to record.
3. Click the programme.
4. Select Record.

Did you know?

To watch a television show you've recorded, simply browse to Recorded TV, and click the recorded show you want to watch! It's just as easy as watching live TV.

Windows Media Center
recorded tv
+ add recording
view scheduled
‹ date recorded ›
title
original air date
shared
TUESDAY
MONDAY
5/21/2009
UNKNOWN
The Sopranos
Matlock
Landscapes
The Sopranos
Rat Pack (Repeat)
Tony reunites with his paroled cousin, Tony Blundetto; Paulie and Christopher relive some bad memories; Carmela launches a film club; Adriana struggles with her guilt.
54 AETV Tue, Jun 02, 2009 65 min
1 | 4

The Mobility Center

11

What you'll do

Explore Windows Mobility Center

Enhance battery life

Turn on and off wireless connectivity

Turn on Presentation Settings

Get started with Sync Center

Connect an external display

Introduction

Windows Mobility Center is only available on laptops and netbooks and offers special features just for users that are on the go. If you own a laptop or notebook computer, tablet PC, smart PC or Ultra-Mobile PC, you've got easy access to power management options, wireless features, presentation capabilities, battery status and sync options.

Many of these features will prove quite useful, and you'll access them often, including selecting a power plan from the Notification area to improve battery life, using presentation settings when playing a slide show or managing some other type of production, and easily turning off wireless capabilities when on an aeroplane (while still being able to use your computer). All of these options and more are available from the Mobility window.

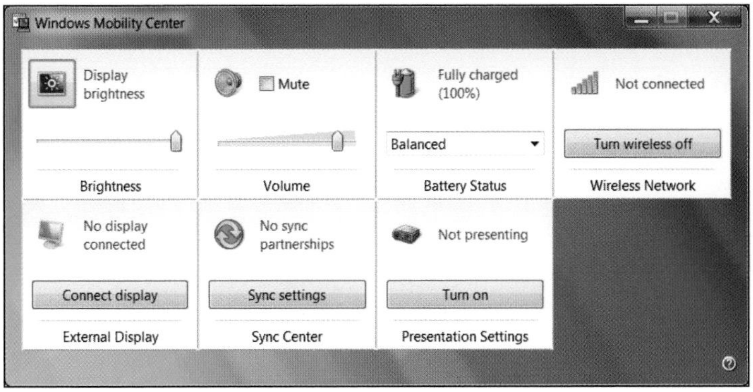
Windows Mobility Center
Display brightness
Brightness
Mute
Volume
Fully charged (100%)
Balanced
Battery Status
Not connected
Turn wireless off
Wireless Network
No display connected
Connect display
External Display
No sync partnerships
Sync settings
Sync Center
Not presenting
Turn on
Presentation Settings

For your information

In this chapter, I use terms such as *portable PC*, *portable computer*, *notebook*, *laptop* and even, occasionally, *tablet PC* to describe mobile computers running Windows 7. For the most part, these terms are largely interchangeable in the context of this chapter unless specifically stated otherwise.

Although Windows Mobility Center was originally created for business users, you don't have to be a businessperson to take advantage of the features. Say you're on a plane, and the captain comes on the speaker and tells you it's safe to use electronic devices, provided you turn the wireless feature off. You can do that in Mobility Center. While there, you might also want to dim the screen to increase battery life, mute the volume so you don't bother the person sitting beside you, and perhaps sync a mobile device while you have the time.

When you first open the Mobility Center you'll see several squares that contain various features. Here's what you'll find in the Mobility Center window:

- Brightness – use the slider to adjust the brightness of your display. This will only change the brightness temporarily. It will not change the brightness as it is configured in Control Panel's Power Settings.
- Volume – use the slider to adjust the volume or the Laptop speakers or check the Mute box.
- Battery Status – see how much life is left in your battery's current charge. You can also change power plans here.
- Wireless Network – turn your wireless adapter on or off.
- Screen Rotation – if you are using a tablet PC, you'll have this option. Use it to change the orientation from portrait to landscape or vice versa.
- External Display – if you're giving a presentation, such as a PowerPoint birthday or reunion slideshow, you can connect an additional monitor to your laptop to show the presentation on. With a secondary monitor, people won't have to crowd around your laptop to see the show.
- Sync Center – perform Sync Center tasks, such as creating a new partnership, syncing or viewing sync progress.
- Presentation Settings – adjust what is necessary for giving a presentation. You can turn off the screensaver, change the volume, speaker volume and select a new Desktop background image. You can also access alternate connected displays.

In the panel titled 'Exploring Windows Mobility Center', you'll learn how to locate and open Windows Mobility Center, change the brightness of your display, and mute the sound or turn the sound up or down.

◀ Exploring Windows Mobility Center

Did you know?

You might also see additional settings that are not listed here, supplied by your computer manufacturer. These settings will be specific to your laptop and are not part of the mobility settings included with Windows 7.

Exploring Windows Mobility Center (cont.)

1. Click Start.
2. In the Start Search dialogue box, type Mobility.
3. Click Windows Mobility Center under Programs.
4. Move the slider for Brightness to the left to dim the display; move to the right to brighten it.
5. Check Mute to turn off all sound, or move the slider to the left to lower the sound; move the slider to the right to turn up the sound.

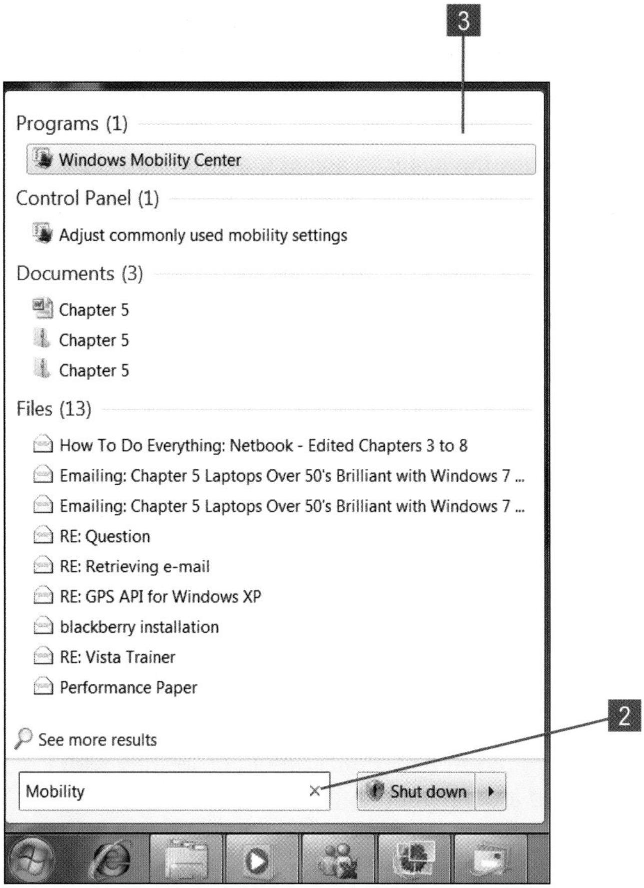

3
Programs (1)
Windows Mobility Center
Control Panel (1)
Adjust commonly used mobility settings
Documents (3)
Chapter 5
Chapter 5
Chapter 5
Files (13)
How To Do Everything: Netbook - Edited Chapters 3 to 8
Emailing: Chapter 5 Laptops Over 50's Brilliant with Windows 7 ...
Emailing: Chapter 5 Laptops Over 50's Brilliant with Windows 7 ...
RE: Question
RE: Retrieving e-mail
RE: GPS API for Windows XP
blackberry installation
RE: Vista Trainer
Performance Paper
See more results
2
Mobility
Shut down

Enhancing battery life

There are lots of ways to improve battery life, although some are more obvious than others. You can lower the display brightness in Windows Mobility Center, opt for a power-saving power plan and turn off animated effects, to name a few. You can change how and when the laptop sleeps or goes into hibernation. You can also choose the Windows 7 Basic theme over those that incorporate Windows Aero. The easiest way to conserve battery power and improve battery life, though, is to use the Power Saver plan, available in Windows Mobility Center (among other places).

?

Did you know?

Power Saver reduces performance, but if you really need to make your battery last, say for a four-hour plane ride, this is the option to choose.

Enhancing battery life (cont.)

1 Open Windows Mobility Center.

2 Click the down arrow for Battery Status to select the Power saver plan.

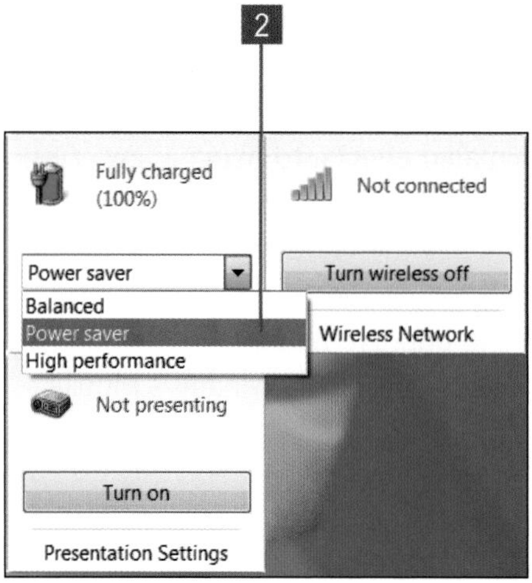

2
Fully charged (100%)
Not connected
Power saver
Turn wireless off
Balanced
Power saver
High performance
Wireless Network
Not presenting
Turn on
Presentation Settings

There are other ways to select a power plan and manage battery usage. For starters, there's a battery metre icon in the Notification area. To see the status of the battery, hover the mouse over the battery icon. The battery icon shows a power metre and a plug. Depending on the status of the laptop and its battery, you'll see different variations on the icon. The pop-up will always offer the status of the laptop and its battery.

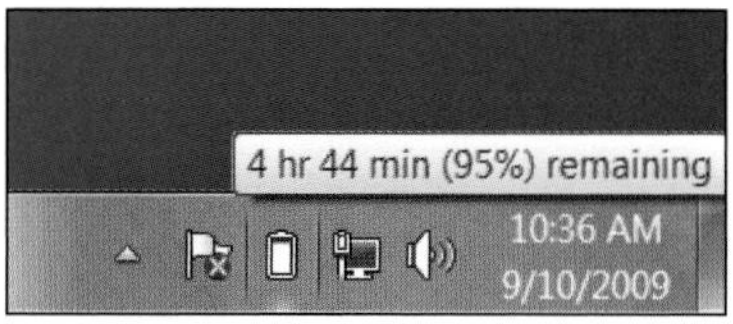

4 hr 44 min (95%) remaining
10:36 AM
9/10/2009

Using the battery metre

If you want to change the power plan from the Notification area, you'll need to click the battery icon. If you click the battery metre icon once, you can select a new power plan, such as Balanced or Power saver. If you right-click the battery metre icon, you'll see a pop-up menu where you can access options including Adjust screen brightness, Power Options, Windows Mobility Center, and Turn system icons on or off.

If you click Power Options, you'll have access to the available power plans. The three built-in power plans include:

Important !

To show the High Performance plan, click Show additional plans (which will change to Hide additional plans after clicking).

Enhancing battery life (cont.)

- Balanced – this is the default power plan. Balanced is meant to imply that the plan balances power use and computer performance. You won't get the best power savings with this plan, and you won't get the best performance either. You will get something in the middle. You can click this plan in Power Options to see how the settings are configured.

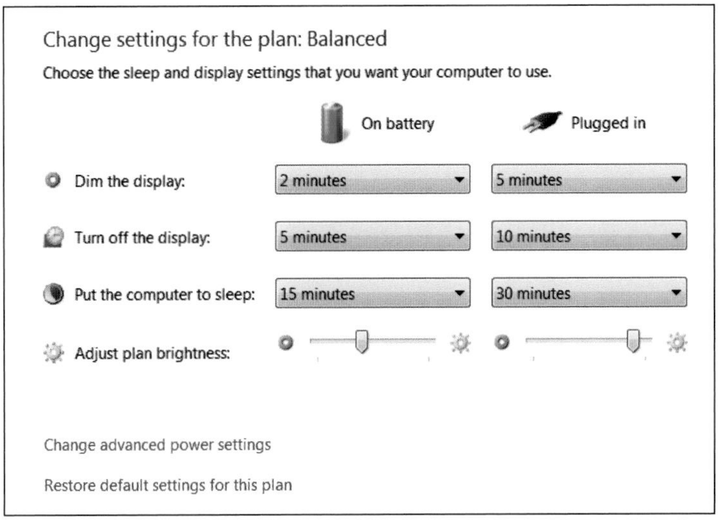
Change settings for the plan: Balanced
Choose the sleep and display settings that you want your computer to use.
On battery
Plugged in
Dim the display:
2 minutes
5 minutes
Turn off the display:
5 minutes
10 minutes
Put the computer to sleep:
15 minutes
30 minutes
Adjust plan brightness:
Change advanced power settings
Restore default settings for this plan

- Power Saver – this plan is all about lengthening battery life. That means in all instances, even when the laptop is plugged in, you'll be able to notice decreased brightness and processor levels, and the computer will go to sleep, turn off hard disks, and turn off the display within minutes of inactivity.
- High Performance – this plan is all about enhancing performance. This power plan doesn't worry about battery life. Here, Windows 7 provides 100 percent of your CPU's processing power, which is necessary for playing games and performing resource-intensive tasks. The computer will still turn off its display, put the hard drive to sleep and put the computer to sleep after a set amount of idle time, though.

Wireless connectivity

You can increase battery life by turning off unnecessary features, including wireless connectivity. If you do not need access to a local network, turning off wireless capabilities will lengthen the amount of battery power you have. When wireless connectivity is turned off, Windows 7 does not continually scan for networks, and this saves computing power.

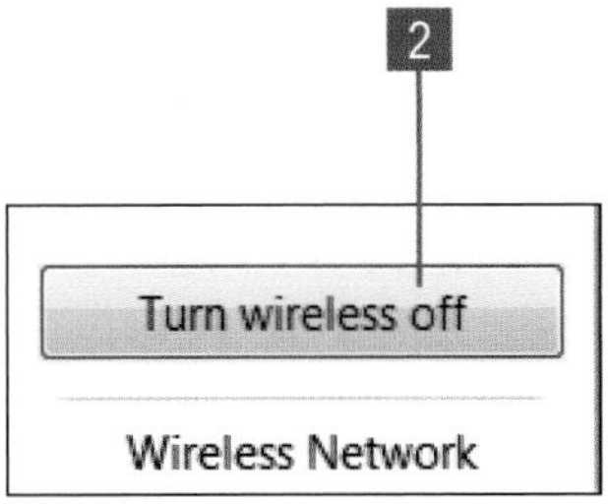

2
Turn wireless off
Wireless Network

Turning on and off wireless connectivity

1 Open Windows Mobility Center.

2 Click Turn wireless off to disable your wireless adapter. (You'll click Turn wireless on to turn it on again.)

11

Exploring Presentation Settings

Mobility Center's Presentation Settings lets you disable your usual power management settings temporarily, to make certain that your system stays awake while you give a presentation. You may think you don't need this feature if you don't give presentations, but if you think outside the box it can actually be quite useful.

For instance, you can create a PowerPoint presentation or a Windows Live Photo Gallery slideshow for a party, and run that presentation (on battery power) without having the screen dim, the hard drive going to sleep or a screensaver coming on. PowerPoint presentations are becoming all the rage in retirement parties, bridal showers and children's birthday parties.

There are presentation settings you can configure too, and they include:

- I am currently giving a presentation – check this option to enable Presentation Settings.
- Turn off the screensaver – check this option to disable the screensaver.
- Set the volume to – use the slider to configure the volume.
- Show this background – check this to change the Desktop background temporarily.

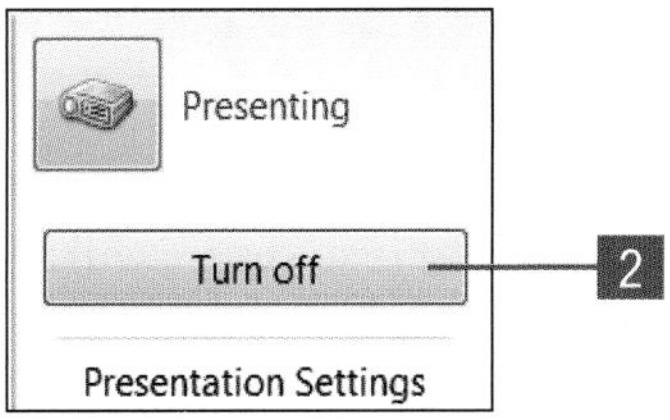

Presenting
Turn off
Presentation Settings
2

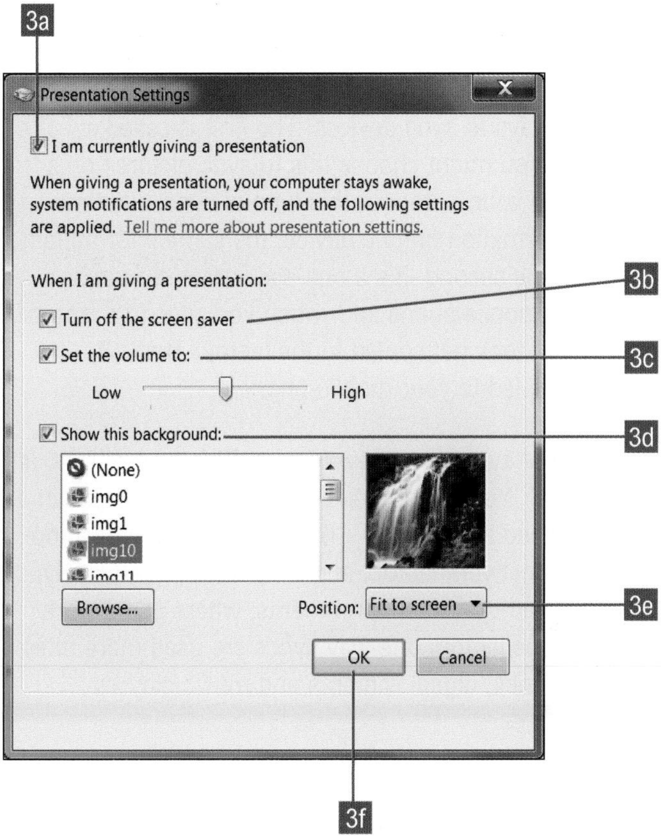

3a
Presentation Settings
I am currently giving a presentation
When giving a presentation, your computer stays awake, system notifications are turned off, and the following settings are applied. Tell me more about presentation settings.
When I am giving a presentation:
Turn off the screen saver
3b
Set the volume to:
3c
Low
High
Show this background:
3d
(None)
img0
img1
img10
Browse...
Position:
Fit to screen
3e
OK
Cancel
3f

Turning on Presentation Settings

1 Open Windows Mobility Center.

2 Click Turn off or Turn on to enable or disable presentation settings.

3 To configure Presentation Settings, click the projector icon in the Presentation Settings window in Windows Mobility Center.
   a In the Presentation Settings window, if desired, click I am currently giving a presentation.
   b Click Turn off the screen saver, to keep the screen saver from coming on during your presentation.
   c Click Set the volume to, to configure volume settings.
   d Click Show this background to select a Desktop background for your presentation.
   e Configure the Desktop background to appear in the centre, as tiles, or to fit it to the screen.
   f Click OK to apply.

4 Click the X in the Windows Mobility Center window to close it.

Sync Center

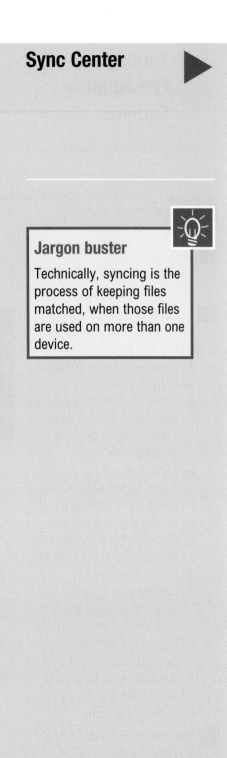

Sync Center can help you keep your files, music, contacts, pictures and other data in sync between your computer and mobile devices, network files and folders, and compatible programs such as Outlook. You only need to use Sync Center if you keep files in more than one location, such as on a mobile PC, music player, thumb drive, PDA or mobile phone, as well as your computer, and you do not have third-party synching software such as iTunes or Blackberry Redirector.

> **Jargon buster**
>
> Technically, syncing is the process of keeping files matched, when those files are used on more than one device.

There are two ways to sync devices. The first is called a one-way sync. You might choose this to sync pictures on a mobile phone to your laptop. In this type of sync, any time you change information on one device, the same information is changed on the second. It's a one-way street. You take pictures with a mobile phone and, when you sync to a laptop, the pictures you took get copied to the laptop. That's it. Nothing gets copied to your mobile phone.

The other type of sync is a two-way sync. This type of sync is a two-way street. You might create a two-way sync between a network folder and a computer. Changes made on the laptop will sync to the network laptop, and vice-versa. Two-way syncs are generally used in work environments, where users work on more than one laptop; one-way syncs are used more often with mobile phones, digital cameras and music players.

Here's a common scenario for a one-way sync. You manage your music collection on your laptop and use a portable music player while away from the computer. You want to configure a sync relationship between the laptop and music layer so that any music you add to or delete from your computer is also added to or deleted from your music player.

Here are some sync rules to remember. If, while syncing data:

- Sync Center discovers two versions of the same file are different, Sync Center selects the most recent version to keep by default.
- Sync Center discovers that a file has changed in both locations since the last sync, Sync Center prompts you

there's a sync conflict and lets you choose which version to keep. You can keep both if you aren't sure.

- Sync Center finds files are identical in both locations, Sync Center doesn't do anything.
- Sync Center finds you added a new file in one location but not the other, Sync Center copies the file to the other location.
- Sync Center finds you have deleted a file from one location but not the other, Sync Center will delete the file from the other location.

Sync Center (cont.)

> **Important**
>
> Sync Center is included with Windows 7 but is often not the best syncing solution. If your music player or mobile phone came with syncing software, use it.

11

Getting Started with Sync Center

1. Open Windows Mobility Center.
2. Click Sync settings.
3. Click Set up new sync partnerships to set up synching between your laptop and your device.
4. Connect the device and the computer using a USB cable.
5. If the device is recognised, follow the directions in Sync Center to sync the device.

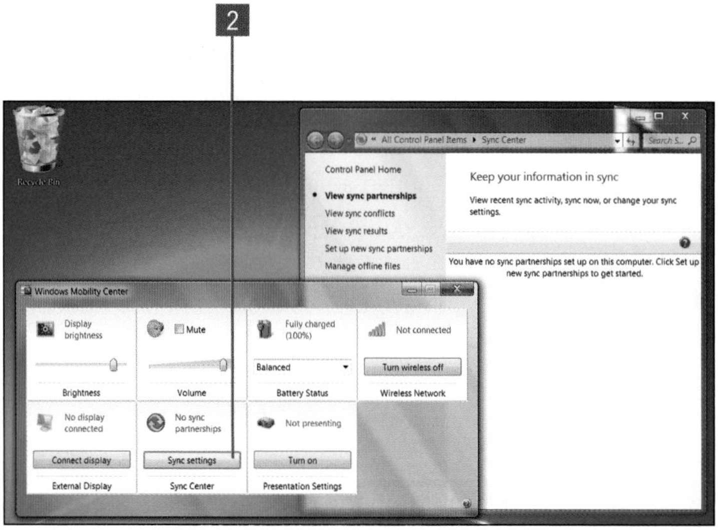

2
All Control Panel Items ▸ Sync Center
Control Panel Home
View sync partnerships
View sync conflicts
View sync results
Set up new sync partnerships
Manage offline files
Keep your information in sync
View recent sync activity, sync now, or change your sync settings.
You have no sync partnerships set up on this computer. Click Set up new sync partnerships to get started.
Windows Mobility Center
Display brightness
Mute
Fully charged (100%)
Not connected
Balanced
Turn wireless off
Brightness
Volume
Battery Status
Wireless Network
No display connected
No sync partnerships
Not presenting
Connect display
Sync settings
Turn on
External Display
Sync Center
Presentation Settings

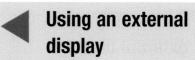

Using an external display

If you use your laptop as a media centre in a motorhome for watching TV and DVDs, if the laptop has a very small screen, or if you just want more screen 'real estate', you can connect an external display. Most laptops offer an external display port. To connect the display, simply connect the display to the proper port on the back of the laptop, plug it in and turn it on. Then, in Windows Mobility Center, you can click Connect Display and configure settings for it.

Connecting an external display

For your information

The display may automatically be enabled and Steps 4 and 5 may not be necessary.

1. Connect the external display to the back of the laptop.
2. Plug in the external display.
3. Turn on the external display.
4. Open Windows Mobility Center.
5. Click Connect display.
6. When prompted how to use the display select one of the following options:
   - a Computer only – this leaves the display connected but does not use it.
   - b Duplicate – this option simply duplicates what you see on your laptop's display on the external display.
   - c Extend – this option will show what's on your laptop's single display across it and the external monitor.
   - d Projector only – this will disable your laptop's monitor and show the display.

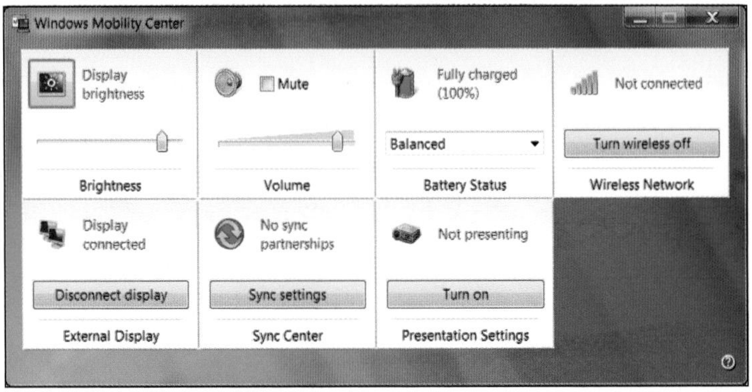
Windows Mobility Center
Display brightness
Brightness
Mute
Volume
Fully charged (100%)
Balanced
Battery Status
Not connected
Turn wireless off
Wireless Network
Display connected
Disconnect display
External Display
No sync partnerships
Sync settings
Sync Center
Not presenting
Turn on
Presentation Settings

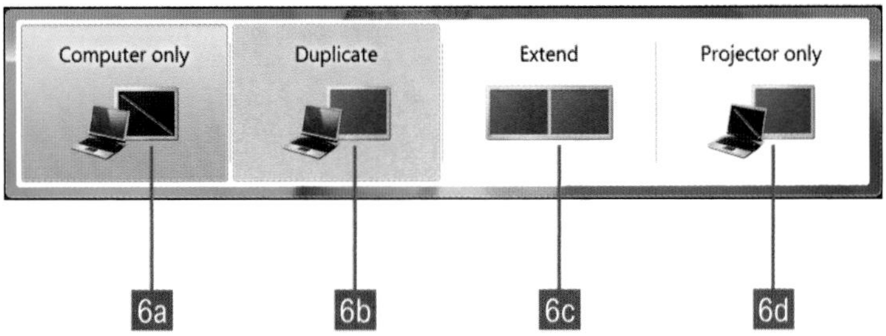
Computer only
Duplicate
Extend
Projector only
6a
6b
6c
6d

Appendix A: Avoiding laptop disasters

Because of the nature of a laptop and how you may use it, it's easy to cause damage to it. While you would have to be extremely negligent to drop a desktop PC into a swimming pool, it's much more likely you'd drop a laptop there, provided you tripped at the proper moment and were standing, well, by a swimming pool. Because of the obvious and not so obvious ways you can cause a laptop disaster, we'll devote an Appendix to avoiding them.

Common sense precautions

After reading the first paragraph, we hope you won't be close enough to a swimming pool to lose your laptop in it any time soon. It is certainly possible for a cruise ship to rock just enough to send the computer sliding off your lap while you're checking email, or to drop it in the water after tripping over a float while walking to your beach chair. That said, there are lots of other common sense practices to be aware of while working on your laptop (or simply walking around with it):

- Always place your laptop on a stable surface. You do not want it falling off. This is especially true when the laptop is in a motorhome or cruise ship.
- Try to keep the laptop away from vibrating surfaces. This could loosen internal parts.
- When you do find a place for your laptop, keep drinks and food away from it. If anything spills on your keyboard, the entire laptop could be ruined. (If you do spill something on your laptop, turn it upside down, with the lid open, and very, very gently position it so the liquid can drain out for a few hours.
- Always allow enough room around the laptop so it can 'breathe'. There are ventilation vents and holes that need space around them. If you feel the computer getting excessively hot, make sure its vents are getting adequate air and put the computer in Sleep mode for an hour.
- Keep cables and power cords away from anywhere people could walk on them or snag them. This could cause the laptop to fall or cause injury to others.
- When in a car, keep the laptop in its case and preferably in the trunk of the car. This will keep the laptop from hitting you in the case of an accident.

Health precautions

There are some precautions you need to take to protect your health too. This includes not using a plugged in laptop near any kind of water. You could get electrocuted! Here are some others:

- Men, using a laptop on your lap for long periods may decrease sperm count. It's the heat your sperm doesn't like. Consider a laptop desk.
- A laptop uses wireless signals to access the Internet and look for open networks (even when you aren't connected to one). Wireless signals are also used in hearing aids, pacemakers and other medical devices. Keep your pacemaker at least 6 inches away from the laptop.
- Don't over load a power strip. Doing so could cause a fire. Be especially careful in motorhomes, hotel rooms and older homes, as the electrical system may not be up to necessary standards.
- Don't compute and drive at the same time. You could cause or get involved in an accident (not to mention getting car sick).
- If you start feeling any eyestrain or headaches, take a break from the computer. In fact, it's best to look away from the computer every 15 minutes or so and focus on something far away to relax your eyes.
- If you start feeling pain in your fingers or hands, you may be using the computer too much, especially if this is a new feeling and not due to an existing condition.

Laptops and physical precautions

Yes, you know you shouldn't force cables into holes they don't belong in, and you should not expose the computer to water, rain or excess humidity. But did you know that you should also keep your laptop away from magnetic fields and direct sunlight? Both could damage it. It's true, and there's more:

- Don't leave your laptop in a place where the temperatures will get extremely hot or cold. This could damage the internal parts.
- If you're on holiday in the desert, shield the laptop from flying dust or dirt particles.
- Close the lid when moving from room to room. Turn the laptop off if you will be moving the laptop by car or bus.
- When possible, keep the laptop with you or inside a home, air-conditioned motorhome or hotel room. This will minimise temperature changes.
- Avoid using the laptop on a bed, couch or blanket as material may bunch up and clog ventilation holes.
- When the laptop's lid is closed, avoid placing objects on it.

Appendix B: Holidaying with a laptop

The main reason you have a laptop may very well be the fact that it's a mobile device. You want to take it with you when you travel for both work and pleasure. You may wish to share photos of your travels with others via email, have a tool for keeping a journal or notes, and the option of doing work on the run. You may want to take a slideshow of your own pictures to your children's homes, or have the option of talking on a webcam with the family while you're away. You may even have an always-on satellite Internet connection where you can access maps, hotel websites and locate camp-site information. Being mobile brings its own set of problems, though, including getting through airport security, having to leave the laptop in a motorhome or hotel room, and going through customs, just to name a few. In this appendix you'll learn how to avoid common problems, keep your laptop secure and use it safely.

What you'll do

Clean up your laptop before leaving on a trip

Move sensitive data off the laptop (USB key or external drive)

Prepare for airline travel

Change the time, language or region

Backup your laptop before you leave

If your laptop is your only computer, you probably have everything of any importance on it. Some of this data may be precious to you, such as family photos, and some may be sensitive like tax information or personal or company documents. When travelling with a laptop, then, you have to ask yourself two things:

- Am I prepared to replace this data if my laptop is stolen, lost or broken? Do I have a valid, tested and working backup?
- What will happen if the personal data I have stored on my laptop gets into someone else's hands? Will the thief be able to steal my identity, access my personal bank accounts or otherwise use my personal information to his or her advantage?

If you keep these two things fresh in your mind while preparing for a trip, I can almost guarantee you'll perform a backup of your data and remove sensitive (and unnecessary) data from your laptop. (It's highly unlikely you'll need last year's tax information while on holiday, for instance, so you should remove it from your laptop, just in case it's stolen.)

Now, with the idea that you need to prepare your laptop in case it is lost or stolen (or broken), here are the tasks you need to complete:

- Make a backup copy of all your important files. Keep the backup at home in a safe place. Here are just a few of the folders you should backup and remove personal information from:
  - Desktop – this folder contains links to items for data you created on your desktop.
  - Documents – this folder contains documents you've saved, subfolders you created and other data.

- Pictures – this folder contains sample pictures and pictures you saved to the laptop.
- Videos – this folder contains sample videos and videos you save to the laptop.

■ After the backup is complete, remove sensitive information from your laptop. Remove everything that won't be needed on your trip. This may include but is not limited to tax spreadsheets, confidential company files, confidential personal files, medical information, letters to lawyers, documents that list passwords or sign-in information for websites, and similar data. I will suggest you create a second backup of this information on a USB key, CD or DVD.

■ Remove and store unnecessary external hardware such as webcams, printers, external drives, Ethernet cables or mice.

■ If you must have access to sensitive information while away from home, consider using a secure online data storage service, such as Google Docs & Spreadsheets, or Windows Office Live Workspace.

Backup your laptop before you leave (cont.)

Clean up your laptop before leaving on a trip

Open
Empty Recycle Bin
Create shortcut
Rename
Properties

1. Delete data that is not longer needed. One way to do this is to drag it to the Recycle Bin, but you can also right-click and choose Delete.
2. Create a backup of important data.
3. Detach any hardware not needed on your trip.

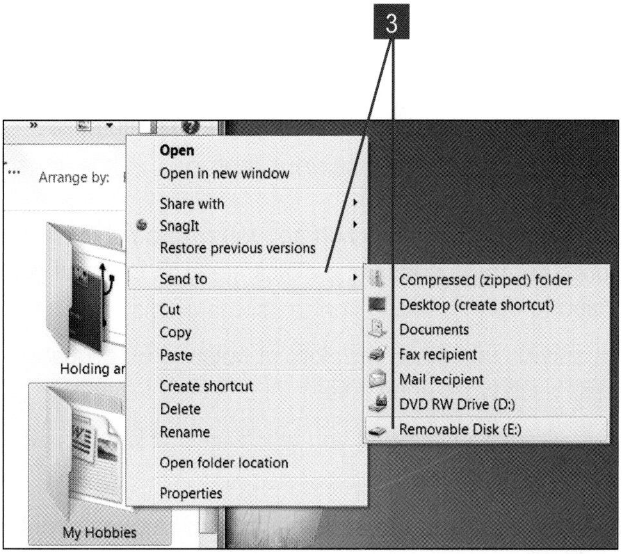
3
Arrange by:
Open
Open in new window
Share with
SnagIt
Restore previous versions
Send to
Cut
Copy
Paste
Create shortcut
Delete
Rename
Open folder location
Properties
Compressed (zipped) folder
Desktop (create shortcut)
Documents
Fax recipient
Mail recipient
DVD RW Drive (D:)
Removable Disk (E:)
My Hobbies

Did you know?

If you are travelling on an aeroplane and need access to a power outlet on the plane, contact the airline and see if you can get a seat close enough to a power outlet to use it.

Move sensitive data off the laptop (USB key or external drive)

1. If you have a USB key, insert it into one of the laptop's USB ports. If you do not, connect the laptop to an external or network drive.
2. Right-click any data you want to move. To select contiguous files, hold down the Shift key while selecting. To select non-contiguous files, hold down the Ctrl key while selecting.
3. Click Send to and locate the Removable Disk. Click on it.
4. Verify the data is on the disk in Computer. Delete the file from the laptop.

Be sure you need your laptop

Have you ever packed a laptop for a trip, lugged it to the airport, got it through security and then never turned it on? It happens all the time. So before you start packing, ask yourself if you will really have time to use your laptop. Here are some questions you can ask yourself, and the answers you provide will help you to decide if you'll have time or need to use your laptop:

- Are you staying with relatives? If so, you may be able to use their computer to go online and check email, if that's all you really need to do.
- Are you staying in a place with lots of noise? You probably won't get much work done if so.
- Is your itinerary so filled that you won't have time to use the laptop?
- If you will have a computer available to you, can you simply take the files you need on a USB key or CD?
- Do you need Internet access to work? If so, do you have Internet service or are there free Internet cafés available?
- Are you going to be too busy camping, swimming, hiking and biking to use your laptop? You can always upload and email the pictures you take once you get home.
- How far are you going to have to carry your laptop bag? Do you have a long walk from where you'll park to the airport terminal, or from the terminal to your hotel? Are you going to be happy carrying it around if so?
- Can you use your mobile phone or a small handheld mobile device such as a PDA instead of a laptop?
- Will you have enough time to get through security with your laptop? Do you know of any problems taking a laptop through customs in your part of the world?
- Do you have the necessary power adapters if going overseas? If not, can you afford to purchase the required adapters?

Packing your laptop

If you've decided you need to bring your laptop on your trip with you and that you'll have time to use it, you'll want to make sure you pack all of the required accessories, and that you pack correctly. No matter how you're travelling, be it by boat, car, aeroplane or motorcycle, you really do need a single, heavily padded carrying bag (or case) that will hold everything you need for your laptop. It's time-consuming, disorganised and unsafe to carry a laptop in one bag, such as a carry-on, while packing everything else in another. Your laptop won't do you much good if the airline loses your checked luggage, which also contains your power cable. Make sure that the bag that contains your laptop also contains required hardware, such as power cables, an extra battery, Ethernet cable and/or wireless network card.

Make sure the bag you choose has padding, but it should also have compartments to keep hardware from hitting each other. When I travel, I prefer to use an expandable backpack that has wheels and an extendable handle for pulling. Expandable backpacks have lots of compartments, almost always fit in an aeroplane's overhead bin, are often padded, and can be stowed easily under a couch in a motorhome or under a bed in a hotel. A backpack on wheels also helps disguise what you're carrying. It doesn't look like a laptop carrying case; it looks like a backpack. This discourages theft.

Here are some things you should carry in your laptop bag:

- power cable
- wireless network card
- Ethernet cable (in case Wi-Fi is not available)
- a USB key for backup
- an extra battery (for long excursions without power)
- power adapters

Timesaver tip

Getting through airport security with a laptop requires you to take it out of the bag, so you'll want to make removing the laptop a quick and easy process. I keep my laptop in a compartment all to itself, so there is no problem removing it.

Packing your laptop (cont.)

- a plastic garbage bag or something similar to wrap your laptop bag in if you have to walk in the rain with it
- a laptop lock if your laptop offers support for one. Check out www.kensington.com for more information.

And here are a few things you can actually pack in your checked luggage, or in a separate bag for a car or boat trip:

- The operating system disk: you may need to recover the laptop if there is a software failure.
- Warranty information: you really only need this if you're going on a long trip.
- Wireless network detector: while Windows 7 will pick up on all wireless local networks, with a wireless network detector, a device you can connect to your keyring, you can check for wireless signals without taking out or turning on your laptop.
- If you prefer, a real mouse, external keyboard, headset, webcam and/or a surge protector.

Finally, here are a few things you probably don't need to bring:

- external speakers
- travel printers: many hotels offer free print services, you can probably find an Internet café that offers one, and you can save anything you want to print to a USB drive and print it when a computer with a printer becomes available.

Taking your laptop on an aeroplane

Since 9/11, airports across the globe have tightened security. You have to take off your shoes, belts and jewellery, and place your mobile phone and laptop (and other electronic devices) in a special bin to be x-rayed. That's what you'd expect, and likely what you've experienced. However, airports in other countries may require security steps you have not yet been exposed to. For instance, you may be asked to turn on your laptop to prove it is a working device. (The same can be true of cameras.) For that reason, you'll want to make sure you have enough power to boot your laptop without having to drag out a power cable and find a plug.

As you would expect, there are plenty of ways to prepare for a trip to the airport with a laptop. Here are a few things to remember:

- Always put your laptop and peripherals in a bag you will carry on the aeroplane with you. Never check in a laptop.
- Keep your laptop bag with you at all times. If possible, keep the bag underneath the seat in front of you once you're on the plane; that way, you are in complete control of it.
- It's OK to send your laptop under an x-ray machine; it won't hurt it. What you must do is make sure you're through security before your laptop is through the x-ray machine. People have been known to steal a laptop from a security line, or that's the rumour anyway!
- Make sure you have some kind of proof the laptop belongs to you. You may want to carry a copy of the original sales receipt, have your full name as an option for a user account when logging in, and place stickers on the outside of the laptop with your name and address.

Taking your laptop on an aeroplane (cont.)

- Regarding the receipt, if you have to go through customs, bring it. You will want to be able to prove, if asked, that the laptop was purchased in your country, not the country you just visited. You don't want to be forced to pay duties or taxes on it. If you are in the US and will be travelling abroad, complete a Certificate of Registration (CBP 4457). This document is valid for as long as you own the mobile items listed on it. You show it to Customs when returning to the US. (You need to find out about similar certificates in your country.)
- If at any time during your stay at the airport or on the aeroplane someone seems a little too curious about your laptop, keep in mind they could be looking for a laptop to steal.
- If possible, once through airport security, lock your laptop bag.

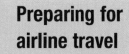

Preparing for airline travel

1. Purchase a heavily padded carrying case, preferably one with wheels that you can pull behind you. Make sure all required peripherals will fit in it (power cables, network cards and Ethernet cables).
2. Pack the case carefully, placing the laptop in a compartment by itself for easy removal. Make sure that other components are secure and cannot touch other peripherals and damage them.
3. If you have to work on an aeroplane but can't get access to a power outlet, carry an extra battery on the plane with you.
4. Remove disks from disk drives.
5. If you are unsure what type of power adapter to bring, call the hotel, airline or campground. Purchase the proper adapter and pack it before leaving.
6. Call your hotel, camp-site, hostel or motorhome park to find out how you can connect to the Internet while there. You may need to bring a phone cord for dial-up, an Ethernet cable for wired connections or a wireless network card for satellite service.
7. Call your insurance company and ask if your laptop will be covered on your trip. If not, consider travel insurance. You can contact a travel agent for advice.
8. Charge your laptop battery completely before leaving for the airport.
9. Avoid having your laptop stolen by monitoring it closely. Be especially aware of where the laptop is as it travels through the x-ray machine. If you're worried, in many airports you can ask for manual inspection.
10. If possible, keep your laptop at your feet during the flight.

Changing the time, language or region

Once you've arrived at your destination, have got off the plane and into the airport (or to your hotel), you should change the Clock, Language and Region settings on your laptop. There are several options including changing the date and time, changing the time zone, showing additional clocks, adding a Clock gadget, and even changing the country or region so that information you obtain online matches your current location. You can also change how numbers, currency, time and date are displayed on your laptop, if you desire.

1. Click Start.
2. Click Control Panel.
3. Click Clock, Language, and Region.
4. To change the time zone, click Change time zone.
5. Select the time zone from the drop-down list.
6. Click OK.

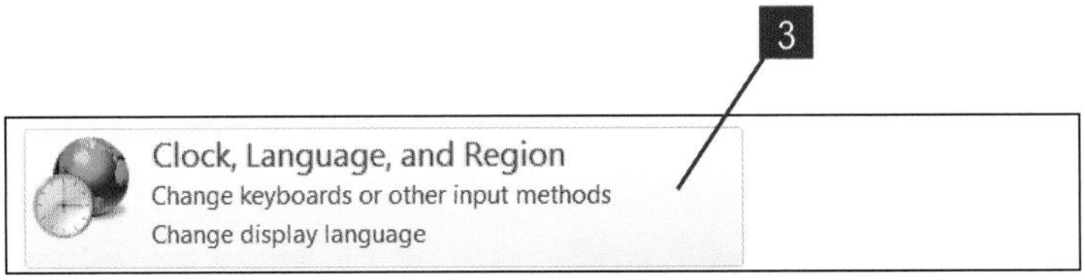

3
Clock, Language, and Region
Change keyboards or other input methods
Change display language

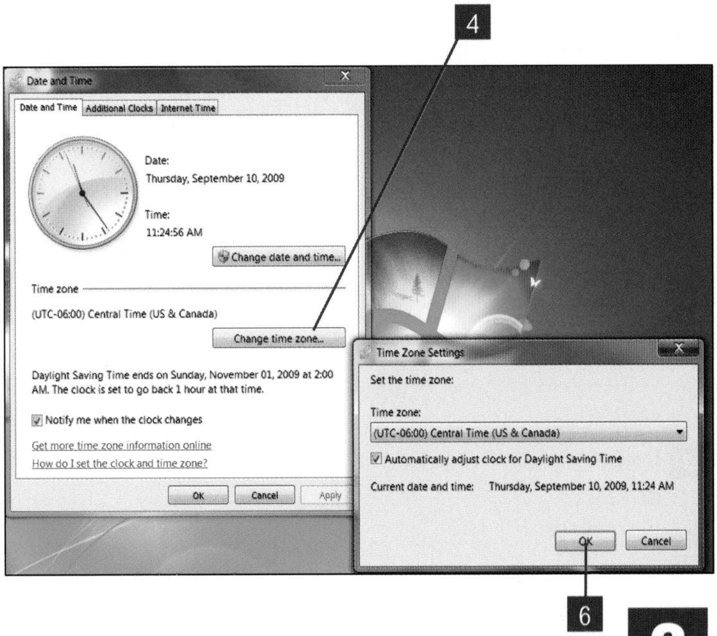

4
Date and Time
Date and Time
Additional Clocks
Internet Time
Date:
Thursday, September 10, 2009
Time:
11:24:56 AM
Change date and time...
Time zone
(UTC-06:00) Central Time (US & Canada)
Change time zone...
Daylight Saving Time ends on Sunday, November 01, 2009 at 2:00 AM. The clock is set to go back 1 hour at that time.
Notify me when the clock changes
Get more time zone information online
How do I set the clock and time zone?
OK
Cancel
Apply
Time Zone Settings
Set the time zone:
Time zone:
(UTC-06:00) Central Time (US & Canada)
Automatically adjust clock for Daylight Saving Time
Current date and time: Thursday, September 10, 2009, 11:24 AM
OK
Cancel
6

Did you know?

You can also change the date and time, among other things.

Getting online access

Travelling with a laptop is not always easy, but the benefit of having Internet access often makes up for the trouble of lugging it around. Having Internet access means you can email friends and family, send photos, keep an online blog of your travels, get local information, and even manage bank accounts and pay bills. Beyond that, you can backup the data you create while travelling to online servers, or even email it to yourself so you'll have it when you get home.

You may be surprised to know that getting online isn't the same in all countries around the world, though. A modem from one region may not recognise the dial tone from other regions. Even if it does, you may be charged long-distance fees for connecting. So, if you use a dial-up connection, make sure to call your ISP before you leave, tell them where you're going, and ask if you'll have Internet access while there and, if so, how you'll log on and what it will cost. Additionally, you won't always have access to an Ethernet jack that offers Internet access and, if you do find one, you'll probably have to have a user name and password. In most places, though, you can obtain Internet access via satellite. Therefore, before taking off on a long journey with your laptop, consider spending the money for a satellite card and subscription.

Staying safe on the Internet

Because you'll likely be in a foreign place during your travels (pardon the pun), you need to take as many precautions as possible when online, especially if you're in a public place such as an Internet café. There is no way for you to know if the connection you have to the Internet is safe, or if others can access your laptop while you're online.

First, when connecting to a public network, make sure you select Public when prompted by Windows 7. When you connect to a network you know, like a network in

Getting online access (cont.)

your home, you select Home (or Work). However, when you're in a public place, when prompted, always select Public Location.

Second, make sure your laptop's security applications and software updates are current, and that includes anti-virus software, your firewall and anti-spyware.

Beyond these two very important precautions are several more. When connecting to the Internet in a foreign place:

- Limit the amount of confidential information you send over the Internet. If possible, do not make credit purchases, travel reservations or input your National Insurance number.
- Set up a remote web mail account to enable email access from any browser, such as Gmail, Yahoo! Mail or MSN Hotmail. Web mail servers have built-in security that you can benefit from while travelling.
- Always sign out of any secure websites you enter, so that the next person can't use your information to make purchases or withdraw funds.
- If possible, delete your browsing history. In Internet Explorer, you'll find this option under Tools.

Travelling without a laptop and getting online

In Europe, Canada and the US, most places that offer Internet access, whether free or for lease, offer drinks, snacks, coffee or even alcoholic beverages, and their main business is to sell these items to you while you are online. There are other places too, including launderettes, print shops and convenience stores. In larger cities, you can use your own laptop to get online but, more and more often, you can use a laptop made available by the establishment. In smaller cities and in less developed countries, you will be more likely to find a computer to use, and won't need to bring your own.

If you do plan to travel (with or) without a laptop you can probably find a list of Internet cafés in a local travel or guidebook, but you can also locate Internet cafés online before you leave. As you research, you may find that some Internet cafés are equipped with microphones and headsets, cater to a specific age group, allow or do not allow the ability to burn CDs, access USB ports, or upload or download data. Most of the time, you'll simply have Internet access, and nothing else. Beyond Internet cafés, there are options that are almost always free. These include public libraries and hotel lobbies.

Carrying online data

There are several important things to bring with you on your trip if you plan to communicate over the Internet. You'll need your contacts' email addresses for one. This information will be on your laptop, but if you're not bringing a laptop make sure to print out your contact list. You'll probably also want a list of your Favorites, the websites you visit often. You'll have to do this by hand, most likely. And while you may also need your user names and passwords, it's ultimately best to commit those to memory (versus writing them down on paper or saving them to your laptop).

Here are some additional options for enabling access to sensitive data such as user names and passwords:

- Store them in an encrypted folder on your laptop.
- Email them to yourself and access the email when you need to retrieve the data.
- Save the information to a USB drive you keep on a keychain that's with you at all times. You may also like to change the information slightly just in case the USB drive gets stolen. For example, if your password is Wx6658#, save the password as Wx6658#np.

Getting online access (cont.)

Important

The most secure places to get online using a rented computer are those where the computer is reset to its default settings each time a person quits a session. Before committing, ask the proprietor if this is the case.

Physically secure your laptop

While away you'll want to make sure your laptop is secure. The easiest way to do that is to keep the laptop in your sight. If it must be left in a hotel room or car, hide it. Better yet, in a hotel room use a laptop lock, and in a car use the boot.

It's also important to know that while it's common for people in the US, Canada and Europe to carry a laptop in plain sight or work on the laptop in public coffee shops and cafés, in less developed countries this can be seen as a sign of wealth. This may make your laptop a target for thieves or, worse yet, you. As you'll have learned in Appendix A, carrying the laptop in a bag such as a generic backpack makes you (and it) far less attractive to the bad guys.

Hard drives can also be damaged if you drop them, or if they are exposed to lots of heavy vibration. So, if you're on a safari in a bumpy jeep, leave the laptop at camp. Laptops are also affected by heat and humidity, and the best way to keep a laptop safe is to avoid these types of weather phenomenon.

Finally, because the power grid is unreliable in many developing countries, always use a surge protector. You may also need to purchase an adapter to use the electrical plug available at your destination.

Appendix C: Cleaning and protecting your laptop

There are a few things you have to do to keep your laptop in tip-top shape for the long term. One is to clean the laptop physically, but it's important to note you can't just scrub it down with soap and water! You have to know what to do and how to do it, so that you don't harm any of the laptop components. It's also important to take precautions such as using a surge protector, and configuring the laptop's keyboard power button to apply the available hibernation and sleep options when you press it.

What you'll do

Clean the outside of the laptop

Clean the keyboard and monitor

Clean the inside of the laptop

Maintain your laptop

Maintaining your laptop, physically at least, doesn't take that much effort. You need to keep it physically clean, make sure it's protected from power surges or lightning strikes, and try to avoid continually turning it on and off (and turning it off properly when you must). Let's start by cleaning the laptop.

Clean your laptop

On the surface, your laptop may look just fine. You may see a few finger prints, maybe a couple of sticky spots or the remnants of a sticker from the laptop's manufacturer, and think all is well. That may not be the case. If you look at the ports on the laptop, including USB and FireWire ports, additional monitor port, the printer port, speaker connections and other areas, you just might find various dust bunnies, cat hairs or even nicotine build-up. If you look closely at the monitor and keyboard, you're likely to find a good amount of dirt there too. Fingerprints, food particles, pet hair and more can all accumulate over time. To keep your monitor and keyboard performing optimally, you'll want to remove the grime. Since it's important to keep these areas dirt free, you should perform steps to clean these areas two to three times a year, or as needed.

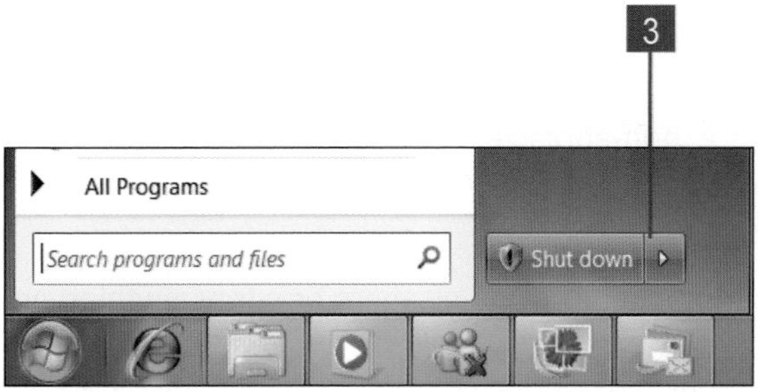
3
All Programs
Search programs and files
Shut down

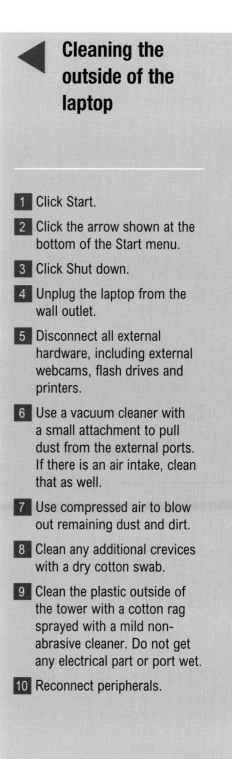

Cleaning the outside of the laptop

1. Click Start.
2. Click the arrow shown at the bottom of the Start menu.
3. Click Shut down.
4. Unplug the laptop from the wall outlet.
5. Disconnect all external hardware, including external webcams, flash drives and printers.
6. Use a vacuum cleaner with a small attachment to pull dust from the external ports. If there is an air intake, clean that as well.
7. Use compressed air to blow out remaining dust and dirt.
8. Clean any additional crevices with a dry cotton swab.
9. Clean the plastic outside of the tower with a cotton rag sprayed with a mild non-abrasive cleaner. Do not get any electrical part or port wet.
10. Reconnect peripherals.

Cleaning the keyboard and monitor

1. Click Start.
2. Click the arrow shown at the bottom of the Start menu.
3. Click Shut down.
4. Unplug the laptop from the wall outlet.
5. Disconnect all external hardware, including external webcams, flash drives and printers.
6. To clean the keyboard, hold the entire laptop upside down with the lid open and shake gently.
7. After shaking gently, and still holding it upside down, use compressed air to remove additional dust and grime. (You may need someone to help you with this.)
8. Turn the laptop right side up, and use a toothpick to loosen dirt that is stuck between the keys.
9. Wipe the monitor clean using the instructions stated in this chapter. Remember, never spray anything directly onto the screen.

When you clean the inside of a laptop you have to deal with two things: the monitor and keyboard. When cleaning the laptop's screen, make sure first to read any instructions that came with your laptop. There may be specific instructions you need to follow. If you don't have any instructions, try looking up the information on the Internet. This is important because monitors can be flimsy and you don't want to damage it.

That said, when cleaning your laptop's monitor:

- Use a soft, dry, non-abrasive cloth. Don't use a paper towel. If you can find one and can afford it, purchase a LCD cleaning cloth kit.
- Never use ammonia or strong cleaners or spray anything on the screen.
- For tough spots, add a touch of vinegar to the cleaning cloth.
- Clean from top to bottom.

The inside of a laptop can also acquire dust, dirt, cat hair and smoke build-up. This build-up can cause your laptop to run 'hot', and running hot can cause problems. Problems related to heat may cause the computer to shut down unexpectedly or, worse, cause permanent damage to the laptop's internal parts. Thus, the inside needs to be cleaned on occasion as well.

I clean the inside of my laptop once a year. However, this involves opening the laptop's case, which voids the warranty. That said, you have three choices regarding this task. You can:

a Never clean the inside of the laptop, but keep the air vents and other openings free of dust with canned air.

b Take the laptop to a qualified technician every 18 months or so.

c Take your chances and clean the inside of the laptop yourself.

If you choose c, the box 'Cleaning the inside of the laptop' shows you how to perform the internal cleaning of a laptop.

Cleaning the inside of the laptop

1. Unplug the computer from the wall and disconnect any connected hardware.
2. Find out how to open your laptop case and obtain the required tools. Most open with a flat head screwdriver these days.
3. Open the battery compartment and remove the computer's battery. There will be instructions on how to do this either in the battery compartment itself or in the computer's documentation.
4. Open the laptop case.
5. Ground yourself and expel any stored static electricity by touching a metal desk (or something similar) before touching anything inside the laptop.
6. Remove dust using a dry cotton swab, a small vacuum attachment or canned air. Be extremely careful not to loosen any parts.
7. Do not detach the monitor, keyboard or force any part of the laptop to open. If you can't reach it easily, dust probably can't either.
8. Replace the battery and cover.

Using surge protection

Lightning strikes, electrical power surges and power outages can wreak havoc on your laptop's power supply and internal parts. One good lightning strike can destroy a laptop, as can a blast from your motorhome's generator or your city's over-taxed electrical grid. To be safe, when your laptop is plugged in, it should be connected to a surge protector, which often comes in the form of a power strip.

Make sure when you purchase your surge protector that you don't end up with a simple power strip. Power strips don't offer protection – they only offer additional electrical outlets. While you may need additional outlets in a hotel room or motorhome, a surge protector offers additional outlets and protection from power surges for any or all of the following:

- electrical cord to the laptop
- cable, DSL or other modems
- coaxial cable inputs.

!

Important

Even the most expensive surge protectors may not protect your laptop if lightning hits your home or motorhome. Since that is the case, it's best simply to unplug your laptop when a lightning storm approaches.

Jargon buster

Activation – The process you must complete to verify you have a valid copy of Windows 7 including a proper product ID. You usually activate Windows 7 online, the first time you turn on the PC. This is mandatory.

Adware – Internet advertisements (which are also applications), which often include additional code that can be used to track a user's personal information and pass it on to third parties, without the user's authorisation or knowledge.

Aero – Windows Aero builds on the basic Windows 7 interface and offers a high-performing desktop experience that includes (among other things) the translucent effect of Aero Glass.

Aero Glass – Added visual reflections and soft animations that are applied when Aero is selected as the display setting.

Applications – Software installed on your laptop other than the operating system. Some applications come preinstalled, such as Internet Explorer. Third-party applications are software you purchase separately and install yourself, such as Microsoft Office or Photoshop.

AV-in – Accepts input from various audio/video devices.

Backup and Restore Center – This feature lets you perform back-ups and, in the case of a laptop failure, restore them (put them back). However, there are other back-up options too, including copying files to a CD or DVD, copying pictures and media to an external hard drive, USB drive or memory card, or storing them on an Internet server.

Bandwidth – Generally this is used to represent how much data you send and receive on a paid connection, such as a smart phone or Internet connection.

Battery bay – This holds the laptop's battery. Sometimes you have to use a screwdriver to get inside the battery bay, at other times you simply need to slide out the compartment door.

Better release latch – This latch holds the battery in place, even after the battery bay's door has been opened. You'll need to release this latch to get to the battery.

Battery lock – This locks the battery in position.

Bluetooth – A technology used to create 'personal' networks for the purpose of connecting devices that are in close range (such as a mobile phone and an earpiece). A laptop may come with built-in Bluetooth capabilities (although this is not common), or you can add it by purchasing and installing a USB

Bluetooth dongle – A small device, about the size of a USB flash drive, that connects directly to a USB port on the outside of the laptop.

Boot up – When a laptop is powered on, it goes through a sequence of tasks before you see the Desktop. This process is called the boot-up process. Laptops can be rated by many factors, and one of those factors is how long the boot-up process takes.

Browse – Browsing for a file, folder or program is the process of drilling down into Windows 7's folder structure to locate the desired item.

Burn – A term used to describe the process of copying music from a laptop to a CD or DVD. Generally music is burned to a CD, since CDs can be played in cars and generic CD players, while videos are burned to DVDs since they require much more space and can be played on DVD players.

Contacts folder – This folder contains your contacts' information, which includes email addresses, pictures, phone numbers, home and businesses addresses, and more.

Control Panel – Available in all Windows 7 editions, a place where you can change laptop settings related to system and maintenance, user accounts, security, appearance, networks and the Internet, the time, language, and region, hardware and sounds, visual displays and accessibility options, programs and additional options.

Cookies – These are small text files that include data which identifies your preferences when you visit particular websites. Cookies are what allow you to visit, say, www.amazon.com and be greeted with Hello <your name>, We have recommendations for you! Cookies help a website offer you a personalised web experience.

Copy command – Copies the data to Windows 7's clipboard (a virtual, temporary, holding area). The data will be not deleted from its original location even when you 'paste' it somewhere else. Pasting Copy data will copy the data, not move it.

CPU – Central processing unit. This is the 'computer chip' inside your laptop.

Cut – To remove the selected text, picture or object.

Cut command – Copies the data to Windows 7's clipboard (a virtual, temporary, holding area). The data will be deleted from its original location as soon as you 'paste' it somewhere else. Pasting Cut data moves the data.

Desktop folder – This folder contains links to items for data you created on your Desktop. Computer, Network and Recycle Bin aren't listed, but shortcuts to folders you create and data you store on the Desktop are.

Dialog Box – A place to make changes to default settings in an application. Clicking File and then Print, for instance, opens the Print dialogue box where you can configure the type of paper you're using, select a printer and more.

Digitizer – This is an add-on to a laptop that accepts and converts handwritten text. You write on the digitiser pad.

Disk Cleanup – An application included with Windows 7 that offers a safe and effective way to reduce unnecessary data on your computer. With Disk Cleanup you can remove temporary files, empty the Recycle Bin, remove setup log files, and downloaded program files (among other things), all in a single process.

Disk Defragmenter – An application included with Windows 7 that analyses the data stored on your hard drive and consolidates files that are not stored together. This enhances performance by making data on your hard drive work faster by making data easier to access. Disk Defragmenter runs automatically once a week, in the middle of the night.

Documents Folder – This folder contains documents you've saved, subfolders you created and folders created by Windows 7.

Downloaded program files – Files that are downloaded automatically when you view certain web pages. They are stored temporarily in a folder on your hard disk, and accessed when and if needed.

DPI – Dots per inch refers to how many dots (or pixels) per inch there are on a laptop's monitor.

Driver – A driver is a piece of software (or code) that allows the device to communicate with Windows 7 and vice versa.

DV – Digital video, generally used as a DV camera.

DVD drive – A physical piece of equipment that can play and often record DVDs.

DVI port – Used to connect the laptop to a television set or other DVI device; for laptops, this is generally an upscale display.

Email address – A virtual address you use for sending and receiving email. It often takes this form: yourname@yourispname.com.

Ergonomics – The science of working without causing injury to yourself. Injury can include back strain, eye strain or carpal tunnel syndrome, among others.

Ethernet – A technology that uses Ethernet cables to transmit data and network laptops.

Ethernet cable– A cable that is used to connect laptops to routers and cable modems, among other things.

ExpressCard slot – Used to insert an ExpressCard where you can expand your laptop's capabilities by offering additional ways to connect devices. ExpressCards are often used to offer wireless capabilities.

Extended warranty – A warranty that you purchase along with the manufacturer's warranty. This type of warranty is supposed to cover everything, including drops and spills. Often, though, extended warranties fail to pay in such an event (which is spelled out in the f ine print).

Favorites Folder – This folder contains the items in the Internet Explorer's Favorites list. It may also include folders created by the computer manufacturer or Microsoft, including Links, Microsoft websites and MSN websites.

Filter Keys – A setting you can configure so that Windows ignores keystrokes that occur in rapid succession, such as when you accidentally leave your finger on a key for too long.

FireWire – Also called IEEE 1394, a technology often used to connect digital video cameras, professional audio hardware, and external hard drives to a laptop. FireWire connections are much faster than USB, and are better than anything else when you need to transfer large amounts of data, such as digital video.

Flip and Flip 3-D – A way to move through open windows graphically instead of clicking the item in the Taskbar.

Form data – In Internet Explorer, this is information that's been saved using the Internet Explorer's autocomplete form data functionality. If you don't want forms to be filled out automatically by you or someone else who has access to your laptop and user account, delete this.

Gadget – In our terms, an icon you can place on the Desktop such as the Weather or Clock gadget.

GHz – Short for gigahertz, this term describes how fast a processor can work. One GHz equals one billion cycles per second, so a 2.4 GHz computer chip will execute calculations at 240 billion cycles per second. Again, it's only important to know that the faster the chip, the faster the laptop.

GPU – Short for graphics processing unit, it's a processor used specifically for rendering graphics. Having a processor just for graphics frees up the main CPU, allowing it to work faster on other tasks.

Hard drive – A physical piece of equipment where your data is stored. Hard drives are inside a laptop, but you can purchase additional, external hard drives to back-up data. Digital music, photos and video take up a surprisingly large amount of hard drive space.

History – In Internet Explorer, this is the list of websites you've visited and any web addresses you've typed. Anyone who has access to your laptop and user account can look at your History list to see where you've been.

Hotspot – A Wi-Fi hotspot lets you connect to the Internet without having to be tethered to an Ethernet cable or tied down with a high monthly wireless bill. Most of the time this service is free, provided you have the required wireless hardware.

Icon – A visual representation of a file or folder that you can click to open it.

Instant Messaging – Text and instant messaging require you to type your message and click a Send button. It's similar to email, but it's instantaneous; the recipient gets the message right after you send it. Instant messaging is the term generally reserved for text communications between two or more computers; text messaging is a term generally reserved for communicating between two mobile phones.

Interface – What you see on the screen when working in a window. In Internet Explorer, for instance, you see tabs, icons and web pages.

Internet – A large web of computers that communicate via land lines, satellite and cable for the purpose of sharing information and data. Also called the world wide web.

Internet Server – A computer that stores data off site. Hotmail offers Internet servers to hold email and data, so that you do not have to store them on your laptop. Internet servers allow you to access information from any computer that can access the internet.

ISP – Internet Service Provider. A company that provides internet access, usually for a fee.

Kensington lock slot – a way to connect the laptop to a lock to prevent it from being stolen when you are travelling.

Line-in jack – An input on a laptop that accepts audio from external devices, such as CD players.

Link – A shortcut to a web page. Links are often offered in an email, document or web page to allow you to access a site without having to actually type in its name. In almost all instances, links are underlined and in a different colour from the page they are configured on.

Load – A web page must 'load' before you can access it. Some pages load instantly while others take a few seconds.

Magnifier – A tool in the Ease of Access suite of applications. You use Magnifier to drastically increase the size of the information shown on the screen.

Mail – Often referred to as Windows Live Mail, a program that's part of the Windows Live Essentials suite of applications. This is the only thing you need to send and receive email, manage your contacts, manage sent, saved and incoming email, and read newsgroups.

Mail servers – A computer that your ISP configures to allow you to send and receive email. It often includes a POP3 incoming mail server and an SMTP outgoing mail server. Often the server names look something like pop.yourispnamehere.com and smtp.yourispnamehere.com.

Malware – Stands for malicious software. Malware includes viruses, worms, spyware, etc.

Menu – A title on a menu bar (such as File, Edit, View). Clicking this menu button opens a drop-down list with additional choices (Open, Save, Print).

Menu bar – A bar that runs across the top of an application that offers menus. Often, these menus include File, Edit, View, Insert, Format and Help.

Mouse keys – Instead of using your mouse, you can use the arrow keys on your keyboard or the numeric keypad to move the mouse pointer on the Desktop or inside programs or documents.

Music folder – This folder contains sample music and music you save to the laptop.

Narrator – A basic screen reader included with Windows 7. This application will read text that appears on the screen to you, while you navigate using the keyboard and mouse.

Network – A group of computers, printers and other devices that communicate wirelessly or through wired connections.

Network adapter – A piece of hardware that lets your computer connect to a network, such as the internet or a local network.

Network and Sharing Center – A collection of features where you can easily access network connections, sharing options, networked computers and devices, and diagnose and repair features.

Network Discovery – A state where computers can find other computers on the network. Network Discovery must be on to locate and communicate with network devices.

Network Map – The Network Map details each of your network connections graphically, and allows you to distinguish easily among wired, wireless and Internet connections.

Notification area – The area of the taskbar that includes the clock and volume icons, and also holds icons for applications that are running in the background. You may see icons for your anti-virus software, music players, updates or Windows security alerts.

Operating System – In this case, the operating system is Windows 7. This is what allows you to operate your laptop's system. You will use Windows 7 to find things you have stored on your laptop, connect to the Internet, send and receive email and surf the web, among other things.

Page Setup button – Clicking Page Setup in a Printer dialogue box opens the Page Setup dialogue box. Here you can select a paper size, source, and create headers and footers. You can also change orientation and margins, all of which are dependent on what features your printer supports.

Parental Controls – If you have grandchildren, young children, or even a forgetful or scatterbrained spouse who needs imposed computer limitations, you can apply them using Parental Controls. With these controls you are in charge of the hours users can access the laptop, which games they can play and what programs they can run (among other things).

Paste command – Copies or moves the cut or copied data to the new location. If the data was Cut, it will be moved. If the data was Copied, it will be copied.

Per user archived Windows Error Reporting – Files used for error reporting and solution checking.

Phishing – A technique used by computer hackers to get you to divulge personal information such as bank account numbers. Phishing filters warn you of potential phishing websites and email, and are included in Windows 7. In other words, an attempt by an unscrupulous website or hacker to obtain personal data including but not limited to bank account numbers, social security numbers and email addresses.

Pictures folder – This folder contains sample pictures and pictures you save to the laptop.

Pixel – The smallest unit of data that can be displayed on a computer. Resolution is defined by how many pixels you choose to display

Playlist – A group of songs that you can save and then listen to as a group, burn to a CD, copy to a portable music player and more.

POP3 Server Name – The name of the computer that you will use to get your email from your ISP. Your ISP will give you this information when you subscribe.

Power cable –The cable that you will use to connect the laptop to the wall outlet (power outlet). You can connect and disconnect the power cable at any time, even when the laptop is running.

Power plan – A group of settings that you can configure to tell Windows 7 when or if to put the laptop to sleep.

Processor – Short for microprocessor, it's the silicon chip that contains the central processing unit (CPU) inside a computer. Generally, the terms CPU and processor are used interchangeably. CPUs do almost all of the computer's calculations and are the most important piece of hardware in a computer system.

Print button – Clicking Print opens the Print dialogue box where you can configure the page range, select a printer, change page orientation, change print order and choose a paper type.

Additional options include print quality, output bins and more. Of course, the choices offered depend on what your printer offers. If your printer can only print at 300 x 300 dots per inch (dpi), you can't configure it to print at a higher quality.

Print Preview button – Clicking Print Preview opens a window where you can see before you print what the print out will actually look like. You can switch between portrait and landscape views, access the Page Setup dialogue box and more.

Programs – See Applications.

Public folder – Folders where you can share data. Anyone with an account on the laptop can access the data inside these folders. You can also configure the Public folder to share files with people using other computers on your local network.

RAM – Short for random-access memory, it's the hardware inside your laptop that temporarily stores data that is being used by the operating system or programs. Although there are many types of RAM, all you need to know is that the more RAM you have, the faster your laptop will (theoretically) run and perform.

ReadyBoos – A new technology that lets you add more RAM (random-access memory) to a laptop using a USB flash drive or a secure digital memory card (such as the one in your digital camera) as RAM, if it meets certain requirements. Just plug the device into an open slot on your PC and, if it is compatible, choose to use the device as RAM.

Recycle Bin – The Recycle Bin holds deleted files until you decide to empty it. The Recycle Bin serves as a safeguard, allowing you to recover items accidentally deleted, or items you thought you no longer wanted but later decide you need. Note that once you empty the Recycle Bin, the items in it are gone forever.

Remote Desktop Connection – A Windows 7 program you can use to access your laptop from somewhere else, such as an office or hotel room.

Resolution – The amount of pixels that are shown on a computer screen. Choosing 800 x 600 pixels means that the Desktop is shown to you with 800 pixels across and 600 pixels down. When you increase the resolution, you increase the number of pixels on the screen.

RF-in – A jack that accepts input signal from digital TV tuners.

Rip – A term used to describe the process of copying files from a physical CD to your hard drive, and thus your music library.

Router – A piece of equipment used to send data from your laptop to a computer on a network. A router 'routes' the data to the correct PC and also rejects data that is harmful or from unknown sources.

Screensaver – A screensaver is a picture or animation that covers your screen and appears after your laptop has been idle for a specific amount of time that you set. You can configure your screensaver to require a password on waking up for extra security.

SD card slots or card readers – Slots on the outside of the laptop used to accept digital memory cards found in digital cameras and similar technologies.

Setup Log Files – Files created by Windows during setup processes.

SMTP server name – The name of the computer that you will use to send email using your ISP. Your ISP will give you this information when you subscribe.

Snipping tool – A new feature in Windows 7 that allows you to drag your cursor around any area on the screen to copy and capture it. Once captured, you can save it, edit it, and/or send it to an email recipient.

Sound Recorder – A simple tool included with Windows 7 with only three options: Start Recording, Stop Recording and Resume Recording. You can save recorded clips as notes to yourself or insert them into movies or slide shows.

Spam – Unwanted email. Compare spam with junk faxes or junk postal mail.

Standard toolbar – A toolbar that is often underneath a Menu bar (in an application window) that contains icons, or pictures, of common commands. Common commands include New, Open, Save, Print, Print Preview, Find, Cut, Copy, Paste, Undo and Date/Time.

Sticky Keys – This setting allows you to configure the keyboard so that you never have to press three keys at once (such as when you must press the Ctrl, Alt and Delete keys together to log on to Windows). With Sticky Keys, you can use one key to perform these tasks. You configure the key to use for three-key tasks.

Sticky Notes – A tool that enables you to create short handwritten or voice notes. Just like a real pack of sticky notes, you can jot down ideas, reminders or create lists using the pen or stylus, or create a voice clip by speaking into the microphone.

Surges – Unexpected increases in the voltage of an electrical current. Surges have the potential to damage sensitive electrical equipment. (Sags are the opposite of surges, equally dangerous, and are a drop in electrical current.)

Surge protector – A piece of hardware you use to protect the laptop from power surges.

S-video – A port or technology used to connect the laptop to a television or other display that also offers s-video connectivity.

Sync – The process of comparing data in one location to the data in another, and performing tasks to match it up. If data has been added or deleted from one device, for instance, synching can also add or delete it from the other.

Sync Center – An application included with Windows 7 that helps you to keep your files, music, contacts, pictures and other data in sync between your laptop and mobile devices, network files and folders, and compatible programs such as Outlook. Technically, syncing is the process of keeping files matched, when those files are used on more than one device.

System Restore – If enabled, Windows 7 stores 'restore points' on your laptop's hard drive. If something goes wrong you can run System Restore, choose one of these points, and revert to a pre-problem date. Since System Restore only deals with 'system data', none of your personal data will be affected (not even your last email).

System Restore Point – A snapshot of the laptop that Windows 7 keeps in case something happens and you need to revert to it because of a bad installation, computer malfunction or incorrect hardware driver.

Tablet PC – A PC that contains a stylus you can use to handwrite notes on a touch screen. Some Tablet PC screens swivel too.

Tablet PC Input Panel – Stores the tablet PC tools. Here you can write notes in your own handwriting and then enter the converted text anywhere text is accepted. If you have a tablet PC with a touch screen, you can write directly in the tablet PC Input Panel using the stylus. If you have a laptop, you can write by moving your mouse.

Tags – Data about a particular piece of data, such as a photo or a song or album. Tags can be used to group pictures or music in various ways. Some tags are applied automatically when you import pictures from a digital camera, including the date they were uploaded, along with any name you applied to the imported group. You can create your own tags.

Taskbar – The bar that runs horizontally across the bottom of the Windows 7 interface, and contains the Start button and Notification area. It also offers a place to view and access open files, folders and applications.

Temporary files – Files created and stored by programs for use by the program. Most of these temporary files are deleted when you exit the program, but some do remain.

Temporary Internet files – Files that contain copies of web pages you've visited on your hard drive, so that you can view the pages more quickly when visiting the page again.

Text messaging – Text and instant messaging require you to type your message and click a Send button. It's similar to email but it's instantaneous; the recipient gets the message right after you send it. Instant messaging is the term generally reserved for text communications between two or more laptops; text messaging is a term generally reserved for communicating between two mobile phones.

Thumbnails – Small icons of your pictures, videos and documents. Thumbnails will be recreated as needed should you choose to delete them using Disk Cleanup.

Touch input – Many newer tablet PCs have screens you can touch with your finger, like you can with an iPhone. With this technology you can perform tasks with your finger instead of a stylus, mouse or keyboard.

Touchpad – A pointing device that is usually located in the centre of the keyboard or at the bottom of it. Place your finger on the touchpad or trackball and move it around to move the mouse.

USB – Universal Serial Bus. A port you use to connect USB devices. USB devices include mice, external keyboards, mobile phones, digital cameras and other devices, including USB flash drives.

VGA port – An external monitor port. With this port you can connect your laptop to a secondary monitor or network projector where you can mirror what you see on the laptop's screen or extend the screen to the second monitor. A VGA port is a 15-pin port.

Video messaging – A form of instant messaging where one or both users also offer live video of themselves during the conversation. Use Windows Live Messenger for this.

Videos folder – This folder contains sample videos and videos you save to the laptop.

Video format – The video file type, such as AVI or WMA.

Virus – A self-replicating program that infects laptops with intent to do harm. Viruses often come in the form of an attachment in an email.

Visualizations – Produced by Windows 7 and Windows Media Player, these are graphical representations of the music you play.

Web browser – Windows 7 comes with Internet Explorer, an application you can use to surf the Internet. Internet Explorer lets you 'surf the web', and it has everything you need, including a pop-up blocker, zoom settings and accessibility options, as well as tools you can use to save your favourite web pages, set home pages and sign up to read RSS feeds.

Webcam – A camera that can send live images over the Internet.

Website – A group of web pages that contain related information. Microsoft's website contains information about Microsoft products, for instance.

Window – When you open a program from the Start menu, a document, folder or a picture, it opens in a 'window'. Window, as it's used in this context, is synonymous with an open program, file or folder and has nothing to do with the word Windows, used with Windows 7.

Windows Defender – You don't have to do much to Windows Defender except understand that it offers protection against Internet threats. It's enabled by default and it runs in the background. However, if you ever think your laptop has been attacked by an Internet threat (virus, worm, malware, etc.) you can run a manual scan here.

Windows Firewall – If enabled and configured properly, the firewall will help prevent hackers (people whose job it is to get into your laptop and do harm to it) from accessing your laptop and data. The firewall blocks most programs from communicating outside the network (or outside your laptop). If you want to allow a program to communicate outside your safety zone you can 'allow' a program by adding it to an 'exceptions' list. This is all very easy to do.

Windows Live Essentials – A Live Essentials suite of applications that's free from Microsoft. It contains Windows Live Mail, Live Messenger, Live Photo Gallery and more. It's a must-have.

Windows Media Center – An application that allows you to watch, pause and record live television, locate, download and/or listen to music and radio, view, edit and share photos and videos, and play DVDs (among other things). It's included with most versions of Windows 7.

Windows Mobility Center – An application that lets you adjust your mobile PC, tablet PC or laptop settings quickly, including things such as volume, wireless and brightness.

Windows Update – If enabled and configured properly, when you are online Windows 7 will check for security updates automatically and install them. You don't have to do anything, and your laptop is always updated with the latest security patches and features.

Worm – A self-replicating program that infects laptops with intent to do harm. However, unlike a virus, it does not need to attach itself to a running program.

Troubleshooting guide

Chapter 1

What are the advantages to owning a laptop over a desktop PC?

Where can I find a place to watch media and play games?

How can I get directions from the Internet?

How do I use my laptop ergonomically?

Chapter 2

What should I look for if I'm in the market for a new laptop?

What questions should I ask while shopping for a new laptop?

Do I need a rugged laptop or an extended warranty?

Chapter 3

What do all of these things on the outside of my laptop enable me to do?

What is Bluetooth?

How do I insert or remove the battery?

Chapter 4

How do I turn up or down the sound, use the microphone, or locate the webcam?

How does the touchpad work?

What are the most common keyboard shortcuts?

Chapter 5

Is there something that is included with Windows 7 that can help me get started?

What edition of Windows 7 do I have?

What are all of these icons on my screen (Desktop)?

How do I find and open programs (applications)?

What are the best programs to explore first?

Where are the accessories, such as Calculator?

What's the best way to turn off my computer?

Chapter 6

How can I change the look of my laptop?

Can I change what's on the Desktop?

I want to create a shortcut to a folder I use a lot, how do I do that?

Can I make the icons on the screen appear larger or smaller?

Chapter 7

Can I make Windows 7 read things out loud to me?

I have a visual impairment, what can I do to make the computer easier to use?

What are the best keyboard shortcuts?

Can I talk to my laptop and have it respond?

Chapter 8

Can I add another user account for my grandchild?

How can I protect my PC from harm?

What security features are available to me?

How do I resolve error messages that pop up on the screen?

How can I protect my data and personal information?

Can I set parental controls for my grandchildren?

How can I perform a simple backup of my data?

Chapter 9

What are my options for connecting to the Internet?

How do I set up a connection to the Internet with Windows 7?

Does my laptop have the wireless hardware required to connect to a free hotspot?

How do I connect to a hotspot?

Chapter 10

How do I listen to music?

Can I rip and burn CDs?

Where is my email program, instant messaging program and photo editing program?

How do I download applications from the Internet?

How do I import pictures from my digital camera or media card?

Can I edit my pictures?

How do I email photos to friends and family?

Can I watch DVDs?

Can I watch TV on my laptop?

Can I record TV on my laptop?

Chapter 11

What is the Mobility Center and what does it offer?

How can I enhance my laptop's battery life?

How much battery power is left right now?

How do I turn off my wireless features when I'm on an aeroplane?

What are 'presentation' settings?

How do I sync a phone, music player or other device?

Can I add a second display?